A Measure of Success

Cleveland, Ohio, in 1834: View from the Buffalo Road, east of the court house (*Courtesy Cleveland Public Library*)

A Measure of Success

Protestants and Public Culture
in Antebellum Cleveland

Michael J. McTighe

STATE UNIVERSITY OF NEW YORK PRESS

Production by Ruth Fisher
Marketing by Fran Keneston

Published by
State University of New York Press, Albany

© 1994   State University of New York

For information, address the State University of New York Press,
State University Plaza, Albany, NY 12246

Library of Congress Cataloging-in-Publication Data

McTighe, Michael J., 1948–1993
     A measure of success : Protestants and public culture in
antebellum Cleveland / Michael J. McTighe.
          p.   cm.
     Revision of thesis (Ph. D.—University of Chicago, 1983)
originally presented under title: Embattled establishment.
     Includes bibliographical references and index.
     ISBN 0–7914–1825–1 (alk. paper). — ISBN 0–7914–1826–X (pbk. :
alk. paper)
     1. Cleveland (Ohio)—Church history—19th century. 2. Ohio—
Church history—19th century. 3. Christianity and culture—
History—19th century. 4. Protestant churches—Ohio—History—19th
century. I. Title.
BR560.C57M38   1994
280'.4'097713209034—dc20   93–26789
                                                                                      CIP

10 9 8 7 6 5 4 3 2 1

For
Clarice Jungck
Leroy Jungck
Elaine McTighe
Carolyn L. Carter
and
Edward Carter McTighe

CONTENTS

LIST OF TABLES

LIST OF TABLES

ACKNOWLEDGMENTS

Many debts, scholarly and personal, have accumulated during the years it has taken to complete this project. Dozens of church secretaries and clergy welcomed me and provided access to their records. Librarians at the Cleveland Public Library, particularly Donald Tipka, the Western Reserve Historical Society Library, the Congregational Church Library in Boston, and the Presbyterian Historical Society in Philadelphia helped provide access to their collections.

The computer work on which much of the argument about the interlocking elite rests was a collaborative effort. Jackie Warren, Lorraine Zimmer, and Kim Cahaus provided help with data entry and record linkage. Jane Huerta and Janice Tobin of Cleveland State University and Carl Spitznagel of John Carroll University helped me sort out some of the general issues involved in producing machine-usable data. Laura Darcy, Louise Boston Mayerik, and Ed McNeeley, of the Cleveland State Computer Services staff, were endlessly patient and resourceful in transforming isolated bits of data into tables which said something about religion in Cleveland.

Through numbers of drafts of papers, articles, and chapters, Janice Hayes of Cleveland State University and Sandra Martin of Gettysburg College have patiently produced many versions of the material which eventually culminated in the book.

I have been blessed with the support, advice and encouragement of many friends and colleagues. Martin E. Marty of the University of Chicago supervised the initial work in its dissertation form. His advice about defining what contribution this might make to the field served to guide my later research and writing. Marian Morton of John Carroll University was a constant inspiration with her own writing and knowledge of early Cleveland. She and I participated on a number of historical panels together, and her comments invariably helped sharpen and focus my argument.

Lee Gibbs of Cleveland State University and Lou Hammann, Buz Myers, and Lisa Portmess of Gettysburg College all provided much welcomed support. Other Gettysburg College colleagues, too, have helped create a setting that made this work possible. At the risk of leaving some out, I would like to mention Frank Chiteji, Norman O. Forness, Michael J. Birkner, Jean Fletcher, Bokin Kim, and Len Goldberg.

Two colleagues at Gettysburg, both in Russian History, have been a constant source of encouragement, criticism, and insight. Chris Ruane, now at Washington University in St. Louis, was present at the "Eureka Moment," when I finally realized what the book was about. Our many conversations over lunch helped clarify the scope and direction of my argument.

Being around Catherine Clay, one can't help but be excited by history. Katy's wide-ranging interests and her ability to conceptualize alternatives have been invaluable in rethinking many of the chapters of the book as it went through its final revisions. A series of friends have been nearby in these years, offering encouragement and having our periodic get-togethers mark the progress of the manuscript. I think particularly of Tom Weeks and Elizabeth Copley, David Dawson and Virginia Dawson, Carol Singer and Danny Singer, and Jean Howard and Jim Baker. To these and the many others who have helped bring this history to completion I offer my deepest thanks.

SUPPLEMENTAL ACKNOWLEDGMENTS

On February 4, 1993, a little more than a month after he submitted the final text of this book to the publisher, my husband, Michael J. McTighe, died of cancer. It is the steadfast support of SUNY Press, Gettysburg College, and Mike's friends and colleagues who have made it possible for this book to be published.

Professor Michael J. Birkner of Gettysburg College selflessly took time out from his own scholarship to edit the book and shepherd it to publication. He cannot be thanked enough for his great generosity and his willingness to devote his time, talent, and experience to the book. Catherine Clay continued her commitment to the book by communicating with the publisher, helping select the illustration, and recruiting volunteers to work on the book. Many other colleagues at Gettysburg College helped in other ways. Thanks to these people, Mike knew before he died that the final work on the book was in good hands.

I would also like to thank Gettysburg College's president, Gordon A. Haaland, its Provost, Baird Tipson, and Mike's two Department Chairs during his tenure at the College, Louis J. Hammann and Carey A. Moore, for their unwavering support of Mike and his scholarly work.

Carolyn L. Carter

PART ONE

Protestants and Public Culture

Chapter 1

Reverend Pickands,
the Bridge War,
and the Public Culture

In 1837, Reverend James Pickands set a standard for religious involvement in public life that few clergy or church members ever matched. Pickands, the minister of the First Presbyterian Church of Ohio City (a rival city on the West bank of the Cuyahoga River, incorporated into Cleveland in 1854), played a prominent role in a violent skirmish known in Cleveland history as "The Bridge War." The bridge in question rankled Ohio City boosters because it diverted traffic coming from the south away from their town and toward Cleveland. One night in 1837, 1,000 protestors armed with guns, crowbars, axes, planks, stones, and other weapons gathered to march across the new bridge, intending to render it impassable. Pickands invoked divine aid as they began their march. According to some accounts, Pickands even led the procession. At the center of the bridge, Pickands and his compatriots confronted a similar army of Clevelanders led by that city's mayor. Three people sustained serious injuries during the ensuing battle. Despite Rev. Pickands's and his "army's" efforts to destroy the bridge, the bridge stood.[1]

Such active, even violent, action in the public arena runs counter not only to popular images of nineteenth-century religion but also to historians' accounts. Even when the pervasive cultural presence of religion is noted, it is most often in terms of the work of moral and benevolent voluntary societies. Pickands provides an indication that Protestants cannot be so easily pigeonholed. His direct involvement in a practical economic issue suggests that a different image for nineteenth-century religion must be developed. With Reverend Pickands in mind, it is the argument of this book that Protestants played an active role in the public life of a

3

developing commercial city. Their reach extended from education, temperance, and benevolence, areas customarily associated with religion, to economics, politics, and rituals of community life, areas where historians have underestimated their impact.

Pickands' participation in the Bridge War, as striking as it is, represents only one, quixotic, instance of Protestant involvement in the public life of Cleveland in the years before the Civil War. Other Cleveland Protestants would exercise their influence in ways less dramatic, perhaps, but no less significant. How can their power and influence be characterized?

Any study of the power and influence of religious communities necessarily enters into a debate about the relationship among ideals, self-interest, and social activity begun by Max Weber's *The Protestant Ethic and the Spirit of Capitalism*. Few issues are more vexing and complex—or more important. Virtually every study of religion in the antebellum years that touches on public life addresses the issue either directly or obliquely. *A Measure of Success* aims to contribute to this debate by describing the power and influence of Protestants in the "public culture" of a specific community at a particular stage of economic and urban development.[2]

By using the term "public culture," the intention is to encompass the widest possible variety of forces and influences that contribute to shaping values, attitudes, and institutions. Analyzing the public culture involves assessing the complex intermingling of political, economic, social, and cultural influences that constitute community life. It includes aspects of social life where values, attitudes, and institutions are established and maintained. The public culture is expressed in formal institutions such as political parties or orphan asylums, as well as in widely shared attitudes toward work, progress, and morality.

In addition to conceiving of the formation of public culture as a process, it might usefully be thought of as the forum or arena where power in its various forms is elaborated and made authoritative. Possessing formal instruments of political and economic power, such as owning businesses or holding political office, are certainly included. But equally, if not more important, is the ability to confer meaning. Those who succeeded in identifying railroads as instruments of moral and material progress, for example, certainly possessed power—they have set the stage for others to accept their understanding of what is important. That those who conferred such significance to railroads also owned the railroads, or led churches whose leading members owned the railroads, indicates the extent to which these two forms of power were often closely related.

Rather than being a fixed entity, the public culture may be more profitably thought of as an arena that changes as participants vie to make their influence felt. It is a forum where power in its various forms is projected, elaborated, and made authoritative. Many individuals and groups vied for influence in antebellum Cleveland, and it is from this process that the public culture of the commercial city takes shape.[3]

Power and influence in this public culture take many forms. Reverend Pickands represents an immediate, direct exercise of power—the ability to prevail through physical force. Yet this is only the most dramatic invocation of power. Power belongs just as much to those who have the ability to confer meaning and importance (identifying railroads as instruments of moral and material progress, for example) as well as to those who possess formal instruments of economic and political power (ownership of businesses or occupying positions of leadership).[4]

Any aspect of social life where values, attitudes, and institutions are developed is part of the public culture. The public culture is expressed in formal institutions such as political parties and orphan asylums, in voluntary associations including those dedicated to benevolence or moral reform, as well as in widely shared attitudes toward work, progress, and technology.

Using the term "public culture" aims to provide focus to the discussion of social power and influence by finding an alternative to terms such as "politics," which is too narrow, and "society," which is too broad and ill-defined. Politics is included in the public culture because politics broadly conceived involves contests for power, authority, and the ability to bestow meaning on public life. But even an expanded definition of politics fails to encompass some crucial aspects of the process of establishing and maintaining power and authority, such as investing railroads with millennial import, or the involvement of churches and church members in July 4th observances. Including the discussion of politics under the rubric of public culture also serves as a reminder that politics functions in the context of ideological and economic concerns which must be accounted for in any full analysis of social life.

At the same time as it seeks to be a term more inclusive than politics, public culture is meant to be more precise than "society."

The concern of the book will be to focus on those aspects of society where values, attitudes, and institutions are established and maintained. To focus on "society" often results in a static portrait of existing social arrangements. It is just as important to highlight the ways society is constantly changing and to notice the individuals and movements vying for influence. Any human society is dynamic and fluid, the ever-changing result of a process. Nowhere is this more true than in an antebellum American city such as Cleveland which made the transition from village to city, and from horse to steamboat to railroad, in barely 25 years.

Using the term "public culture" underscores this dynamic process. The public culture emerges as the result of a contest between diverse groups and interests over public policies and values. It is always being created, revised, and defended. This concentration on the process by which the public culture is formed and maintained is particularly appropriate when applied to the public activity of Protestants, since they consciously sought to establish their influence and spread their message not only in Cleveland but throughout antebellum America.

In addition to being an alternative to "politics" or "society," focusing on the process by which the public culture was shaped directs attention to activities often seen as private, such as religiously inspired schools or voluntary societies. The work of these groups was ultimately part of the process by which the city's values, attitudes, and institutions were formed. In the world of the antebellum Protestant, the distinction between public and private had little meaning since the ideals formed in the church were assumed to be applicable to all society and the virtues of the home were seen as appropriate for the public world. Thus, the public culture is visible just as much in benevolent projects conducted by women, which are often considered private, as it is in businesses and political parties dominated by men. Benevolent projects such as the Ragged and Industrial School received public funds, even though they were "private" projects—in this case by the women of First Methodist Church—because they inculcated values considered appropriate for the developing commercial city. Using public culture as an analytical tool, then, allows appropriate recognition of the ways in which the work of women, usually described as "private," helped shape the "public" world of antebellum America. Since women constituted two-thirds of the membership of Protestant churches, any account of religion and public life that neglects the often informal, indirect ways women shaped the city would be incomplete.

Measuring the power of a religious group in the public culture is a delicate task. Power and influence defy precise measurement. Some indices of power and influence used in this book, such as office-holding, filling of leadership positions, wealth, and occupational status, begin to suggest the extent of Protestant influence. To supplement this, much of the argument about Protestant power and influence in the public culture rests on another sort of evidence—particular "moments" when the tangle of motives and the variety of forces at work can be observed and analyzed. Three types of moments are particularly illuminating—moments of Protestant priority-setting, moments of participation and cooperation, and moments of social decision-making.

Moments of Protestant priority-setting provide an occasion to assess the internal state of the Protestant community. These are moments when Protestants juggled conflicting commitments, attempting to decide which to keep and which to revise or abandon. The salient example was the conflict between their Sabbath principles and the imperatives of an economic development of which they were prime beneficiaries. The convenience, efficiency, and profitability of running steamboats and railroads on the Sabbath tempted Protestants to abandon strict adherence to the Sabbath. In instances such as this, it is possible to evaluate the ways Protestants resolved their religious ideals, self-interest, and class interest.

In moments of participation in the broader society and cooperation with other people and institutions within it, we can glimpse at the relationship of Protestants to those outside their community. Protestants joined in public life by establishing a presence for themselves in a variety of ways, often in alliance with public officials. These instances of participation and cooperation occurred when Reverend Pickands led his bridge charge, when Protestant ministers led celebrations marking the completion of railroad lines, when churches took the lead in July 4th parades, when business leaders incorporated religious ideals in their advice to young men entering business, when benevolent institutions promoted the Protestant agenda, when churches were used for business meetings and public school commencements, and when public officials joined Protestants in benevolent and educational projects. At these moments, Protestants legitimated aspects of public life and, in return, the community incorporated Protestants and acknowledged their centrality and their role in meaning-giving.

Moments of social decision-making, too, offer a window on Protestant power and influence in the city. Analyzing the moments when Protestants worked to pass and enforce temperance laws, or when they asked the city to supply money for a teacher for the Protestant Orphan Asylum, makes it possible to assess the extent of their ability to translate their wishes into social policy. Moments of social decision-making reveal which attitudes, forces, groups, and individuals held sway in forging the values and institutions that shaped the city's public culture.

Essential features of the role of Protestants in the public culture emerge most clearly when these various "moments" can be seen to coalesce into "patterns" of Protestant priority-setting, participation and cooperation, or social decision-making. Such indications of Protestant involvement appear, for example, when the city government continually cooperates in supporting Protestant benevolent institutions, or when Protestants invariably give priority to the imperatives of economic development rather than to their religious ideals.

Since using public culture as an analytical tool directs attention to patterns of cooperation as well as occasions of confrontation, an often-overlooked aspect of Protestant involvement in economic life becomes more visible. Protestant church members and ministers rarely confronted society's economic and political arrangements in obvious or systematic ways. The impact of Protestantism on antebellum America would have been more obvious if there had been a pattern of confrontation. Instead, church officers, members, and ministers had few criticisms to make of the emerging commercial and industrial economy. They applauded the public culture they in large measure created and maintained. Their crucial role in the process of public culture formation was to bestow their approval on a particular form of economic life. To put it another way, they privileged entrepreneurial capitalism. In the process, they made an element of their own ideology, the ideal of stewardship, an integral part of the new ethos. Looking for evidence of the process by which the public culture is created thus provides a way to evaluate not only direct, formal, and institutional exercises of power but also the more subtle, amorphous, and pervasive modes of power that constituted the dominant method of Protestant influence.

When all these indications of Protestant influence and power in the public culture are accumulated, a portrait of the extensive involvement of Protestant church members and ministers in the public culture emerges that extends far beyond the brief appearance of Reverend Pickands during the Bridge War. It is not surprising to find extensive Protestant influence in the public culture of Cleveland. Accounts of antebellum culture, particularly religious histories, have tended to stress, if not overestimate, the impact of Protestantism as a culture-shaping force. Many histories have focused on the national level, where the proliferation of voluntary societies and the prominent role of religious leaders in the antislavery movement have created an image of a pervasive cultural Christianity.[5]

Yet national visibility does not directly translate into immediate influence over the day-to-day growth and development of an urban settlement such as Cleveland. With the role of religion within a particular local community under the microscope, notions of a Protestant Empire or a Christian Commonwealth must be qualified, if not abandoned. When it came to shaping the public culture of Cleveland, Protestants found themselves one of many groups contesting for influence. Given the substantial role Protestantism played throughout the antebellum United States, what is most surprising about the history of Protestants on the local level is their limited influence. Whether it was the only partially successful temperance crusade, the loss of their central role in public rituals, or the accommodation, if not capitulation, to the imperatives of the commercial economy, Protestants often lost contests for power and influence.[6]

Another image that has dominated histories of antebellum religion is of a Protestantism secure and beyond challenge in its private sphere of home, family, morals, and character formation, and at the same time shunted to the margins, if not completely excluded, from political and economic life. It has been easy to pigeonhole religion in the private sphere because, once again, much of the attention in histories of antebellum religion has been on ministers and national voluntary organizations. Ministers did not own businesses, run for political office, or become mayors of cities. National voluntary societies, too, were largely confined to the private sphere. When they attempted to pass laws or elect candidates, temperance, antislavery, and Sabbath activists made forays into the public sphere, but these have usually been described as an extension of religion's role as moral guardian rather than as an integral part of the Protestants' conception of religion. Turning attention to the involvement of Protestants in the public culture highlights their persistent interest in seeing their religious views embodied in public life. Working to pass temperance laws can best be interpreted not as an extension of their core function of supervising private morality, but as a reflection of their conviction that religion belonged at the center of all aspects of life, both public and private.[7]

When the focus is shifted away from ministers and national organizations to churches and church members on the local level, and from major, dramatic confrontations to the quiet, informal, and indirect spreading of influence and exercise of power that can be brought out by focusing on the public culture, the extensive public involvement of antebellum Protestants is apparent. While they did not dominate the culture, neither were they shunted to its margins. In the years from 1836 to 1860 Cleveland's Protestant ministers and church members took stands on political issues, led July 4th observances, played a prominent role in civic celebrations, and commented on the changes brought by technology and economic development. Churches used their disciplinary powers to set standards for moral conduct and business integrity. Protestant-based voluntary societies helped pass temperance laws and they enlisted the help of local authorities in benevolent projects. In addition, church members themselves took prominent leadership roles in a wide range of reform, business, and political organizations. All of these activities rested on the conviction that religion generated ideals appropriate to every aspect of social life, and they undermine any portrait of Protestantism which relegates it to the private sphere.

A Measure of Success argues that Protestants in antebellum Cleveland continually, and in many instances, successfully, vied to shape the public culture of the developing commercial city along lines favorable to their interests as members of an economically successful, well-connected leadership elite.[8] Protestants brought to this effort an ideology beset with tensions and ambiguities which they never fully resolved. This ideology was fashioned out of a number of influences—their acceptance of the imperatives of economic development, their interests as a social elite, and their religious convictions, particularly the insistence that religion generated ideals appropriate for all aspects of public and private life. Consequently, Cleveland's Protestant leaders created and then

applauded the developing commercial city and worked to inculcate some of the attitudes and behaviors needed for its economic
expansion. At the same time, they did not completely embrace the
ideology of economic development. Influenced by their religious
ideals, they sustained the notion that they were part of an organic
community where the most favored bore responsibility for the welfare of others. This attitude incorporated some restraints on laissez-
faire capitalism's tendency to create a society of individualistic
profit-seekers. With their sense of obligation to others, Protestants
styled themselves stewards of the city. Much to their dismay, fewer
and fewer Clevelanders welcomed their guidance in the increasingly pluralistic city Cleveland had become by 1860.

The title of the book, *A Measure of Success*, points to the two
major purposes that have guided this examination of religion in
antebellum Cleveland—to sum up the extent of Protestant power
in the commercial city and to suggest a methodology that can be
used to assess that power. As regards the extent of their power, after
a quarter-century of effort, by 1860 Protestants had achieved "a
measure of success" in planting their values, attitudes, and institutions in the public culture. They had established a substantial presence, but not a dominant one. The methodological contribution of
this history of antebellum Cleveland Protestants is exemplified in
the variety of ways it seeks to measure power and influence, and in
the focus on the process of the formation of the public culture as
an appropriate context for assessing power and influence.

Above all, *A Measure of Success* is an account of how people's
lives, values, attitudes, and institutions were shaped by Protestant
religion and economic and urban development. The city's Protestants actively participated in the contest over the values and
arrangements which would prevail in Cleveland, one of many similar commercial cities emerging in early nineteenth-century America. Whatever the wisdom of the example he set in the Bridge War
of 1837, Reverend Pickands, in blessing the march of the protest-
ing West Siders and then joining in the battle, at least dispelled the
notion that religion was separate from the strife and contention of
public life. But Pickands' role was small and his impact was minor.
Other Cleveland Protestants played a steadier, more permanent,
and ultimately more decisive role in shaping the values, attitudes,
and institutions that dominated the public culture of the expanding commercial city in the antebellum years.

Chapter 2

The Emerald City of the Lakes

The Bridge War and Reverend Pickands' role in it, although not fully representative of the variety of ways Protestants exercised power and influence, epitomize much about religion and urban development in antebellum Cleveland. The rivalry between the settlements on either side of the Cuyahoga River points to the boosterism and economic ambition that provided the constant backdrop against which urban development proceeded in antebellum Cleveland. Private speculators and developers built the bridge, just as they built the city, hoping to profit from the trade expected to flow through this prime location at the junction of the Cuyahoga River and Lake Erie.

The Bridge War also highlights the fluid line between public and private in the era before the Civil War. Public officials and private entrepreneurs cooperated, a pattern made easier because they were often the same people. When Ohio City at first boycotted the bridge, Cleveland's city council came to the aid of the city's merchants by removing Cleveland's half of the only other bridge across the river, thus cutting off Ohio City's major trade route. This pattern of private-public cooperation typified the relationship of government not just with business but with Protestant churches as well, for the city contributed to salaries for teachers associated with religious schools and aided religious institutions such as the Protestant Orphan Asylum.

Pickands' role, too, can be taken as emblematic. Amidst the strife, both practically and symbolically, was religion, in the person of Reverend Pickands, first blessing the mob's assault, then joining the fray himself. In fact, these two motifs—blessing and joining—recur throughout this history of antebellum Cleveland. Protestants blessed the boosters' plans for economic development and joined actively in efforts to bring the plans to fruition. By and large, Protestants lent their sanction to the commercial city and

13

the values, attitudes, and institutions that drove it. They actively participated in the city's institutions, playing leadership roles in a wide variety of business, political, moral reform, and benevolent activities.

To be sure, there were Protestant critics of commercial development, including many who sought to blunt some of its harsher implications, but they represented a minority voice in a religious community generally convinced that the new city had found the formula for the achievement of moral and material progress. Indeed, it is the argument of this book that the city's Protestants played a decisive role in creating and maintaining the values, attitudes, and institutions that pervaded the city's public life.

The city whose public life Protestants sought to shape was little more than a village when it was incorporated in 1836. The location, at the juncture of Lake Erie and the Cuyahoga River, offered access to the north, east, and the Ohio hinterland. The permanent white settlement of Cleveland resulted from a land venture by a private concern, the Connecticut Land Company, which first sent surveyors in the late 1790s.[1] The town grew slowly. By 1825, only 500 people had settled in Cleveland, on the east bank of the Cuyahoga. Even fewer occupied the settlement on the west bank, known as Ohio City.

Although growth was slow, hopes were high. Antebellum Cleveland was one of many small American communities whose ambitious citizens were eager to turn their small village into a thriving metropolis. The city's boosters were acutely conscious of being one of a number of cities fighting for survival and, ultimately, economic supremacy in the "Great West." Newspapers kept up a constant stream of good publicity and editorial boosterism, designed both to convince the city's residents of their good fortune and to lure emigrants. The papers cited the city's convenient location for trade, its fertile soil, its pleasant living conditions, its "population proverbial for enterprise and industry" and its destiny—to be the most important settlement on the Western lakes. Boosters searched for nicknames to capture their optimism about the city's destiny. Cleveland was early known as "the Forest City," for its tree-lined streets. But that was not grandiose enough, so other names were proposed: "the Emerald City of the Lakes," "the Queen City of the Lakes," the "Emporium of Northern Ohio," or, modestly, "the City of the West."[2]

The exaggerated slogans of the boosters contained a kernel of truth, for Cleveland was one of the winners in the city-building sweepstakes. It succeeded in establishing political and economic dominance over its neighbors in northeast Ohio. Political prominence came by designation when Cleveland was named the county seat in 1810. Economic supremacy accompanied canals. Ohio's most ambitious canal project, the Ohio & Erie Canal, linked Cleveland on Lake Erie to Portsmouth on the Ohio River. The Cleveland-to-Akron section was finished in 1827, and the entire 308-mile canal was completed five years later. The canal provided the early impetus to the city's economic growth by establishing Cleveland as a major link in the transportation system which moved the goods of the Ohio Valley east and the products of the East to the West.[3]

By 1860 Cleveland was a full-fledged commercial power, the center of a network of canals and railroads which linked the city and the Ohio hinterland to the rest of the nation. Its location midway between the coal of Pennsylvania and the ore of upper Michigan made it an ideal place for industrial development built on iron, and, later in the century, steel.[4]

Cleveland's population reflected its economic growth. When it was incorporated in 1836, Cleveland was still a small town, with a population of approximately 5,000. Ohio City's population was close to 2,400. The 1840 Federal Census put the Cleveland population at 6,071. Ten years later, the population had more than doubled, to 17,034. By 1860, following the 1854 merger of Cleveland and Ohio City, the population had more than doubled again, to 43,417, making Cleveland the nation's nineteenth largest city. It was comparable in size to Milwaukee and Detroit, but well behind Cincinnati and Chicago among Western cities (Table 2.1).[5]

Because Cleveland's economic development and population growth paralleled that of many of the nation's new commercial centers, generalizations drawn from the Cleveland experience can, with some confidence, be applied to other cities and to the nation. No one city could be said to be "typical." The nation already contained a variety of established cities, from the substantial metropolitan centers of the northeast such as New York, Philadelphia, and Boston, to the port and trading centers of the South, such as Charleston and Richmond. Cleveland fits another model, the early nineteenth-century urban newcomer. Its pattern of settlement, economic development, and population growth largely paralleled that of a number of what were to become the largest of the indus-

Table 2.1   Population of Cleveland and Selected American Cities

	1840	1850	1860
Cleveland	6,071	17,034	43,417
Ohio City		6,375	
Boston	85,475	113,721	133,563
Chicago	4,470	29,963	109,260
Cincinnati	46,382	115,438	161,044
Detroit	9,192	21,019	45,619
Kingston, NY	6,000 est.	10,000 est.	16,640
Los Angeles		1,610	4,385
Milwaukee	1,712	31,177	45,246
New York	312,710	515,547	813,669
Newark, NJ	17,290	38,894	71,941
Rochester, NY	20,191	36,403	48,204
Richmond		27,500	
Springfield, MA	11,000	18,000	

Sources: Allan R. Pred, *The Spatial Dynamics of Urban Industrial Growth, 1800–1914* (Cambridge, Mass.: M.I.T. Press, 1966); Stuart M. Blumin, *The Urban Threshold: Growth and Change in a Nineteenth-Century American Community* (Chicago: University of Chicago Press, 1976); Blake McKelvey, *Rochester, The Water-Power City, 1812–1854* (Cambridge, Mass.: Harvard University Press, 1945); *Rochester, The Flower City, 1855–1890* (Cambridge, Mass.: Harvard University Press, 1949); David R. Goldfield, *Urban Growth in the Age of Sectionalism: Virginia, 1847–1860* (Baton Rouge, La.: Louisiana State University Press, 1977); Michael H. Frisch, *Town Into City: Springfield, Massachusetts and the Meaning of Community* (Cambridge, Mass.: Harvard University Press, 1972); Kathleen Neils Conzen, *Immigrant Milwaukee, 1836–1860: Accommodation and Community in a Frontier City* (Cambridge, Mass.: Harvard University Press, 1976).

trial cities of the midwest—Chicago, Detroit, Milwaukee, Buffalo, and Pittsburgh.[6]

The religious landscape of the city, too, resembled other cities of the "Great West." As the bulk of the earliest white settlers, Protestants dominated the religious scene in the formative years of the city's development. Baptist, Congregational, and Presbyterian churches formed the majority until the 1850s when German Protestant, German Catholic, and Irish Catholic churches deprived New England-based Protestants of their religious monopoly. At the time of the city's incorporation in 1836 there were 10 New England-derived and English-speaking Protestant churches, two German Protestant churches, and no Catholic churches or Jewish synagogues. By 1860, English-speaking Protestant denominations had 28 churches which now shared the city with 12 German Protestant churches, nine Roman Catholic churches, four Jewish synagogues, and one A.M.E. church (Table 2.2).

Membership statistics tell a similar story. English-speaking Protestant churches claimed an estimated 1,400 members in 1840, 1,900 in 1850, and 3,900 in 1860 (Tables 2.3 and 2.4). Comparable membership statistics for the city's Roman Catholic churches are difficult to arrive at, since the Catholic Church considered all those with Catholic heritage, whether or not they attended or affiliated with the church, as members. The Roman Catholic church claimed 3,000 members in 1836, although the city directory reported 1,000 Catholics. The Church claimed 20,000 members in 1860 (Tables 2.3 and 2.4). If nothing else, such numbers reminded Protestants that they no longer held the monopoly over the city's religious life they had enjoyed in the first few decades after the city's founding. Taking into consideration the problematic nature of the membership statistics, it is likely that Roman Catholics constituted approximately 30 percent of Cleveland's population in 1860 (Table 2.4).[7]

Table 2.2   Cleveland Churches

	1836	1840	1850	1860
English-speaking Protestants, major denominations	3	4	16	32
English-speaking Protestants, other denominations	1	1	3	8
All English-speaking Protestants	4	5	19	40
Jewish	0	1	1	3
Roman Catholic	0	1	1	9
German Protestant	0	1	3	8

Sources: See Appendix.

Table 2.3   Church Membership Totals

	1836	1840	1845	1850	1855	1860
BAPTIST						
Erie Street	-	-	-	-	226	207
First	145	306	335	314	281	364
Third	-	-	-	-	90	136
CONG. & PRESBYTERIAN						
Associate Presbyterian	-	-	x	x	x	x
Euclid Street Presbyterian	-	-	-	-	50	141
First Congregational (Avery)	-	-	-	-	x	x
First Presbyterian	176	283	380	311	254	277
First Presbyterian, Ohio City	40	189	144	x	163	250
Plymouth Congregational	-	-	-	30	100	235
Second Presbyterian	-	-	58	212	254	398
Westminster Presbyterian	-	-	-	-	26	x
EPISCOPAL						
Grace	-	-	x	63	111	202
St. James	-	-	-	-	-	x
St. John's	20	78	82	87	126	196
St. Paul's	-	-	-	90	108	172
Trinity	100	130	160	140	155	207
METHODIST						
Bridge Street	-	-	-	-	39	85
Church Street	x	78	158	123	96	123
Erie Street	-	-	-	81	100	128
First	x	x	x	160	134	260
Perry Street	-	-	-	-	50	30

(Table 2.3 con't.)

	1836	1840	1845	1850	1855	1860
Wesleyan	-	60	x	x	x	x
OTHER ENG.-SP. PROT.						
Bethel	x	x	55	x	x	x
Disciples	-	-	x	x	87	x
Friends	-	-	-	-	x	x
Prospect St. Univ.	-	-	x	x	x	x
Society of 2nd Advent	-	-	100	-	-	-
St. John's A.M.E.	x	x	x	33	44	x
True Bible Christian	-	-	-	-	x	x
Unitarian	-	-	-	-	x	x
Universalist Inst.	x	x	x	x	x	x
GERMAN (selected)						
Salem Evangelical Assn.	x	x	19	x	x	x
Schifflein Christian	x	x	500	x	x	x
Zion Evangelical Lutheran	x	x	100	x	x	x
CATHOLICS (est.)	x	x	4000	x	x	13135
JEWISH						
Ansche Chesed	x	x	57	x	x	x
Israeltic	x	x	15	x	x	x
TOTAL, ENGLISH-SPEAKING PROTESTANTS	481	1124	1472	1644	2494	3411

Sources: Records of individual churches and their denominational supervisory bodies and city directories (see Bibliography).

Notes: Totals are for communicants or full members. In cases where a membership total was not available for a given date, a total for membership for one year before or after was used. An "x" indicates that none of these was available. There is one exception, however: the 1845 Catholic membership figure is from 1847. A "-" indicates that the church did not exist. Given the number of churches for which statistics are unavailable, and the unreliability of membership statistics, totals should be considered

(Table 2.3 Sources con't.)

approximate. If missing membership statistics were available, the English-speaking Protestant total would be increased by 100–400 for each year.

The membership statistic for Catholics for 1847 is from Wm. Stephenson, comp., *Smead and Cowles General Business Directory of the City of Cleveland for 1848–49* (Cleveland: Smead and Cowles, 1848), p. 2, and the total for 1860 is an estimate by Thomas Kremm, "Cleveland and the First Lincoln Election: The Ethnic Response to Nativism," *Journal of Interdisciplinary History* 8 (Summer, 1977): 79. Kremm's estimate of about 13,000 members is in my judgment more reliable than the 20,000 figure bruited by the church in the late 1850s.

Unlike the growing Roman Catholic presence, the Jewish community was relatively small, ethnically circumscribed, and little threat to Protestant influence. The first synagogue was established by the Israeltic Society in 1839. In 1847, after a split and a subsequent reunion, the new Israeltic and Anshe Chesed Society numbered 62 members. By 1860, there were three Jewish congregations, with a total membership of approximately 200, or approximately 1/2 of one percent of the city's population[8] (Tables 2.2, 2.3, and 2.4).

Unbelievers are the wild card in any assessment of the religious contours of the city and the potential extent of Protestant influence over social life. In 1846, the year for which there are the most complete records, approximately 38 percent of the population over 18 belonged to New England-derived Protestant churches, 30 percent belonged to Catholic parishes, and 2 percent were Jews. That leaves approximately 30 percent of the population unchurched. Not all these would have been hostile to religion. Undoubtedly, there were more passive nonbelievers than fervent infidels. Nevertheless, the unchurched population constituted a group relatively distant from the orbit of Protestant influence (Table 2.4).

More troublesome for Protestant pretensions for social influence than the sheer numbers of Roman Catholics, Jews, and the unaffiliated, was the trend. New England-derived Protestant church members were an ever smaller proportion of the city's population—approximately 18 percent in 1840, 10 percent in 1850, and 8 percent in 1860 (Table 2.4). Protestants could not help but sense that their share of the population was declining. They were a substantial presence in the city but not necessarily, just based on size, a dominant influence. Catholics and the religiously unaffili-

Table 2.4   Church Membership as a Percentage of Population

	1840		1850		1860	
	N	%	N	%	N	%
Total Population	6,071		17,034		43,417	
Engl.-Speaking	1,400	(23.1)				
Protestant (est.)			1,900	(11.2)	3,900	(9.0)
Catholic			4,000	(23.5)	13,135	(30.3)
Jewish			62	(0.4)	2,000	(0.5)

Sources: See Tables 1 and 2.

Notes: Estimates for English-speaking Protestant churches are based on Table 2. They have been adjusted upward to account for the churches (mostly smaller congregations) whose membership totals were unavailable.

ated could be expected to resist some of their efforts to attain influence in the public culture.

The growth of the Catholic churches and the beginnings of Jewish synagogues were signs that the natural audience of the city's New-England-derived Protestant churches was limited and declining. The censuses tell the same story. In the 1850 Census sample, 18.5 percent listed one of the German states as their birthplace, and 14.0 percent listed Ireland. These residents were likely to be attracted to Catholic or German Protestant churches (Table 2.5). The increasing diversity meant that Protestants could not dictate the attitudes, values, and institutions which would make up the evolving public culture, as they might have been able to do in a more homogeneous environment. They needed to entice as much as coerce, and to operate informally as much as formally. They would have to work through a variety of institutions, both governmental and voluntary, to spread their influence. Whatever method they employed, the growing pluralism of the city augured ill for Protestant power and authority, especially in the 1850s.

Residents of the newly incorporated cities of Cleveland and Ohio City could not help but be optimistic. For the city's Protestants, the crucial question was how they might shape what could be "the Emerald City of the Lakes," or, even, if things turned out well, "the City of the West." How might their religious ideals and their social and economic interests shape the new commercial city? In their quest for power and influence over the process of establishing and maintaining Cleveland's public culture, much would depend on their ability to marshal their considerable, though not unlimited, resources.

Table 2.5   Birthplace, 1850 Census

	1850 Census Sample (N=2423)	
BIRTHPLACE		
Ohio	654	(27.2%)
OTHER WEST		
Indiana	3	(0.1%)
Illinois	1	(0.0%)
Iowa	1	(0.0%)
Michigan	11	(0.5%)
Wisconsin	3	(0.1%)
TOTAL	19	(0.8%)
NEW ENGLAND		
Connecticut	75	(3.1%)
Maine	6	(0.2%)
Massachusetts	75	(3.1%)
New Hampshire	13	(0.5%)
Rhode Island	4	(0.2%)
Vermont	38	(1.6%)
TOTAL	211	(8.8%)
MID-ATLANTIC		
Maryland	6	(0.2%)
New Jersey	6	(0.2%)
New York	311	(12.9%)
Pennsylvania	42	(1.7%)
TOTAL	365	(15.2%)
SOUTH		
Kentucky	4	(0.2%)
Louisiana	1	(0.0%)
Virginia	14	(0.6%)
South—Other	3	(0.1%)
TOTAL	22	(0.9%)

(Table 2.5 con't.)

	1850 Census Sample (N=2423)	
BIRTHPLACE		
EUROPE AND OTHER		
Canada	69	(2.9%)
Caribbean, Central & South America	2	(0.1%)
England	195	(8.1%)
France	10	(0.4%)
Germany	446	(18.5%)
Ireland	337	(14.0%)
Isle of Man	20	(0.8%)
Scotland	20	(0.8%)
Wales	11	(0.4%)
Europe—Other	25	(1.0%)
TOTAL	1153	(47.2%)
UNKNOWN	17	

Source: 1850 Manuscript Census Sample (See Appendix).

Note: The people whose birthplace was unknown or not listed were not included in computing the percentages.

Chapter 3

The Contests Within the Contest: Defining and Mobilizing the Protestant Community

Even as they entered the contest for influence in the public culture, Protestants faced contests within their own ranks. They found their path to dominance blocked not only by "outsiders"— Catholics, Jews, and the religiously indifferent—but also by divisions within their own community. Protestants had first to decide who they were. How would they define themselves? Would they accommodate themselves to their evolving identity as a privileged, well-connected segment of the population? Would they reassess their choices in response to concerns that the poor would feel unwelcome in the lavish edifices? In debating their identity, they risked division. Could they mobilize their resources in the service of common goals, or would their efforts be dissipated by internal bickering?

The way Cleveland Protestants would resolve these contests concerning their identity would determine what interests they would serve when they left their pews and how effectively they would be able to pursue those interests. Particularly in the debates about the implications of building ostentatious churches and the propriety of selling pews, Cleveland's Protestants defined their identity through the choices they made. These moments when Protestants fought over their collective identity crystallized their self-understanding. If these contests could be settled without bitterness or schisms, Protestants would be able to unite to more effectively tap their resources and project their values into the public culture.

Potentially, Protestants could call on substantial resources in terms of facilities, talented clergy, and accomplished members, not to mention that all-purpose social lubricant, money. If they could forge a unified community capable of directing these resources to a common goal their power would be hard to resist.

Two particular issues provided moments which forced Protestants to define themselves in ways that shaped their activity in the public culture. First, in reacting to criticisms that churches had buried their message beneath elaborate and lavishly appointed edifices, Protestant churches faced the question of their class alignment and sympathies. Would they identify themselves with the wealthy? Would they risk having middle and lower income people feel unwelcome? The second issue, whether money would be raised by the sale and renting of pews or by voluntary contributions, raised similar questions. In the pew-selling and renting system, seating depended on paying a substantial sum of money, with only a few pews, always in the back, available to non-contributors. Would this make the church the sanctuary of the well-to-do? Would church positions on public issues be tied to the interests of those who bought the pews?

The increasingly elaborate churches Protestants built forced them to resolve the tension between their religious ideals and the attractions of wealth. In answering critics, Protestants confronted questions about their priorities and their place in the new commercial economy. In deciding whether they felt comfortable settling into velvet-cushioned pews in imposing buildings, Protestants constructed their self-image, determined the signals they would send to others about who they were, and made clear the type of people they expected to become members.

Lavish buildings were the most obvious indication that Protestant churches acted as the gathering place of the privileged. The exteriors were magnificent—large, substantial "edifices" (a mere "building" would not do) with graceful spires and gothic turrets. The lush interiors of the churches duplicated the splendor of the exteriors. Cushioned and carpeted pews with silver name plates, organs with pipes as big as trees, stained glass windows, and castle-like pulpits, with a nearby Bible resting on a crimson velvet stand, were the standards of the day, said the *Plain Dealer*.[1]

The *Plain Dealer* made a habit of calling attention to the extravagance and ostentation of the buildings, and the consequent submergence of the church's social concern under the weight of so much wealth. The complaints were given concrete form in stories of church members and their servants. Every Sunday the pattern was the same for the church member, claimed the *Plain Dealer*:

> Entering the sanctuary with an air of reverence, he treads the soft carpet of the aisle to his pew, seats himself upon the velvet cushion, opens the gilt-edged, morocco-bound hymn books, and goes through the entire service, to the inward satisfaction of himself, and the admiration of all.

Outside, even in the bitter cold of winter, this same man's carriage driver had to wait, stamping his feet trying to maintain circulation. The driver can't help but think, concluded the *Plain Dealer*, "that his master has precious little religion, and less kindness."[2]

A letter from "X" complained that the leading ministers, with their fashionable coats and salaries, didn't bear much resemblance to the original disciples, "and it is doubtful in my mind whether Christ himself, if again on earth, would be invited or called to the Euclid Street charge." When a worthy cause went unaided, the charge that the churches misdirected their spending on buildings was always available. Such was the case in 1853 when a black man needed to raise $50 to buy his son from slavery in Kentucky. The man labored all day, but collected only $5, which led the *Daily True Democrat* to ask, "Does this reflect credit upon the generous spirit of our citizens?—citizens who will spend thousands and thousands to build churches, and yet not help a man to buy his own son!"[3]

An article about $1,000 subscriptions for improvements at Trinity Episcopal Church, including expensive bells, brought an outraged reply from "Volney" about the incompatibility of such lavish displays of wealth with "true religion." Members of Trinity professed to be followers of the meek and lowly Jesus, "Volney" observed. Where did they find authority for spending so much money on a high pile of brick and mortar? "Does a church, with all its costly trappings and furniture, feed the hungry or clothe the naked?[4]

Three days later "A Christian" replied that Cleveland was a city of rapid growth, and it was reasonable to improve the style and convenience of the city's churches. Besides, the building Trinity erected wasn't extravagant, but a plain, substantial, convenient structure, "having of course all the modern improvements," and big enough to meet the demands of a rising population. Church buildings should be equal at least to secular buildings, since they are for the glory and worship of God. Further, it was not true that religion had neglected the poor. The morality, humanity, sympathy, and charity inculcated in churches benefited the poor, "A Christian" argued.[5]

Religion had become a business, "Volney" responded: "preaching is a trade; the Bible, the word of God, the merchandise. The Pastor is chief salesman, and a church the warehouse where the goods are offered at retail, in lots to suit purchasers." Such churches excluded the poor, since the poor could not afford the pew rents, and if they did enter, they would not feel comfortable. As for morality and charity, which "A Christian" had pointed to as a help to the poor, had he ever tried them for dinner, or as protection against inclement weather? If so, "Volney" suggested that "A Christian" apply at once for a patent—it would be the most valuable one ever obtained.[6]

"Volney's" criticisms notwithstanding, Cleveland's Protestants persisted in spending large sums on lavish buildings. In doing so, they defined their identity and clientele. They were willing to risk the possibility that only the well-to-do would feel welcome. Protestant church members were the city's elite, and their religious surroundings faithfully reflected that social identity.

A second controversy, about the selling of pews, gave Protestants another chance to debate their priorities. Churches depended on pew sales and rents to pay for the bulk of their expenses. (The system of supporting churches through weekly or monthly voluntary offerings did not prevail in Cleveland until well after the Civil War.) Some churches made full membership contingent on buying a pew. Under Trinity Episcopal Church's Articles in 1839, voting was open to those who subscribed to the Articles, occupied a pew, and were not behind in their pew payments. In 1847 the by-laws were amended to require that a voter for the vestry must have been a member for six months and to have paid at least $2 per year for a pew or sitting. Third Baptist Church resolved that no one was to receive a letter of dismission, which was a necessity if the person intended to join a church in a new city, without a financial accounting. Requirements such as these meant that meeting financial obligations was added to a confession of faith, continued piety, and moral conduct as integral parts of church membership.[7]

Potential churchgoers unable to afford the cost of buying a pew had two options—renting a pew or occupying a "free pew." Pews that were not sold could be rented, usually for $5 to $30 per year. The number of pews available for renting is unclear. Some churches were able to sell only a third of their pews, while others such as Euclid Street Presbyterian Church sold all 173 of its available pews in 1852.[8]

Most Cleveland churches set aside four to ten "free pews," always at the back of the church. For example, in 1834 Trinity Episcopal Church made 4 of its 76 pews available as free pews and in 1855 First Baptist Church made 17 of its 168 available. Trinity Episcopal Church's provision for free pews was grudging in 1840. The vestry resolved that no pews would be designated as free until they were offered for sale and not sold.[9]

As Protestant churches grew in membership and embarked on extensive building campaigns, pew prices increased to meet the growing expenses and aspirations of the congregations. Pew prices were moderate in the 1830s and 1840s, generally under $100. By the 1850s buying a pew at one of the major Protestant churches usually cost $200–$400 or more. When First Presbyterian sold its pews in 1855 almost half cost more than $400, and eight sold for $1,000.[10]

Buying a pew did not end one's financial obligations. Assessments were made yearly, at a rate of 5–10 percent of the pew cost. When special needs arose, further assessments were made. Such costs were beyond the means of most manual workers, even those in skilled trades, whose incomes in 1850 would have been in the $300 a year range.[11]

Churches sometimes found the implications of pew selling troublesome. In 1847 First Presbyterian Church recognized that a widow who had recently shared a pew with her husband now had no seat in the church and could not pay for one. The church voted that a pew would be held for her and for other members of the church unable to pay. The rent would be paid out of church funds. Elisha Taylor, a leading member, protested. One-fourth of the seating in the church was already free, he pointed out, and more than a score of members already sat in the free seats. The church should not show partiality to this widow, and, he argued, there were no funds for such a purpose. The dispute was resolved when one of the deacons bought the pew for the widow.[12]

First Baptist Church records report another case where pew prices inconvenienced a committed member. The member had become poor and was unable to pay his pew rent. As a result, although he was still a Baptist and his children attended Baptist School, he attended St. Paul's Episcopal Church.[13]

Critics of the pew-selling system thought the problem ran even deeper than these individual cases of hardship. Relying on pew sales and rents to finance church construction gave credence to the alarming charge that religion was for sale and that the poor were not welcome. The *Plain Dealer* was as critical of pew prices as it was of the wealth and extravagance of the churches. When First Presbyterian Church moved into its new building in 1852 the *Plain Dealer* reflected on the consequences of what it termed "exorbitant" pew prices:

> At the present rate at which slips are rented, it is utterly and totally impossible for poor people, and even those in moderate circumstances, to provide seats for themselves and their families. This ought not to be. It is wrong, unquestionably wrong, and brings disrepute upon the cause of religion. We know several families who have attended services under Dr. Aiken for years, who find themselves wholly unable to pay the prodigious expense it is now necessary to do, in order to remain among his people.[14]

Two Episcopal ministers, Alexander Varian of Grace Church and James A. Bolles of Trinity Church, issued the strongest indictment of the pew selling system. The system made no provision for the poor and needy, Varian charged. They were virtually shut out from the house of God. For Varian, purchasing the exclusive right to a seat in a church was much like being involved in a joint-stock company.[15] He argued for voluntary offerings as the appropriate way to finance a church. Grace Episcopal Church, founded in 1844 under Varian's direction, adopted a system of free will offerings as a way of reaching seamen and immigrants. With such an arrangement, Varian explained, the privilege of uniting in God's worship was not for sale. With free will offerings "it has been our aim to make this place exclusively the house of God, and not the property of man." According to Varian the seats would be as free as the Gospel preached by Christ, who had opened the kingdom of heaven to all believers. Unfortunately for Varian, Grace's new system of free will offerings did not raise enough money, and many of the members disliked being subject to collections every Sunday. In 1850 free sittings were abolished.[16]

Bolles, too, turned his criticisms of pew rents into a slashing indictment of the way wealth had corrupted the mission of the church. As far as Bolles was concerned, the system of selling and renting pews was unchristian, "hostile to the free and expansive and universal invitations and proclamations of mercy." In a characterization that must have raised unpleasant echoes in Protestant minds, Bolles referred to the selling of pews as an "unholy traffic," like selling the church's blessings for money.[17]

Selling and renting pews made raising money for churches a business transaction, Bolles charged. It introduced into the church "all the frauds and trickeries and miserly calculations of trade, making the house of God, not a 'house of prayer,' but, in awful and horrible reality and truth, a 'house of merchandise.'" The principle that should guide the church, said Bolles, was that all were equally poor in the eyes of God. Houses of prayer should be for all people, rich, poor, high and low. People should not be driven out of church or discouraged from attendance simply because they could not pay.[18]

Selling and renting pews virtually closed the door to whole classes of people, and not only the poor, Bolles feared. Young men working in stores and offices, businessmen whose jobs kept them on the move, and families not permanently settled, were also discouraged by the system. The people shut out the most, though, were the less well-to-do. Servants and laborers, who in the next generation would be the lords and ladies of the land "are just as completely and effectually excluded from the House of God, as though it was written upon the door, *No admittance for servants and laborers here.*" Bolles cautioned that there was a growing feeling among the masses that "*Religion is not for the likes of us; it is for the great and rich people.*" The pew-selling system, he said, practically told people "that the key to unlock the storehouse of spiritual blessings must be made of gold." Bolles feared it gave rich people the feeling "that they are justly and rightfully the *monopolizers* of the blessings of the Gospel."[19]

Bolles could write from personal experience about how this affected ministers. According to him, ministers felt themselves the hirelings of only one class and had to gratify the vanity of a "fashionable congregation." Under the pew system ministers worked for wages, not the salvation of souls.[20]

Bolles, like Varian, was confident that free will offerings were the answer, but Bolles never got to form such a church in Cleveland. Trinity Episcopal Church's vestry rejected his proposals to adopt a free pew system. In 1859 he accepted a call from Trinity Church of the Advent in Boston, a free-will-offering church.[21]

Varian and Bolles expressed a viewpoint shared in other denominations. Discord over pew prices and the principle of selling pews played a role in a number of schisms. The high price of pews sold by First Presbyterian Church in 1837, and the desire that more of the poor might hear the gospel preached, led to the formation of the short-lived First Congregational Church. The product of a later schism, Free Presbyterian (later Plymouth Congregational) Church, picked its name in 1850 to emphasize its disagreement with First Presbyterian Church over slavery and its intention to be a free pew church.[22]

The free pew ideas of Varian, Bolles, and Free Presbyterian Church, although they were the wave of the future for religion in the United States, did not carry the day in antebellum Cleveland. Only three churches adopted free church principles before the Civil War. Varian and Bolles, with their criticisms of the effects of wealth on piety, were out of the mainstream of the Protestant accommodation to wealth and progress.[23]

The moments of Protestant self-definition occasioned by the disputes over lavish buildings and pew selling evidenced a clear pattern. Protestants cast their lot with those who enjoyed the fruits of the commercial economy, even if they ran the risk of discouraging other potential members.

The resolution of these conflicts over their identity at once honed and dissipated Protestant power. The debates opened class, theological, and ideological fissures within the Protestant community that prevented Protestants from being a homogeneous, united force. At the same time, the debates about who they were, especially in terms of wealth and social identification, were necessary steps in shaping Protestants into a self-conscious community with something to say to the new city and with a relatively united voice capable of making itself heard in the public culture. These two countervailing forces—the unity provided by shared religious commitments and common social characteristics, and the disunity brought by religious, class, ideological, and personal rivalries—molded the Protestants of Cleveland who would contest for power in the public culture.

The Protestant community's resolution of the controversies over ostentatious wealth and pew rents in favor of the well-to-do arose quite naturally from the social characteristics of the Protestant community. In forging their identity in these contests within the larger contest over influence in the public culture, Protestants did not start with a blank slate. The social characteristics of the community had already largely defined them as a relatively privileged segment of the population. Cleveland Protestants were numerous, prosperous, and well-situated in the social structure.

The Protestant community's social characteristics decisively shaped the identity it formed and its activity in the public culture. The city's Protestants were securely established on the top rungs of society's ladder. The male members of the Protestant community were a prosperous, well-connected segment of the population which occupied leadership positions across a broad range of public organizations, including business and government. Churches invariably presented themselves as being constituted by members of moderate means. Benjamin Rouse, a founder and leading member of First Baptist Church, described the social composition of the early church in a memoir in 1883:

> The membership of the church was made up of young men, tradesmen, mechanics, lawyers, clerks, etc., who had come to the rising city hoping to make money. They were all comparatively poor; there was not a wealthy man among them; but they were brave, and trusted in God, believing He would help them, if they would make a strong effort to help themselves.[24]

This gives a misleading picture. Although this may have described the members in 1833 when the church was organized, by the mid-1840s Protestant church joiners were a well-to-do segment of the city's population and they were heavily represented in leadership positions in Cleveland's business, political, educational, and reform organizations.

In terms of wealth and occupation, Cleveland's male Protestants were perched at the top of society. Males over the age of 18 who joined churches from 1836–1860 and were located in the 1850 Census were more likely to have real property (29 percent) than other males over the age of 18 (16.3 percent). (No males under the age of 18 were listed as owning property.) Not only were church joiners more likely to own property, they owned more of it. The mean amount of property for the general sample of 115 real property-holders was $2,724, while for the 9 church-joiners it was $11,833[25] (Table 3.1).

Table 3.1 Age and Property-Holding, 1850 Census, for Sample
Population and for Those Who Joined Churches, 1836–60

	MEAN AGE	REAL PROPERTY Individual Mean	N	Head of Household Mean	N
CENSUS SAMPLE					
Male and Female					
1850 Census (N=2423)	22.3	$ 2,775	119	$ 1,304	1313
Joined Church 1836–60 (N=90)	30.2	$11,833	9	$ 3,749	61
Joined Church 1846–50 (N=23)	34.7	$19,833	3	$ 3,805	17
Joined Church 1851–55 (N=26)	26.7	$ 1,500	2	$ 1,987	16
Female					
1850 Census (N=1143)	22.2	$ 4,250	4	$ 1,777	515
Joined Church 1836–60 (N=48)	29.5			$ 5,775	28
Joined Church 1846–50 (N=15)	34.7			$ 6,470	10
Joined Church 1851–55 (N=14)	25.6			$ 1,971	7
Male					
1850 Census (N=1279)	22.4	$ 2,724	115	$ 1,000	797
Joined Church 1836–60 (N=42)	30.9	$11,833	9	$ 2,030	33
Joined Church 1846–50 (N=8)	34.8	$19,833	3	$ 19,833	7
Joined Church 1851–55 (N=12)	28.0	$ 1,500	2	$ 2,000	9
Female Over Age 18					
All (N=659)	32.3	$ 4,250	4	$ 1,765	321
Joined Church 1836–60 (N=39)	33.7			$ 6,166	24
Joined Church 1846–50 (N=15)	34.7			$ 6,470	24
Joined Church 1851–55 (N=10)	30.1			$ 2,760	5
Males Over Age 18					
All (N=707)	34.0	$ 2,724	115	$ 495	564
Joined Church 1836–60 (N=31)	37.7	$11,833	9	$ 1,807	26
Joined Church 1846–50 (N=8)	34.8	$19,833	3	$19,833	7
Joined Church 1851–55 (N=8)	35.0	$ 1,500	2	$ 1,500	6

Sources: See Appendix.

Information about the property-holding of church joiners underestimates the role of the two-thirds of church members who were women, since they were much less likely than men to own property. For church joiners who were women, or those joiners who were under the age of 18, information about the property-holding of their head of household can give an indication of their socio-economic status. The property-holding of the heads of the households of church joiners reinforces the impression that church members were a relatively wealthy segment of the population. Heads of households of church joiners were more likely to own property (67.8 percent as opposed to 54.2 percent of the census sample) and they owned more of it ($3,749 to $1,304)[26] (Table 3.1).

The occupations of male church joiners as listed in the 1850 Census sample reinforce the portrait of a well-to-do group. Those who joined a church in the years from 1836–1860 and whose occupations appeared in the 1850 Census were more heavily represented in the professional occupations (41.4 percent) than were the members of the general population (9.5 percent). Male church joiners mirrored the general population's percentage of skilled white collar workers (24.1 percent compared to 22.5 percent of the general population), and they were less likely to hold skilled blue collar (24.1 percent vs. 38.8 percent), unskilled (3.4 percent vs. 9.8 percent), or laborer (6.9 percent vs. 19.3 percent) jobs. The heads of households of church joiners repeat the same patterns.[27]

Male church joiners were also disproportionately represented in particular sectors of the economy. A majority of church joiners (60.0 percent) worked in the commercial sector of the economy, while 36.7 percent worked in manufacturing. For the general population a majority worked in the manufacturing sector (54.0 percent) rather than the commercial (40.5 percent). Similar patterns, though slightly less pronounced in terms of holding occupations in the commercial sector, marked the occupations of the heads of households of church joiners.[28]

Protestants exhibited a level of civic involvement befitting their prominent economic status. Male Protestant church members were so extensively involved in the city's social organizations that they formed an interconnected urban elite that penetrated virtually every aspect of the city's life. A substantial percentage of those who were officers or leaders in city organizations in the years from 1836–1860 can be found in lists of those who joined a Protestant church in the years before the Civil War. For men, the level of church joining was highest for business officers (39.0 percent), and educational administrators and teachers (38.7 percent), with somewhat lower percentages for those active in benevolence (25.3 percent) and moral reform (28.3 percent) and for government officeholders (25.2 percent), political party candidates (23.7 percent), and social and fraternal society officers (18.1 percent) (Tables 3.2 and 3.3).[29] As was true for Cleveland's male church joiners, women joiners were active in a variety of organizations. But in the case of women, all the activity was confined to benevolence, education, and moral reform (Tables 3.4 and 3.5). Given the incompleteness of Protestant church records (only three-fifths of members' names survive) and the difficulties of matching names from membership lists with those of lists of civic and social leaders, this is a substantial level of activity to find for church joiners. Had complete membership lists been available and if name matching were not so problematic, the percentages could have been 15–25 points higher (see Appendix).[30]

These patterns of property-holding, employment, and civic involvement help explain some of the power Protestants would have in the city, and the ways they might deploy that power. Male Protestants constituted a well-connected elite with access to money and formal institutional power, so they were poised to exercise authority in setting the economic and legislative agenda of the city. They vied to shape the public culture from a position of strength. They occupied a station inside the city's most influential institutions, so their customary way of operating would be to define the society's institutions and values, hoping to crowd out alternatives proposed by others outside the Protestant community.

Another social characteristic of the Protestant community that played a significant role in their identity as a community, is that its committed membership was two-thirds female. This demographic characteristic was fraught with significance for the identity of the Protestant community and for the ways their power might be established and maintained. Of those who joined from 1816 to 1860, 3/5 (60.6 percent) were women. For those who joined from 1836–1860, two-thirds (66.9 percent) were women. The percentages are similar for each of the five-year periods from 1816 to 1860. In these years, women made up less than one-half of the total Cleveland population (47.2 percent in 1850) (Table 3.6).[31]

This gender distribution prescribed the channels and strategies available to the Protestant community. Churches and religious life,

Table 3.2 Church Joining and Office-Holding for Men Active in Organization Types

	CHURCH JOINERS, 1816–60		CHURCH OFFICERS, 1836–60	
	N	%	N	%
OFFICERS IN ORGANIZATION TYPES				
Benevolence 1837 . . 60 (N=88)	44	50.0	25	25.3
Business 1837 . . 60 (N=172)	62	39.0	50	29.1
Education 1837 . . 60 (N=155)	60	38.7	40	25.8
Government 1837 . . 60 (N=254)	69	27.2	35	13.8
Government 1836–60 (N=396)	100	25.2	49	12.4
Temperance 1837 . . 60 (N=99)	39	44.3	23	26.1
Politics 1837 . . 60 (N=265)	72	27.2	35	13.2
Politics 1836–60 (N=553)	131	23.7	65	11.8
Social and Fraternal 1837 . . 60 (N=304)	55	18.1	21	6.9

Sources: See Appendix.

Notes: Church joiners are those who were traced to Protestant membership lists. Dates given in the form "1837 . . 60" are drawn primarily from the city directories of 1837, 1845, 1850, 1853, 1857, and 1860. Dates given in the form "1836–60" and 1816–60" come from newspapers, local histories, and church records, and are based on year by year lists. Individuals active in more than one organization in a particular organization type were counted only once. Those who joined more than one Protestant church were likewise counted only once.

with the allied tasks of character formation and informal education, were part of "women's sphere" in the early nineteenth century. It would be an exaggeration to say that churches were women's institutions since men still occupied the leadership positions. Men were the ministers, trustees, and other church officials.

Table 3.3 Church Joining for Men Who Participated
in Specific Organizations

	JOINED PROTESTANT CHURCH, *1816–60*	

OFFICERS AND PARTICIPANTS IN SPECIFIC ORGANIZATIONS

Benevolent Society Officers, 1837 . . 60

Mona's Relief (N=14)	1	(7.1%)
Protestant Orphan Asylum (N=9)	7	(77.8%)
Western Seamen's Friend Society (N=42)	20	(47.6%)
YMCA (N=21)	20	(95.2%)

Business Officers, 1837 . . 60

Banks (N=72)	42	(58.3%)
Boards of Trade (N=16)	5	(31.2%)
Railroads (N=18)	8	(44.4%)
Other Businesses (N=109)	34	(31.2%)

Education, 1837 . . 60

Business, Administrators (N=22)	8	(36.4%)
Industrial School Administrators (N=15)	10	(66.7%)
Public & Other Administrators (N=96)	35	(36.5%)
Public Schools, Teachers (N=15)	7	(46.7%)
Other Schools, Teachers (N=19)	8	(42.1%)

Government Officers, 1836-60

Cleveland, Major (N=188)	35	(18.6%)
Cleveland, Minor (N=107)	24	(22.4%)
County (N=51)	8	(15.7%)
Courts (N=36)	8	(22.2%)
Ohio City, Major (N=73)	38	(52.0%)
Ohio City, Minor (N=20)	12	(60.0%)

Government Officers, 1837 . . 60

Cleveland, Major (N=83)	16	(19.3%)
Cleveland, Minor (N=68)	20	(29.4%)
County (N=50)	8	(16.0%)
Courts (N=34)	7	(20.6%)
Ohio City, Major (N=38)	21	(55.3%)
Ohio City, Minor (N=14)	10	(71.4%)

(Table 3.3 con't.)

	JOINED PROTESTANT CHURCH, *1816–60*	

OFFICERS AND PARTICIPANTS IN SPECIFIC ORGANIZATIONS

Moral Reform Society Officers, 1837 . . 60

Cleveland Bible (N=13)	9	(69.2%)
Temperance (N=88)	39	(44.3%)

Press, 1837 . . 60

Herald and Herald & Gazette (N=9)	2	(22.2%)
Other Papers (N=23)	2	(8.7%)

Political Candidates, 1836–60

Citizens', Major (N=21)	6	(28.6%)
Citizens', Minor (N=29)	10	(34.5%)
Democrat, Major (N=110)	19	(17.3%)
Democrat, Minor (N=174)	24	(13.8%)
Free Soil, Minor (N=16)	6	(37.5%)
Liberty, Major (N=30)	16	(53.3%)
Liberty, Minor (N=25)	12	(48.0%)
People's, Major (N=29)	13	(44.8%)
Republican, Major (N=38)	12	(31.6%)
Republican, Minor (N=65)	23	(35.4%)
Union, Major (N=9)	3	(33.3%)
Union, Minor (N=27)	12	(44.4%)
Whig, Major (N=82)	19	(23.2%)
Whig, Minor (N=76)	17	(22.4%)
Workers', Major (N=18)	3	(16.7%)
Workers', Minor (N=49)	10	(20.4%)

Political Candidates, 1837 . . 60

Citizens', Major (N=9)	2	(22.2%)
Citizens', Minor (N=29)	10	(34.5%)
Democrat, Major (N=31)	5	(16.1%)
Democrat, Minor (N=78)	9	(11.5%)
Liberty, Major (N=12)	6	(50.0%)
Liberty, Minor (N=7)	6	(85.7%)
Republican, Major (N=18)	8	(44.4%)
Republican, Minor (N=40)	17	(42.5%)
Union, Major (N=9)	3	(33.3%)
Union, Minor (N=27)	12	(44.4%)

(Table 3.3 con't.)

	JOINED PROTESTANT CHURCH, 1816–60	

OFFICERS AND PARTICIPANTS IN SPECIFIC ORGANIZATIONS

Whig, Major (N=19)	4	(21.0%)
Whig, Minor (N=10)	3	(30.0%)
Workers', Major (N=18)	3	(16.7%)
Workers', Minor (N=22)	4	(18.2%)

Social & Fraternity Organization Officers, 1837 . . 60

Fire Companies (N=160)	33	(20.6%)
Masons (N=36)	7	(19.4%)
Military Companies (N=51)	2	(3.9%)
Odd Fellows (N=33)	4	(12.1%)
St. Andrew's (N=25)	9	(36.0%)
St. George's (N=16)	4	(25.0%)

Other Organizations, 1837 . . 60

Anti-Mexican War (N=8)	5	(62.5%)
Anti-Slavery, Officers (N=11)	7	(63.6%)
Culture, Officers (N=62)	29	(46.8%)
July 4 Committee (N=69)	15	(21.7%)
Science, Officer (N=10)	5	(50.0%)
Spiritualism (N=10)	1	(10.0%)
Workers', Officers (N=32)	6	(18.8%)

Sources: See Appendix.

Notes: The category "Anti-Mexican War" included participants in anti-Mexican War meetings. The category "Spiritualism" refers to supporters of spiritualism. The category "Press" includes only newspaper editors and publishers. The category "Other Businesses" includes incorporated companies and non-Cleveland railroads. "Major" political offices are Mayor and members of the Common Council. All other city officers are included in the category of "Minor" offices. For additional notes, see Table 3.2.

Still, women played a larger role in churches than in many other areas of social life. Churches were institutions that offered women a socially sanctioned arena for their activity. Although women were consigned to churches by men because this was considered an

Table 3.4   Church Joining for Women Active
in Organization Types

CHURCH JOINERS, 1816–60

OFFICERS IN ORGANIZATION TYPES

Benevolence 1837 . . 60 (N=88)	18	(20.4%)
Education 1837 . . 60 (N=141)	45	(31.9%)
Moral Reform 1837 . . 60 (N=15)	4	(26.7%)

Sources: See Appendix.

Notes: See Table 3.2.

appropriate, subordinate sphere for their activities, women turned this confinement into an opportunity to create avenues for social influence and power through moral reform and benevolent work. Voluntary organizations devoted to these efforts became the major public, visible avenue through which Protestants sought to influence their society. The predominant form of Protestant social activity, then, can be attributed to the initiative taken by women to exercise their influence within the only sphere society allowed them.[32]

When it came to exercising influence in the public culture, the predominance of women as members and the expectation that women would exercise their influence in the moral and spiritual realm meant that the nature of Protestant involvement was weighted toward the moral and persuasive approaches characteristic of voluntary societies. As a consequence, then, of the Protestant community's identity as a predominantly female group, religion's influence would tend toward the informal and the quasi-public, rather than the more direct and formal power available to business leaders and government officials.[33] Together, male and female Protestants represented an imposing array of potential power, both indirect and direct, that ran the gamut from moral instruction to city legislation.

For this Protestant community, which had begun to define itself in its various contests, particularly those over lavish buildings and pew rent, and which occupied such a prominent place in the community, influence in the public culture would depend to a considerable extent on the way they marshalled the resources at their command. The ministers who presided over the predomi-

Table 3.5   Church Joining for Women Who Participated
in Specific Organizations

	JOINED PROTESTANT CHURCH, 1816–60	
OFFICEHOLDERS AND PARTICIPANTS IN SPECIFIC ORGANIZATIONS		
Benevolent Society Officers 1837 . . 60		
Female Moral Reform (N=26)	4	(15.4%)
Martha Washington & Dorcas Society (N=18)	5	(27.8%)
Protestant Orphan Asylum (N=13)	6	(46.2%)
Religious Miss. & Sewing (N=37)	8	(21.6%)
Education, 1837 . . 60		
Public & Other Administrators (N=68)	20	(29.4%)
Public Schools, Teachers (N=78)	24	(30.8%)
Other Schools, Teachers (N=14)	9	(64.3%)
Moral Reform Society Officers, 1837 . . 60		
Temperance (N=15)	4	(26.7%)
Other Organizations		
Female Protective Union (N=25)	4	(16.0%)
Spiritualism (N=13)	0	(0.0%)
Sources: See Appendix.		

Notes: The category "Female Protective Union" includes both officers and members. For additional notes, see Table 3.2. Dates given in the form "1837 . . 60" are drawn primarily from the directories of 1837, 1845, 1850, 1853, 1857, and 1860.

The figures given are for those who joined an English-speaking Protestant church. Individuals who were officers of more than one society in a particular category were counted only once. Individuals who joined more than one Protestant church were counted only once.

nantly female, well-to-do, and civically involved Protestant church membership were themselves a formidable force. They had been educated at the best Eastern schools and seminaries. A few enjoyed the sort of long service that would allow them to cultivate influence in the city. Samuel Aiken presided over First Presbyterian Church for 23 years (1835–1858), James A. Thome served First Pres-

Table 3.6   Church Joiners by Sex

	Women		Men		Unknown
YEAR JOINED					
1836–40 (N=1277)	777	(63.1%)	454	(36.9%)	46
1841–45 (N=793)	482	(63.2%)	281	(36.8%)	30
1846–50 (N=865)	543	(66.8%)	270	(33.2%)	52
1851–55 (N=1219)	764	(65.7%)	399	(34.3%)	56
1856–60 (N=1956)	1300	(69.5%)	571	(30.5%)	85
1816–60 (N=6773)	4242	(65.5%)	2236	(34.5%)	295
1836–60 (N=5682)	3626	(66.9%)	1793	(33.1%)	263
1850 Census					
Sample (N=2422)	1143	(47.2%)	1279	(52.8%)	

Sources: See Appendix.

Note: Individuals who joined more than one church are only counted once.

byterian Church, Ohio City, for 12 years (1848–1860), Lewis Burton served St. John's Episcopal Church for 13 years (1847–1860), and James McGill served Associate Presbyterian Church for 12 years (1849–1861). The substantial salaries commanded by ministers of the city's leading churches testified to their security. Trinity Episcopal's minister earned $2,000 in 1859, and salaries in the $1,000–1,500 range were common.[34]

The buildings within which these ministers gathered their flocks embodied both symbolic and material resources for spreading Protestant influence in the city. Protestant churches were often built in prominent places around the public square or major intersections, and they became increasingly more elaborate and imposing. The landscape was becoming sacralized. The costs of First Presbyterian Church's buildings tell the most dramatic story of increasing wealth. The church's 1834 building cost $9,500. After a fire destroyed the building in 1853, the church spent $60,000 for a structure completed in 1855 that featured a 230 foot high steeple.[35]

Buildings were a valuable resource in the quest for public presence and influence in the early nineteenth century. Basements could be lent to public schools, church rooms served as congenial quarters for meetings of bank trustees, and the sanctuaries themselves might be made available for major civic celebrations, such as the arrival of a railroad linking Cleveland with Columbus and Cincinnati. By 1860, the Protestants' buildings, like the Protestants themselves, were becoming established as respectable, solid, and influential presences in the city.

The growth in the number of churches, the substantial size of membership, the length of service of a few leading ministers, and the opulence of buildings marked a degree of security and stability which left Protestants poised for influence. If Protestants could act in concert, and so form a united interdenominational front, the extent of their influence in the public culture would be magnified.

Harmony, cooperation, and unity did pervade much of Cleveland Protestantism, both within denominations and among churches and members of different denominations. Within denominations, cooperation was the rule. Many churches owed their founding to the help and cooperation of a "parent" church. Churches of the same denomination shared affiliations to local, regional, and national societies. Established ministers presided at the installation of new ministers of other churches, thereby giving their practical and symbolic approval. Churches were in the habit of inviting ministers of other city churches to preach, especially for holidays and special occasions, and the churches often held common services. When members transferred from one church to another, the new church required a letter certifying that the applicant was in good standing at the former church.[36] Relations between different Protestant denominations were generally smooth as well. Cleveland's Protestants generally followed the advice of J. Hyatt Smith of Second Baptist Church: "let us cultivate with religious industry a spirit of holy charity TOWARD ALL *who love our Lord and Savior Jesus Christ*. . . . May we labor together for the upbuilding of Zion. . . . " One indication that the city's Protestants took these words to heart is that churches invited ministers from other denominations to preach. This happened particularly when national denominational organizations met in Cleveland. When the New School Presbyterian Synod met in 1857, representatives preached at five Presbyterian churches (including one Old School one), three Methodist churches, three Baptist churches, one Congregational church, and one A.M.E. church.[37]

Other occasions brought Protestants from many denominations together. In the early years, especially, the need for buildings led churches to cooperate. Churches sometimes shared their quarters with beginning congregations. When church buildings were destroyed by fire, other churches offered space. Dedication ceremonies for new church buildings involved representatives of the city's various denominations in a ritual joining together. At a more personal level, ministers and their spouses paid visits to each other, thus maintaining cordial relationships with the leaders of other Protestant churches.

Of all the realms where Protestants from many denominations cooperated, none had more public impact than voluntary organizations. Societies organized for benevolence, moral reform, or evangelization often linked Protestants from many denominations in common cause. Whether it was concern for orphans, temperance, or tract distribution, Cleveland's Protestants joined hands in an affirmation of a shared Christian purpose.

Despite these cooperative efforts, there were serious obstacles to Protestant unity. Within denominations, and even within individual churches, theological controversies, organizational rivalries, personality disputes, and conflicting denominational loyalties drove Protestants apart. The resulting contests diminished the possibility that the Protestant community would be able to forge a united front when it came to imprinting their values on the public culture.[38] These disputes fleshed out some of the theological and organizational characteristics of the community that constituted such an important part of their understanding of themselves as religious institutions.

Although a widely shared evangelical theology united most Cleveland Protestants, there was enough divergence to undercut the possibility that a clear, consistent, widely accepted theology could be uniformly applied to social matters.[39] The most divisive controversy involved perfectionism. Samuel Aiken of First Presbyterian Church and Sherman Canfield of Second Presbyterian Church waged a campaign against the Oberlin Perfectionism represented by James Thome of First Presbyterian Church, Ohio City. Canfield served on a committee of the Cleveland Presbytery appointed in 1841 to refute "Oberlinism." He charged Oberlin Perfectionism with teaching that a state of entire sanctification was possible in this life, that some individuals have met all the demands of the divine law, and that the converted were competent witnesses to their own sanctification. Such doctrines, said Canfield, fostered spiritual pride and carnal security, and they brought contempt for pastoral instruction and advice. They led to antinomianism, where the law of love was obeyed but not the moral law in which it was embodied.[40] Underlying this dispute, as so often is the case when the charge of antinomianism is levelled, loomed the anxiety of established, moderate, and comfortable institutions about the disruptive potential of a more socially active, volatile theology and church unwilling to acknowledge the leadership and authority of the city's more established, Presbyterian churches.

Similar disputes about theology and controversies about church organization and practices bedeviled many congregations. Everything from what position to take on slavery, to who to choose as a minister, to whether a choir singing in the gallery had Scriptural support, brought controversy and schism.

First Presbyterian Church, founded in 1820, is a case in point. The church's location on Public Square in the center of the city symbolized its potential for influence. Yet the church was continually wracked by controversy and division which, if nothing else, precluded a completely focused, united effort by the congregation to marshal its resources to shape the public culture. The earliest disputes involved whether the church would be organized along Congregational or Presbyterian lines. First Presbyterian Church was one of many "Plan of Union" churches resulting from the decision of Congregationalists and Presbyterians in New England to unite to missionize the West. Despite the efforts of the early Congregationalist missionaries and the church's early Congregationalist majority, the church tilted toward Presbyterianism, lending some credence to William S. Kennedy's contention in his history of the Plan of Union that "the milk from Congregational cows is being turned into Presbyterian butter." With the arrival of Samuel Aiken as minister in 1835, an uneasy truce was established regarding the church's form of government.[41]

The price paid by First Presbyterian Church for its uncomfortable merger of Presbyterian and Congregational elements was repeated turmoil. Every change in the balance of members, and every new issue that revived latent differences, threatened a schism. Congregational leanings played a part in the schisms that led to the founding of First Presbyterian Church, Ohio City (1834), and Free Presbyterian Church (1850).[42]

The organization of these two new Presbyterian churches illustrated some of the other issues that increased the likelihood that theological or organizational disagreements would ripen into schism. When First Presbyterian Church, Ohio City, was formed in 1834, its thirty-seven members were drawn largely from First Presbyterian Church (Cleveland). The First Presbyterian Church (Cleveland) records mentioned the convenience of a closer church as the reason for the split. Later histories of First Presbyterian, Ohio City, however, contend that it was formed as a result of the weak antislavery position of First Presbyterian Church's minister, Samuel Aiken. The Ohio City church's first minister, James A. Thome, whose perfectionism had worried Aiken, enjoyed unassailable antislavery credentials; he had been one of the students who left Lane Seminary in Cincinnati after complaining of its lukewarm antislavery stance.[43]

An attempt in 1837 to establish Second Presbyterian Church was a reaction not only to Aiken's conservative antislavery principles, but also to the high prices of pews. The church developed from a series of meetings held by Asa Mahan and Charles Grandison Finney, the nationally known evangelist. The church was abandoned after one year, and the members returned to First Presbyterian Church.[44]

A second try at forming a church to be known as Second Presbyterian Church was made in 1841, again by members from First Presbyterian Church dissatisfied with Aiken's moderate position on slavery. The new church was no more successful than its predecessor. It was divided by disputes over Millerism and perfectionism and lasted just three years.[45]

The final antebellum schism from First Presbyterian Church was successful. Free Presbyterian Church was founded in 1850 after revival meetings conducted in First Presbyterian Church. Benajah Barker was converted, and he joined with other members dissatisfied with Aiken's continued moderation on the slavery issue. By taking the name Free Presbyterian Church, the church highlighted not only its antislavery principles but also its intention of having free pews as opposed to the high prices charged for pews in First Presbyterian Church.[46]

Although the issues were different, Episcopalians, too, suffered through a wrenching series of schisms that makes it difficult to imagine them as part of an evangelical united front. The central figure of the disputes was a minister, Gideon B. Perry. The saga of Perry and the Episcopal churches began in 1846 when Perry was asked by the bishop to fill in while Trinity Episcopal awaited the arrival of its new minister, Lloyd Windsor. For the next ten years Perry was a loose cannon rolling around the deck of Cleveland

Episcopalianism. Perry's interim ministry at Trinity was so well received by many in the congregation that they wanted Windsor's invitation withdrawn. Trinity's vestry refused, so some of Trinity's members left in 1846 to form St. Paul's Episcopal Church under Perry's leadership. Theological differences lay at the heart of much of the controversy. Grace and Trinity were more High Church, while Perry was Low.[47]

A later history of Grace Church captures the bitterness that the founding of St. Paul's Church engendered. The history contends that some of the prominent members of St. Paul's Church were indiscreet enough to say that its object was to break down Trinity and Grace Episcopal Churches. Grace Episcopal Church's official history also took a jaundiced view of Perry's methods. It noted what must have seemed to them so damning as to need little elaboration—Perry had been a Baptist before taking Holy Orders. The indictment of Perry was extensive:

> By private conversations with sundry members of the two existing parishes, by calls at their house[s], by representations to them of questions of partizan [sic] character which had not hitherto been well understood, by his manners which were attractive to some, and finally by his pulpit eloquence, he succeeded in alienating the minds of a considerable number of persons from their parochial connections.[48]

Trinity and Grace protested the founding of the new church to Ohio's Bishop McIlvaine. They expressed their distaste for Perry, and maintained that there was no need for another Episcopal church in Cleveland. Trinity called the establishment of St. Paul's "a measure that appears to us to be not only wrong in itself but fraught with evil to the peace, prosperity, and growth of the church here." Grace and Trinity invoked a church canon that required approval of the town's existing Episcopal ministers for a new church to be established.[49]

Despite the canon, Bishop McIlvaine declined to interfere in St. Paul Episcopal Church's founding. He noted that canon law was unenforceable in this instance since civil law sanctioned the founding of the church. The dispute highlighted the limits of denominational control in antebellum America. Civil law, not ecclesiastical, prevailed and sheltered Perry and his church from the complaints of the existing Episcopal churches.[50]

Perry was the center of another maelstrom a few years later. After serving St. Paul's Church for six years, Perry left with 45 of his parishioners in 1852 to rejoin Grace Episcopal Church as associate rector. Grace's minister was Lawson Carter, who was chosen, according to a later account, because the church was in debt, and Carter was "reputed to be a gentleman of large pecuniary means and his friends had intimated that he possessed a benevolent disposition." Because of Carter's age and health, the church named Perry as associate rector. Although in taking the job Perry had given "earnest protestations of the harmony which it would be his care to cultivate," he again brought controversy in his wake.[51]

As associate rector, Perry went his own way, conducting services and sponsoring activities without Carter's approval. A committee of the vestry acquiesced, saying that Carter and Perry both had the power of the rector. When Carter appealed, Bishop McIlvaine had another decision to make. This time he ruled against Perry, deciding in 1856 that Carter had sole power. But again, ecclesiastical law did not provide the basis for the decision. McIlvaine decided that relations between the two were covered by a specific civil contract, the agreement they made when Perry joined, and not by ecclesiastical authority or common law. Despite losing the decision, Perry remained at Grace Episcopal Church, and so did controversy.[52]

True to his reputation, Carter proved to be a financial guardian angel. He gave the church a $5,674.93 loan with interest that was secured by a mortgage. In 1856 the church decided to take out a loan to pay the interest owed to Carter. Because of a new state incorporation law, the vestry felt a new vestry election was necessary in 1856 to make sure the new loan agreement by them would be valid. This set the stage for yet another Perry-led controversy. When Carter refused to read the notice for the election in a way Perry approved, Perry objected. When the election was held, Perry's supporters captured control of the vestry. The vestry proceeded to vote to sell the church building and its land to pay off the church debt to Carter, even though they had no definite plans for a substitute building.[53]

In November, Carter sent a letter to the members of the church in which he said the sale was "an abuse of power, unnecessary, contrary to the wishes of the congregation, and if consummated will defraud the parish of several thousands of dollars." Carter protested that negotiations for the sale were conducted secretly, without telling anyone of the names of the buyers or the proposed terms of the sale. The vestry, charged Carter, refused to entertain an offer to pay half the debt to prevent the sale.[54]

A week after Carter's letter, 41 pew owners and donors protested that no sale should be made until the congregation specifically approved. Since an Ohio law prohibited the sale of church property without a vote of the parishioners, the sale was stopped for a time. In a move that further tangled an already confusing situation, Carter transferred his loan to Samuel Mather, a leading member of the church and a figure prominent in business, sometime in this period. Mather now sued the vestry to force the sale. Eventually, the building was sold to Westminster Presbyterian Church.[55]

Such was the turmoil and division brought by Gideon Perry. In fifteen years as an Episcopal minister in Cleveland, Perry had disrupted the two oldest Episcopal churches in the city, created a third church, then had taken over one of the churches that had earlier opposed him. This exacted a considerable cost in terms of denominational unity. It is hard to imagine Gideon Perry and Lawson Carter joining hands in a benevolent reform or a moral crusade to form a Protestant evangelical united front.

There is a way, however, in which the disruption brought by Perry and the disputes swirling around First Presbyterian Church may not have been as debilitating as on the face of it they seem. Instead of being divisive and a hindrance to exercising influence, contests such as the ones over pew rents and antislavery can be understood as ways Protestants went about clarifying their values and establishing their place in social life. A minority of Cleveland's Protestants favored a system of voluntary contributions in order to broaden the appeal of the churches to the middle and lower classes. The majority cast their lot with pew rents and sales, which brought the kinds of members which located the Protestant churches at the top of the social pyramid with well-connected, high income Clevelanders.

The rifts and tensions within individual churches, denominations, and the Protestant community that generally endangered unity were not the only internal constraints on the Protestants' ability to unite in deploying its resources. Most of Cleveland's ministers did not enjoy the longevity and security of First Presbyterian Church's Samuel Aiken. Only a half-dozen Cleveland ministers served longer than 5 years. Methodist ministers customarily served only a year. The average stay of the 168 Protestant ministers who served in the years before 1860 was 1.8 years, scarcely long enough to build a following, become familiar with the community, and develop influence.[56]

The ability of the Protestant churches to mount a sustained effort to shape the city's development was also limited by financial instability. Congregations needed to provide for their own economic needs first. For all their lavish building programs, churches were seldom financially secure. As they constructed and maintained larger and larger buildings, churches were driven deeper into debt. Trinity Episcopal Church's vestry records testify to the worry over indebtedness. In 1843 the vestry met "to take into consideration the indebtedness of the Church & to devise (if possible) some means of escape from *everlasting disgrace*."[57]

Even when they prospered, Cleveland's churches were not able or willing to bring all their resources to bear on the city. The churches' broad national and international concerns diverted their attention and money away from Cleveland. They engaged in mission work abroad and in the West, and they addressed national issues such as slavery. Unlike controversies over wealth and ostentation, these multiple loyalties occasioned no debate but were an unexamined expression of the wide concerns and commitments of the city's Protestants. Later in the century urban churches would focus more of their efforts on the immediate environment, but in the antebellum years the commitment of Protestant churches to the city was hedged by these diffuse loyalties. This is evident in the projects to which churches contributed money, as reported in their denominational records. Protestant church contributions (excluding money spent for building and operating expenses) can be divided into three types: "international" contributions to foreign missions; "national" contributions to home missions, Bible and tract societies and Sunday School unions; and "local" contributions within the city, including efforts to build and sustain existing and mission churches and support for city moral reform and benevolent projects such as poor relief, the Bible Society, the Orphan Asylum, and the Industrial School. Denominational records and the more detailed records of four leading churches provide a rough estimate of the financial commitments of Cleveland's Protestant churches. The churches' contributions to local efforts were substantial, but still less than their outlays for national and foreign projects.

Approximately 40–60 percent of their donations went to local concerns, such as the Protestant orphan asylum or poor relief societies; 20–30 percent was spread over the rest of the continent, supporting Indian missions in Wisconsin, black churches in Michigan, churches in other areas of Ohio, Bible distribution, or Sunday School unions; and 20–30 percent left the nation for "steamy Calcutta," "Greenland's icy shores," or other foreign mission stations.[58]

Given their internal divisions, financial constraints, and concerns outside the city, the Protestant community which entered the city-shaping arena was something less than an evangelical united front. But the contests over their social, ecclesiastical, and theological identities did not fracture them to such an extent that they were powerless as they moved into the contest over the public culture outside their doors. Their potential for influence was circumscribed but not negligible. Protestants were neither a cohesive bloc nor an atomistic conglomeration of individual worshippers. Despite all their differences and disputes, they could marshal substantial resources. Their numbers, their money, their accomplished ministers, and their well-to-do, prominent, and motivated membership all provided a foundation for shaping the city's public culture.

In the contests over self-definition, Protestants created the foundation for substantial, though not unbounded, influence in the larger contest for power in the public culture. Because Protestants accommodated their identity to their social characteristics, their power would be exercised along particular lines. As a leadership elite with connections in all areas of the city's life, the men had a stake in the developing institutions and values of the commercial city that aligned them with the city's boosters. They would not need to adopt the prophetic role of confronting the powers-that-be with religious demands—they were the powers-that-be. Being enmeshed in the city's power structure meant that they could establish and maintain influence by the more subtle means of working out an accommodation between their religious ideals and the developing values, attitudes, and institutions of the public culture of the commercial city.

The predominately female church membership also shaped the contours of the public role of Protestants. Many of the spouses of women members were part of the male leadership elite of the city, so women could exercise their influence indirectly on them. Even more importantly, Protestant women tirelessly worked to enlarge the sphere allotted to them and in the process moved more deeply into the public culture. Their prime vehicle would be the voluntary society. Although often described as private institutions, voluntary societies worked in public settings, so much so that they must be considered public, or at least quasi-public institutions. The voluntary society served as women's route into the public world. Women had been allotted the seemingly private task of being moral guardians and character-formers. They carried that assignment beyond the narrow confines of the family out into society in a variety of societies dedicated to poor relief, orphans, and temperance. These organizations promoted what they considered to be appropriate values and attitudes as well as providing model institutions for organizing society. Their creative private–public hybrid set the tone of Protestant social involvement. Unable to invoke the direct and massive power Protestants might have enjoyed had they been a state-established church, been completely unified, or if the members had been predominantly male, Protestants concentrated on exercising influence through an array of official and unofficial channels—voluntary societies, laws, benevolent institutions, moral reform societies, participation in public ceremonies—which relied on indirect and informal uses of authority as much as direct and formal ones. Because of their social characeristics and because of the way they resolved their internal contests Protestants developed a curious but potent mixture of strategies—official and unofficial, direct and indirect, formal and informal, public and private—as their means of shaping the values and institutions of the public culture of the nascent commercial settlement outside their walls.

PART TWO

Vying for Power

Chapter 4

Anointing the
Commercial Economy

The contests within the Protestant community honed their identity: as a well-connected leadership elite with extensive involvement in the business life of the city, Protestant church members were prone to look on the development of the commercial economy with favor. Nevertheless, the extent of their support and the form that support might take was not predetermined. At issue was the degree to which they would embrace the commercial economy. Their predisposition to applaud an economy in which they were so well-situated clashed with traditions about wealth and the sabbath inherited from New England Protestantism. Their attitude to the commercial economy was thus beset with tensions, which they resolved over the course of the quarter-century before 1860 partly through a series of conflicts—over keeping the Sabbath, most importantly—and partly through an accommodation to features of the economy such as factories and railroads. In a gradual process throughout these years, they adjusted their ideas and practice to their social status as the city's elite.

Some of these issues they faced had already been resolved, and some of the adjustments already made, in the "contests within the contest" over lavish buildings and pew rents (chapter 3). In a Protestant community containing members from all ranks of society, it was the well-to-do who had managed to set the tone for Protestants as a group. This laid the basis for an ideology that they would take outside the churches in the contest over the formation of the public culture. They would enter this public arena convinced that the values and institutions that served the interests of the leaders of the commercial society would carry all the members of the society to moral and material glory.

The city's first bank and its first church were founded in the same year, 1816, symbolically establishing the close relationship that would develop between Protestants and Cleveland's economic development. For the most part, their activity was not as dramatic as when Reverend Pickands led Ohio City boosters in the Bridge War. The role of the Protestant elite in shaping the public culture was more subtle. Leading Protestants stamped their imprint on their society in a variety of ways, most of them informal and indirect. But if the means were seldom as dramatic as Rev. Pickands's, the result was along the same lines—Cleveland Protestants joined forces with city boosters to promote economic development and material progress.

Protestants assumed that they necessarily must address the new economic world emerging all around them. Such a central part of the public culture as economic development and the values, attitudes, and institutions associated with it could not escape their concern. Samuel Aiken, minister of First Presbyterian Church, argued that Christians, especially Christian ministers, needed to "watch the signs of the times." They should "see God, and lead the people to see Him, in all the affairs of the world, whether commercial, political, or religious."[1]

When they watched the signs of the times in the 1830s and early 1840s, many Protestants worried. Their concerns centered on the destructive impact of the commercial economy. Cleveland Protestants inherited a gnawing worry that mammon would attract the loyalty properly due to religion. The Cleveland Presbytery feared that the new economic order might lead to a loss of piety similar to what had happened in the days of their ancestors. The religion of the Pilgrims had produced industry and frugality, the Presbytery noted. This in turn brought wealth, and in two or three generations wealth "[a]te up vital piety." The Presbytery feared that a similar process was under way in the nineteenth century: "In clearing farms and building houses; in multiplying flocks & herds; making plank-roads & rail-roads & building manufactories & steamboats, speculating in lands and stocks & flying about the country for profit or pleasure,—the time and heart of man are engrossed,—the soul, eternity and God are forgotten; the gospel dispersed is like seed among thieves & on a rock, & the preacher labors in vain, & spends his strength for naught." Others shared the Presbytery's worries. According to Gideon Perry, an Episcopal minister, "the present is an age of business, of enterprise, of bustle,

experiment, of daring and laborious adventure. The love of pecuniary gain is the presiding spirit."[2]

First Presbyterian Church's Rev. Samuel Aiken, in a lecture on
"Commercial Honesty" in 1854 at the Euclid Street Presbyterian
Church, shared Perry's distaste for the overemphasis on money
making. Aiken was uncomfortable with the ethos of his era: "This
inordinate desire to become suddenly rich was the sin of our time.
People were not content with the hum-drum monotony of the
farm, or the store, or the workshop. . . . "[3]

The suspicion that devotion to money making undermined
moral constraints was further ground for discomfort with the new
economic order. In 1860 the Cuyahoga County Temperance Society noted that professed temperance supporters and members of
evangelical churches owned buildings which they leased for selling
liquor. The Society considered these individuals nothing less than
"joint partners in guilt." The lesson the Society drew was a harsh
one: "the devotion of such men to temperance principles is secondary and subservient to their pecuniary interests."[4]

To many, business and economic life were part of a worldly
arena that competed with the spiritual demands of religion. In his
twenty-fifth anniversary sermon, Aiken recalled that during the
business depression of 1837 people went to work to recover what
they had lost and many forsook the duties of religion to pursue
their worldly gains. In professing his experience for First Baptist
Church in 1853, Charles Wheeler admitted that "he had for a long
time had a desire to know and love the savior. His business had
prevented him from taking a decided stance. About three months
since he lost a child, and he felt it was a direct call from God, and
he could now say with truth, he had come to a decision to serve
him."[5]

The fate of the Bethel Church building in 1850 represented
both the literal and the symbolic fulfillment of the worry that religion would be displaced by mammon. The Bethel Church's Chapel
was on ground needed by the Cleveland, Columbus and Cincinnati Railroad, so the church sold its building to the railroad for use
as a car house. The *Plain Dealer* suggested the dimensions of the
change: "when the big doors are thrown open, exposing the full
form of an iron horse snorting steam from its nostrils, it forms a
great contrast between the mild and good Father Day, who for-
merly occupied its pulpit." The newspaper of the Western Seamen's
Friend Society, a group founded and dominated by Presbyterian

Church members as an evangelical project to reach the seamen, noted that there were those who loved the Bethel, "[b]ut this is an age of improvements, and even churches must make way for their onward march."[6]

Such soaring hopes about the benefits of progress and improvements brought by the technological fruits of the developing economy eventually overcame the worries of Cleveland Protestants. They adjusted to the commercial society through countless decisions and small accommodations typified by the Seaman Society's acquiescence in the replacement of the Bethel Church by a railroad building, and by the many Cleveland ministers who waxed euphoric about new technological developments such as telegraphs and railroads. Speaking of the Atlantic Telegraph in a sermon in Boston, Rev. E. H. Chapin of First Presbyterian Church, Ohio City, contended that "it is not man's glory but God's glory that is unfolded in the gradual development of human knowledge and human power." He found God's hand "sweeping through events." Chapin's approach brought the Atlantic Telegraph out of the economic and scientific realm, and into a higher one: "In this view, scientific achievement, expanding beyond all mercenary uses, becomes the Shekinal of the living God—at once His awful veil of mystery, and the signal of His presence." When the nation's first gaslights were turned on in 1849, the *Plain Dealer* welded together boosterism and religion with a familiar religious metaphor: "We are soon to be a city on a hill whose light cannot be hid."[7]

The railroad, especially, excited Cleveland's leading Protestants. In this, they were not alone. For many Americans the railroad was the symbol of the new era. Clevelanders, like others, described railroads using "the rhetoric of the technological sublime"—imputing to the machine qualities formerly reserved for objects of religious power and grandeur.[8]

Samuel Aiken, the dean of Cleveland's ministers, put the seal of approval on the new era in remarks celebrating the arrival of the Cleveland, Columbus, and Cincinnati Railroad in 1851. Aiken saw "the hand of the Almighty" at work in the vast system of railroads, despite their commercial intent. Aiken did not let the doubts of others cloud his sunny view of the benefits of this new technological wonder for religion and for the rest of society:

> Some good people, I am aware, look with a suspicious eye upon the iron-horse. They fancy there is a gloomy destiny in it—a

power to subvert old and established customs;—to change the laws and ordinances of God and man;—to introduce moral and political anarchy, ignorance and impiety, and to make our degenerate race more degenerate still.

Now, I am not troubled with such spectres. I look for evils to be multiplied with the increase of travel. But order will reign—law will reign—religion will reign, because there will be an increase also of counteracting agents. If the effect should be the increase of wealth only, we might well predict fearful consequences. To look upon the railroad simply as an auxiliary to commerce—as a great mint for coining money; is to take but a superficial and contracted view of it. If we would contemplate it in all its bearings, we must consider it as a new and vast power, intended by Providence to act upon religion and education—upon the civilization and character of a nation in all the complicated interests of its social organism.[9]

Aiken had worried that the era was being corrupted by the "inordinate desire to become suddenly rich" and was concerned that people would not be content with the "hum-drum" monotony of the farm, or the store, or the workshop, yet he applauded the railroad, the instrument of all these changes.[10]

The approval by prominent Protestant ministers of the new technological developments of the commercial society set a pattern of accommodation that typified Protestants' contribution to the formation of public culture. Religious worries about mammon were overcome by the conviction that moral and material progress necessarily coincided.[11]

Nevertheless, many antebellum Protestants' anxieties about wealth and loss of piety coexisted with millennial hopes that each new discovery heralded the Kingdom. Somehow the tensions had to be resolved, and Protestants had to establish some priorities that would allow them to address the new era in a consistent, effective way. A series of controversies forced Protestants to determine their priorities. By spending lavishly on new church buildings and selling pews instead of adopting a voluntary donation system, Protestants had already decided within their own community to accept much of the ethos of the commercial economy. A controversy outside their doors, over the keeping of the Sabbath, raised the same issues in the public arena. No other issue so starkly raised the issues of God and mammon, the reconciliation of which went far toward determining the shape of the public culture being formed.

Attempts to maintain the Sabbath tested the resolve of Protestants on nettlesome issues, such as the appropriate degree of observance, or the allowable accommodations which could be made to the forces of material progress. For many Protestants, keeping the Sabbath was the litmus test by which they would judge the developing city. Any society whose practices endangered the Sabbath would be morally suspect. Sabbath-breaking confirmed many church members' suspicions that the pursuit of wealth and progress were proceeding at the expense of religion. Rev. L. D. Mix of First Methodist Church despaired in 1843 of the desecration of the Sabbath brought by those unwilling to have their religious ideals restrain their self-interest: "We live in a world in which men are operated upon by their interests. There are many who are pretty good Christians, so long as religion does not come in contact with their interests."[12]

Sabbath observance would assure that economic development was conducted with due acknowledgment of the priority of God and religion. For Episcopal Bishop Charles McIlvaine, the Sabbath was the anchor that kept Americans from succumbing to the "almost insane excitement after worldly gain." Didn't the morality and religion of the land, and the bodily and mental soundness of its people, depend on "that sudden stop in the pressure, that resting place in the struggle, that sweet opportunity to think of something better and purer than earthly gain, when time is given for voices from another world and the calls of the God of grace to be listened to?" Conversely, refusing to adhere to the Sabbath would lead to ruin. Truman P. Handy, an active Baptist and bank president, was sure that most of the recent bank failures in Ohio could be attributed to a habitual disregard of the Sabbath by their officers or managers.[13]

That the Sabbath should be observed was the consistent testimony of Cleveland's ministers, churches, and church members. The sticking point was how. Underneath all the rhetorical affirmations of Sabbath observance lay difficult decisions about what was appropriate in individual cases. These more complex issues were the substance of a considerable number of church rulings and disciplinary cases. Out of the give-and-take between churches, members charged with transgressions, and the economic life outside the doors of the church there emerged a Protestant resolution of the competing demands of God and mammon.

In 1837 First Presbyterian Church drew the line at owning stock in a business that operated on the Sabbath. The two poles of the dilemma emerge clearly in their resolution, which combined a hearty endorsement of railroads and canals with an admonition to refrain from investing in Sabbath-breaking enterprises:

> Resolved that in view of the great increase of Railroads Canals and other objects of internal improvement we deem it our duty both as citizens and Christians to lend them our means and influence, believing as we do that they are to be sources of great moral benefit or evil to our land; and that while we regard such objects as worthy [of] our attention We deem it a paramount duty (recognizing the principles of the fourth Commandment as obligatory) to decline taking stocks in such railroads, Canals and business associations, unless those associations will respect the Sabbath by making it a day of Sacred rest. . . . [14]

Many of the church disciplinary cases involved retailers selling goods on Sunday. In a First Presbyterian Church case in 1839 a member was called on by a committee concerned that he had sold meat to the stewards of steamboats on the Sabbath. The problem was solved, said the committee, because the member "had sold out," or so arranged his interest in his business so that he could personally avoid selling meat on the Sabbath. In this and other cases the solution was not to insist on strict compliance—the member did not close up shop on Sunday—but rather demand only that actual work by the member cease.[15]

The case of S. N. Herrick, of First Presbyterian Church, Ohio City, also brought out the ambiguities of enforcing Sabbath observance. Herrick appeared before the church in 1839 after being cited for selling milk on the Sabbath. In his defense, he claimed that some people, particularly babies, needed milk every day. The church might have found this acceptable. Unfortunately for Herrick, it concluded that he served all his customers on the Sabbath, not just those with infants, and that he had been seen passing through the streets ringing his bell. Herrick was suspended from membership, but the case did not end there. In December of 1841 the Cleveland Presbytery affirmed the view that delivering milk on Sunday was improper, but stated that, "in the present divided state of opinion," it was against suspending anyone for that purpose if the transgressor's Christian character was otherwise unexceptionable. Once again, a church had compromised its insistence on keeping the Sabbath, in this case by treating the violation as a minor transgression.[16]

Another dilemma in terms of Sabbath enforcement was raised by the situation of Henry Stevens, the president of the street railway. He had a convenient answer to complaints of running on Sunday—he was delivering people to church. He put on extra cars before and after services, but ran no cars during the meeting hours of 10:30–12:00 noon, and 7:30–9:00 p.m. He was allowed to continue operations.[17]

Allowing compromises such as these left Protestants open to charges of hypocrisy. According to the *Boatman's Magazine*, "Some men, of whom better things might be expected, enter into churches retired from the waters, and leave their capital, their counting houses, clerks and servants, to keep up the hum of business and the jargon of profaneness where the stillness of judgment ought to prevail."[18]

No more telling example exists of the conflict between the euphoria about technological progress and the fear that Sabbath observance was threatened than the response of one of the city's leading ministers, First Presbyterian Church's Aiken. He acknowledged that the Sabbath, "this sacred season of rest, . . . is shamefully desecrated by steamers, rail-cars and other modes of conveyance." Aiken did not find this reason to withdraw his approval, though. He argued that religious principles would survive through both the good intentions and the self-interest of the railroad owners. Not only would railroad operators heed the Bible out of religious conviction, but they would also find that their workers would be refreshed and invigorated by a day of rest. "The truth is," argued Aiken, "the law of the Sabbath is written, not only in the Bible, but upon the constitution of man; and such are the arrangements of Providence that it cannot be violated without incurring loss." Providence, in short, guaranteed that human nature and economic incentives would mirror divine injunctions to ensure the harmony of the new economic imperatives and religion.[19]

The Sabbath cause faced an uphill battle. Sabbath advocates struck a central nerve in a city built on commerce. The Cleveland Presbytery diagnosed the weakness of the Sabbath cause in observing that "the business enterprise of the nation seems universally to disregard it." In the Sabbath fight, economic interest and convenience overwhelmed religious injunctions. The technological and economic advantages of running steamboats and railroads seven days a week made the Sabbath vulnerable. Undermined by their own ambivalence and pushed by the weight of the forces of economic development, the Protestant Sabbath campaign enjoyed only minimal success. Sometimes agreements were reached with individual owners, but the city's transportation network largely ignored the Sabbath.[20]

A pattern of accommodation to economic development, implicit in the resolution of the Sabbath controversy, characterized Protestant decision-making in the process of the formation of the public culture of the commercial city. Interconnections between business leaders and church members furnished one of the foundations of the accommodation. Protestants were a central part of the business elite which had a stake in commercial development. They were the owners and directors of the railroads, banks, and other business organizations of the city. Thirty-nine percent of those identified as officers of business organizations between 1837 and 1860 can be found on lists of those who joined New England-derived Protestant churches (Table 3.2). The percentages are even higher for railroad directors (8 of 18, 44.4 percent) and bank officials (42 of 72, 58.3 percent) (Table 3.3).[21] Church members such as Truman P. Handy, George Mygatt, and Benjamin Rouse were influential and active in religion as well as business. Their presence in the pews, along with others like them, guaranteed that Protestant churches would reflect, to some degree, the interests and vision of the leaders of the city's commercial life.

The leadership elite fashioned an antebellum version of the Protestant ethic as their instrument for shaping the public culture in ways that would appeal to all ranks of society as well as reassure Protestants of their own righteousness. There is no better example than the remarks T. P. Handy presented before the Cleveland Bible Society in 1856. A prominent banker and an active member of the city's Baptist churches, Handy spoke in favor of the resolution "The Bible, the only sure basis of our prosperity in business life." Handy was conscious of the theological danger of attributing success to faith, and of identifying faith with works. In supporting the resolution he "would not by this, assert that wealth is certain [to] follow to all who follow its teachings, nor is this world a state of final retribution, nor does wealth of itself bring happiness." Having made his bow to theological distinctions, Handy rushed headlong into a glorification of business and a complete blurring of the lines between faith, work, and success: "Covenant blessings were promised God's chosen people of old, in proportion to their observance of His laws, and no less are those blessings in store for us, just in proportion as we follow the Bible as the basis of our conduct."[22]

The lessons Handy drew from the Bible would have warmed Max Weber's (and Ben Franklin's) heart. Handy claimed to have found the following truths demonstrated in every age: "That a life of *honesty* in our dealings with our fellow-men, habits of *industry* in our daily pursuits, a sacred *regard* for the *Sabbath*, *temperance* in all things, *prudence* and *economy*, *liberality* in the cause of religion, and *kindness* to the *poor*, are the virtues upon the exercise of which, wealth is most frequently promised, and upon which our happiness and prosperity chiefly depend."[23]

When Handy included kindness to the poor as one of the elements on which happiness and prosperity depended, he embraced another crucial element of the Protestant accommodation to economic development—the doctrine of service and stewardship. The pre-Civil War years raised the notion of service to unaccustomed prominence. Appeals for benevolence were continually aimed at the wealthy with the argument that the fruits of their success must be used in service to others. As James A. Bolles argued in appealing for funds for the Trinity Church Home for the Sick and Friendless, wealth was a blessing when it could be employed for the permanent benefit of mankind. Giving money to a worthy cause would be a chance "for some individual to become the instrument of the greatest possible happiness to his race."[24]

By engaging in service, well-to-do Clevelanders could rest assured that wealth would not undermine their religion. In the final analysis, Cleveland's Protestants were critical not of wealth, which could be turned to pious uses, but of the devotion to wealth, which deflected attention from religion. As Rev. Samuel Aiken of First Presbyterian Church said, "wealth is power, and when properly used, is a source of unspeakable good."[25] By putting their wealth to use in benevolent organizations, wealthy Clevelanders could quell any doubts they or others might have had that their riches, or the manner in which those riches were accumulated, were unchristian. (See Chapter 5 for a detailed discussion of benevolence.)

The ideology of service provided a vehicle to spread their influence in the public culture. It allowed Protestants to appeal to middle- and lower-income groups and so attract converts to their commercial ideology and interests. The ideology of service also allowed them to resolve ambiguities in their commercial ideology as well as their consciences. They could appeal to all ranks of society while remaining unapologetic advocates of a commercial economy that worked in their interest.[26]

A climate of cooperation and shared objectives established between businesses and Protestant churches formed another part of the accommodation of the city's Protestants to the wealth and progress of the new era which set the tone of the evolving public culture. In a symbolic moment of cooperation right at the start of the railroad era, in 1839, the members of First Methodist Church were among the official groups welcoming the arrival of the first locomotive. Rev. Samuel Aiken of First Presbyterian Church presided over the celebration marking the completion of the Cleveland, Columbus, and Cincinnati Railroad. Aiken spoke in his church on "The Moral View of Rail Roads" to an audience including the governor, members of the legislature, and other dignitaries. This moment, as much as any other, epitomizes the alliance between Protestants and the early nineteenth-century commercial economy.[27]

There were other instances of a pattern of cooperation between Protestants and business.The result at its vaguest is encapsulated in the injunctions incorporated in 1857 into the statement of principles of Cleveland's Board of Trade, a forerunner to the Chamber of Commerce: "The objects of this association are, the promotion of integrity and good faith, and just and equitable principles in business transactions, and generally to protect the rights and advance the commercial, mercantile, and financial interests of the city." The coupling of the economic interests of the city with integrity, good faith, and just and equitable principles represented an affirmation that there was no inherent conflict between the dynamic of business and the dictates of religious principles.[28]

Cooperation sometimes took curious forms. In an ironic twist to the Biblical story of Jesus finding the money-changers in the temple, a visitor to Cleveland on the night of June 14, 1844, would have found the temple in the office of the money-changers. On that evening, the trustees and the session of Second Presbyterian Church met at the offices of T. P. Handy and Co. At the time, Handy, the formulator of the Protestant ethic described above, was operating as a commission merchant and banker. Trinity Episcopal

Church's officers often met in the offices of Samuel L. Mather, another prominent local businessman.[29]

In addition to supporting benevolent projects, businesses provided a number of other practical services to churches and their members. Leading railroads carried delegates to the state temperance convention in Columbus in 1860 for half fare, just as they had earlier taken Republicans to their convention in Chicago. Closer to home, Henry Stevens, who had escaped church discipline over the issue of running his Omnibus line on Sundays, furnished rides to picnics for Sunday School students and donated some of the profits to the erection of Third Baptist Church.[30]

Cleveland's two business colleges incorporated religion in their studies, which reinforced the pattern of Protestant participation in the commercial economy. In the mid- and late-1850s they customarily included lectures by ministers on commercial ethics as part of their courses of study. The business colleges also sponsored lectures by ministers on topics such as "Dangers to the Republic from Commerce," political economy, and commercial honesty and dishonesty. All these instances of cooperation linking piety and profit formed part of the milieu that set some of the directions for the emerging public culture.[31]

What the pattern of cooperation might mean for the individual—and the nation, given the individual involved—is clear from the experience of John D. Rockefeller. As a young man, Rockefeller benefited from his contacts at Second Baptist Church and the YMCA. Three YMCA officers eased the way for Rockefeller. With the encouragement of George Mygatt, two bank officers, Truman P. Handy (President of the Commercial Bank) and Daniel P. Eells (cashier of the Commercial Bank), concluded that Rockefeller was worthy of their help. Consequently they lent him $2,000 to get a start in business. Handy and Mygatt also knew Rockefeller from Second Baptist Church. Rockefeller's story offers an example of one route to mobility—sponsorship by a church-going elite and the cultivation of contacts made in churches.[32]

A curious side to the climate of cooperation is that, with growing wealth, churches took on many of the attributes of businesses. Churches became heavily involved in concerns about money and how to handle it. Churches, usually through the legal entity of their trustees, took out loans and mortgages to finance debts or expansion, maintained bank accounts, owned land and paid mortgages, and worried about their debts. Churches raised revenue in the form of pew sales and rents, building subscriptions, or donations.[33]

Pews were sold much as any expensive commodity. The terms were similar at the Euclid Street Presbyterian Church (1852), Trinity Episcopal (1854), and First Presbyterian (1855): 25–30 percent down, with the rest spread out over nine or eighteen months, to be paid with interest. If money was short, churches often took a cue from business by holding a sale. In 1856 Euclid Street Presbyterian offered unsold pews for 60 percent of their appraised value—in the language of the marketplace, 40 percent off.[34]

Churches turned to banks when individual contributions were insufficient. When Trinity Episcopal Church wanted to borrow $7000 "on as reasonable terms as the state of the money market will admit," they appointed their minister, James A. Bolles, and one of their most influential and wealthy members, Samuel L. Mather, to correspond with "Eastern capitalists," and, if necessary, to visit the East to get the money. Churches also borrowed substantial sums from Cleveland banks. In moments like these, the churches were dependent on banks, not just equal partners in a pattern of cooperation.[35]

A final element of the alliance between Protestants and others who placed a priority on economic development was implied in Protestant activities that distanced them from the growing working class. The cooperative efforts of workers received little support even though some of the labor organizations promoted notions of equity that would be expected to resonate in a Protestant community familiar with the notions of a just price and fair labor. Groups such as the Female Protective Union, the Ohio Protective Union, or the Workingmen's Association of 1858, did not enjoy the voluntary society support enlisted in behalf of other groups, such as orphans or "ragged" children.[36]

Workers had one champion, Rev. James A. Thome of Ohio City's First Presbyterian Church. His chief concern was the imbalance between capital and labor. He alluded to "the usurpative encroachments of capital," and "the inalienable right of labor to its own gains." Thome, for all his rhetoric, is not mentioned in accounts of the efforts of workers to fight for their rights to organize. Antislavery dominated his reform work.[37]

The public culture rested in part on close ties between Protestants and the commercial economy. The interconnections between

Protestants and business officials, the endorsement of technological progress, the antebellum version of the Protestant ethic, the
doctrine of service, the climate of cooperation and shared objectives between churches and business, and the general lack of concern for workers together gave Protestants an identity as a group
which was a part of, and highly supportive of, the city's economic
development.[38]

From the lofty ideological heights of the doctrine of service
down to the mundane practice of using business offices for the
meetings of church leaders, Protestants and the commercial economy were knit together in antebellum Cleveland. By mid-century,
Protestant churches and ministers had not only helped build a
public culture around the commercial economy, they promoted its
preferred patterns of conduct, they sang its praises, they lent it
their sanction, they encouraged conduct conducive to it, and they
reaped its rewards.

Protestants had entered the antebellum years fearful that
wealth would erode vital piety and that mammon would replace
religion. The Sabbath compromises, the plush churches, the pew
sales which made the churches resemble joint stock companies,
the extensive interconnections of business leaders and church
members, the paeans to technology and progress, the antebellum
version of the Protestant ethic, and the practical cooperation of
religion and businesses, gave evidence that their fears were legitimate. Wealth may not have completely eroded vital piety, but
when churches relied on pew sales for their funding, when they
made meeting financial obligations a condition of membership,
and when they compromised on Sabbath observance, piety was
attenuated. Mammon may not have replaced religion, but when
church meetings were held in bank offices loyalties became
blurred. These priority-setting moments and the pattern of cooperation established with the business community put Protestant
influence and power at the service of commercial values and institutions. This conferred legitimacy on commercial values as central
elements of the public culture.

It is not enough, as critics such as "Volney" did, to point to the
hypocrisy of church discipline decisions allowing owners to meet
their obligations to the Sabbath by being in church while their
businesses and workers kept on working, or to sneer at the gilt-
edged Bibles and the plush pews. For the historian, these merely
symbolize the difficult transition between earlier, deeply held reli-

gious beliefs and the Protestants' social identity as a leadership elite in a city with economic ambitions.

It was, it must be emphasized, an accommodation, not a complete surrender. While the new economy received religious sanction, it also incorporated the admonition to serve, which retained the notion that the fortunate bore some responsibility for others. In casting their lot with the commercial economy which they led and benefited from, Protestants created a mutually reinforcing relationship between religion and economic life. Economic development received religious sanction and was invested with religious hopes. As long as the leaders of the commercial economy made it clear that loyalty to mammon was not going to replace loyalty to God, religious criticism of wealth and progress was defused, and anxieties about the effects of wealth, technology, and economic progress were assuaged.

The appeal of the accommodation for Protestants was that they made a place for religion in the ethos and practices of the marketplace. Federal and state constitutions precluded an official establishment of religion. By linking piety and profit, Protestants moved toward creating a de facto establishment where religion would be embedded deep within the city's public culture.

Antebellum Protestants in Cleveland and throughout the country became a prime shaping force in the public culture at the decisive moment when the distinctive style of American capitalism was forged. Thus, it was the nation's public culture, not just the city's, which was being created. Protestants anointed American economic development and infused it with millennial hopes. In return, the commercial ideology incorporated the conviction that material progress would be constrained by religious values, particularly by a sense of responsibility for those less fortunate. During the antebellum years these became the working assumptions that guided the formation of the nation's as well as the city's public culture.

Cleveland's—and the nation's—Protestant ministers and church members paid a price for this alliance with the dominant economic ethos. Although they succeeded in incorporating benevolence into the public culture, they did little to challenge the underlying attitudes and values of the commercial economy. Protestants surrendered their capacity to make independent, critical judgments about urban and national economic development. The "latent subversiveness" of antebellum evangelicalism, which might have criticized the replacing of God by Mammon, was not tapped. The doubts Protestants expressed in the 1830s and early 1840s about wealth and its corrosive effects dissolved. When the city's Protestants saw society through the eyes of the banker and the railroad owner, aspects of their religion critical of wealth and exploitation were soft-pedaled.[39]

In failing to raise a prophetic voice to judge economic development, Protestants forfeited the initiative in shaping the process of economic expansion and industrialization that played such a major role in determining the shape of the public culture. In return for a few bows toward personal Sabbath observance, maintaining moral standards, and supporting benevolent projects, entrepreneurs reaped a wholehearted endorsement of railroads, progress, and the existing economic system. In effect, Protestants anointed the new commercial economy. Protestants still had a voice in this crucial area of the public culture, but they did not take the lead. They conflated the gospel with their own interests and an appealing commercial ideology. When they identified Christianity with a particular economic system, they forfeited the ability to judge that system, and the public culture which it in large part generated, in the light of their religious ideals. If colonial New England ministers might be characterized as watchmen on the walls of Zion, antebellum Cleveland churches and ministers might be aptly described as junior partners in the offices of the city's commission merchants.

Chapter 5

Benevolence
and the Establishment of
an Ethos of Obligation

Benevolence offered Protestants a supple instrument capable of establishing and nurturing their influence in the public culture. In benevolent projects directed toward the poor and children, they could shape the characters of the recipients of aid, and, at the same time, establish within the culture the value of accepting moral responsibility for those less fortunate. This promoted at both individual and social levels the values, attitudes, and institutions appropriate to a commercial economy. Benevolence served to assuage their consciences as they anointed the commercial economy by making the clear point that the public culture held as one of its central values that the unfortunate were not to be ignored.

Unlike economic life, which was largely the preserve of men, women set the pace in benevolence. In a pattern typical throughout the nation, women conducted most of Cleveland's benevolent efforts, using voluntary societies as their chief instrument. These voluntary societies and the institutions they founded, such as the Protestant Orphan Asylum and the Industrial School, bridged the boundary of public and private, exercising the kind of informal, persuasive power available to women in a society that reserved formal and official power for men.

Benevolence was firmly established in the Protestants' own minds as one of their claims to moral power and influence in the city. More than any other activity, benevolence allowed Protestants to reconcile the conflicting aspects of their ideology. In benevolence they merged their two chief concerns, moral and material progress. The bridge between these two elements of their ideology was the ideal of stewardship and service. By embracing benevolence, Cleveland's Protestants could be both boosters and Christians, and so quell whatever doubts they might have that commercial and urban development were inconsistent with Protestant values. If beggars and rascally boys confounded their expectation that moral and material progress coincided, benevolence would vindicate their vision by turning such "miscreants" into useful citizens and workers. The firmly established expectation that civic leaders were, at the same time, Christians with a conscience, had two major implications for the public culture: the sense of responsibility for others engendered by benevolence set limits on individualism and the headlong pursuit of profit, and the model of service was incorporated as an essential element of the ethos of the new society.

Reinforcing the attractiveness of benevolence for Cleveland's Protestants was the conviction that benevolent activities promoted virtues appropriate to an industrial economy while at the same time affirming a vision of community at odds with the harsher implications of the individualism on which the economy rested. The benevolent projects of Cleveland Protestants promoted the values of self-discipline, restraint, and diligent labor. They dispensed aid to individuals in the expectation that temporary relief would allow the individual to take her or his place as a productive member of the economy. Yet within the Protestant ideology of benevolence there were divergent strains that asserted values which served as a counterweight to economic development and the dislocations it seemed to bring. Many of the projects were dominated by the desire to restore families, or re-create, within an institution, a family environment. Implicit in benevolent projects was the assumption that all Clevelanders comprised a community whose members recognized obligations to each other; they were not just a collection of individuals pursuing personal advancement.

The nature of benevolent activity shifted in the early 1850s. More and more, the city government was called in at key moments—to help Protestant—but not Catholic—institutions. Institutions, with their more regimented style, became the dispensers of benevolence. What was lost was the characteristic form of the earlier "women's benevolence": face-to-face, small scale, nurturing, relatively non-coercive, flexible, and non-judgmental aid. Women's benevolence had the seeds of another vision of the city—one in which truly organic connections prevailed, where humane values at least held their own with commercial ones. This was a vision lost when "male benevolence" overtook "female benevolence" at the end of the antebellum era.

Cleveland's Protestants placed benevolent activity at the center of their definition of what it meant to be Christian. James A. Thome, minister of Ohio City's First Presbyterian Church, was typical in describing "the true idea of Christianity as a union of piety and philanthropy."[1] For the newly redeemed individual, benevolence was part and parcel of what it meant to be Protestant. S. B. Page, minister of Third Baptist Church, recommended "pure and disinterested benevolence" with these words: "We are therefore not only to trust, to have faith, but to do good." Page's dictum was a reflection of the notion popular in antebellum America of being "saved for service." Doing works of benevolence was a natural outgrowth of Christian commitment. Benevolence would have an ennobling effect on the giver as well as the recipient, explained J. Hyatt Smith, minister of Second Baptist Church. All the other graces would be worthless without this crowning glory:

> charity is Godlike in its holy dispensations. It strips wealth of its robes, and want of its rage, and throws over the naked shoulders of every faithful believer, black or white, pauper or prince, bond or free, a spotless mantle of holy beauty. This is the golden link of christian union in the Church—the bright evidence of discipleship.[2]

True to this vision, members of Protestant churches filled the leadership positions of benevolent organizations. Half of the men who were officers of benevolent societies in the years from 1837 to 1860 (44 out of 88) were traced to lists of those who joined Cleveland and Ohio City English-speaking Protestant churches through 1860. Had more complete lists been available, it is likely that more than 80 percent of the men active in benevolence would have been found to have joined a Protestant church (Tables 3.2 and 3.3). The same number of women as men, 88, were identified as officers of benevolent groups from 1837 to 1860. Tracing women officers of benevolent societies to church lists is more difficult, since many names are listed only by initial (see Appendix). Of the 88, 18 (20.4 percent) were found in lists of Protestant church joiners. Given the incomplete records and the difficulties of identifying women's names it is likely that a far higher percentage of female benevolent society officers were members[3] (Tables 3.4 and 3.5).

The Protestants' social situation provided two essentials for benevolence, money and time. Almost alone among the city's communities, Protestants could afford to become involved in benevolent projects. The city's Catholic, German, Irish, and black residents had neither the resources nor the leisure to make major organized efforts to reach out a helping hand to others. Only the city's Protestants and wealthy had the economic security, organizational stability, and time to devote themselves in an extensive way to the needs of others.[4]

At least in the early years of the community, benevolence was the work of Protestant women. Benevolence allowed Cleveland women a socially sanctioned route into the world outside the home, and a way to translate private piety into social activity. The Protestant women of Cleveland organized, staffed, and supervised a wide variety of mission, sewing, maternal, and other voluntary societies.[5] It was in benevolent activities that women had the most visible impact on the public culture. Concerned members of the city's leadership elite such as Rebecca Rouse found in benevolence an entree to public life and potential influence over the developing public culture. Benevolent activity brought women into the public arena in roles of authority. Lori Ginzberg refers to this as the ideology of "benevolent femininity," which demanded that women act to heal or transform the world.[6]

Most of the city's benevolent organizations were run by women officers. The Martha Washington and Dorcas Society and most of the church mission and sewing societies were controlled entirely by women. Other organizations had parallel sets of male and female officers. The Cleveland Orphan Asylum had a popular structure—an all-female board of managers who supervised the facility combined with an all-male board of managers who offered general guidance and access to money. A history of the women of Cleveland written in 1893 described the general pattern of such organizations. At the founding of the asylum in 1852 at the First Presbyterian Church, "a committee of gentlemen drew up a plan for work, which was handed to a committee of ladies to be executed." Despite the subordination of women implied in this structure, Protestant women carved out a public role through such voluntary associations, because these organizations gave their roles as character-formers and moral guardians a public outlet.[7]

Cleveland Protestants brought to benevolence concerns reflecting their social characteristics. Their particular concern was not just for suffering, but for suffering of a particular kind—the plight of those who were not sharing in the material progress the Protestants extolled. In these moments of concern directed especially toward children, we can isolate the particular concerns that guided benevolence. Poverty and the situation of children elicited a response from Protestants both in their role as boosters and as Christians. The dislocations and deprivations of early city life affronted the boosters' image of "the Emerald City of the Lakes" just as much as it did the Protestants' millennial hopes for a transformed society.[8] A letter to the *Plain Dealer* from "God Help the Poor" in 1857 expressed a common sentiment: "There is not a street, alley, or lane within the corporation, inhabited, but you will find destitution in its worst form." Residents complained of "swarms of beggars" and "rowdy" and "rascally" boys infesting their streets. The progress symbolized by the arrival of the Cleveland, Columbus, and Cincinnati Railroad in 1851 seemed only to highlight the misfortune and misery as well as to call into question the triumph of the official version of the public culture. The *Forest City Democrat* summarized the anomaly in 1857: "Destitution and ignorance riot in our lanes and alleys, in our most fashionable streets, crawl in filthy rags past the mansions of the rich, past the gorgeous fronts of temples dedicated to a god of mercy."[9]

The response to these conditions reflected the concerns of the Protestant, interconnected elite which dominated benevolence. Even when their concern might be attributed to a general sympathy for those in straitened circumstances, aid was given with the needs of a commercial economy in mind. Donors inquired into the circumstances of potential recipients in order to identify the "deserving"—those willing to work, but because of circumstances beyond their control, unable to do so. When they set up institutions, Protestants established regimens for residents that inculcated values and conduct suitable for a commercial economy. Even benevolence conformed to the dictates of a public culture saturated with commercial values.[10]

Relief to the poor was the most prominent antebellum benevolent activity. Economic and urban development was leaving growing numbers of Clevelanders behind. This forced the benevolently inclined to look for alternatives to the personal, ad hoc, and small-scale benevolence that had characterized the city since its founding. By the 1850s charity offered by individuals or mutual aid societies receded in importance as more systematic, institutional, and public efforts became widespread. This was a decisive step in the process by which religion developed a substantial presence in the public culture. When benevolent societies developed systematic and coordinated approaches to poverty, they enlisted the aid of public authorities who to some extent displaced their efforts.[11]

Voluntary poor relief societies that had concerns beyond helping their own ethnic or religious group were slow to emerge. It was not until the formation of a women's organization in 1843, the Martha Washington and Dorcas Society (MWDS), that a concerted voluntary effort was made in the area of general poor relief. The society's objectives indicate an interest in not only aiding the poor, but in having a broad moral and social influence. According to its constitution, the society was organized "for the retarding of intemperance, to which is added, systematic labor for the inevitable result of the vice, namely, poverty of every description."

The MWDS modeled a poor relief effort consistent with the early public culture rather than the later commercial one—its aid was personal, small-scale, flexible, and minimally coercive. For the term of its existence, the MWDS was the major provider of poor relief in Cleveland outside the poorhouse. The society's aid was designed to be temporary. As its report for 1847 stated, "our object has been to assist those families, who by long and protracted sickness, are temporarily in distress—and who, with a little help at such time, are soon able to take care of themselves."[12]

The prime mover of the MWDS and its only president, Rebecca Rouse, conducted most of the work of the society. Rouse often made daily visits to comfort and aid sufferers. She provided families with wood, food, medicine, nurses, and beds. The society found jobs for men and widows, and arranged to have children who needed care taken into homes. It also sent clothes to the hospital for cholera victims whose own clothes had to be burned.[13]

The MWDS disbanded after six years of work, largely because Rouse, in the course of her visitations, became concerned with the plight of poor children and turned her energies toward the organization of an orphan asylum. But other factors were also involved in its demise which point to a moment when Protestants shifted to a benevolence suitable to the commercial economy's public culture. The *Daily True Democrat* attributed the folding of the MWDS to "the increase of pauperism and the added burden of aiding paupers without assistance from the local government." It was, like many voluntary societies, a group with a narrow base and limited resources faced with a social problem that had grown beyond its capacities.[14]

The collapse of the MWDS brought a reassessment of benevolence for the poor. The secretary of the society, Catharine Lyon, set the terms of the debate in her report for 1849. "Who will replace Rouse?" she asked. "Who would visit? Who would 'have our homes besieged at all hours of the day by the sick, the lame, the halt and the blind?' Can we not have some permanent form of relief?" Lyon pleaded. All the elements of the benevolence of Cleveland's last antebellum decade are present in Lyon's laments. More public involvement, insistence on a permanent form of relief, a greater reliance on institutions, and a lurking fear of being besieged by the needy were the marks of late antebellum benevolence in Cleveland, a benevolence in tune with the public culture of the commercial economy.[15]

After the collapse of the MWDS, benevolent activities were directed more intentionally toward efforts to shape the values, behavior, and institutions of the public culture. Those interested in benevolence decided that they no longer lived in a small-town society where personal, face-to-face almsgiving of the MWDS-type sufficed. As a result, their aid began to reflect their desire to shape the direction of the new commercial economy through systematic measures which would inculcate their preferred values. The chief mechanism for furthering their aims was a new strategy based on ordered and discriminating giving. Concern for the "deserving" reached fever pitch in the late 1840s and in the 1850s. The newspapers reported a concern for "a more systematic assessment" or of "systematic measures." Aid would be targeted to the "deserving," as determined by the dispensers of the aid. Like Boston, and unlike Charleston, South Carolina, purposeful work was the criteria for receiving benevolence. Terms handy in distinguishing some poor from others, such as the "deserving" poor and the "worthy" poor, became staples of the discussion of relief. Cleveland benevolence rushed toward what one Episcopal minister called "the *substitution of a system* in the dispensation of your charities, for the more promiscuous and consequently less satisfactory mode of alms-giving which must prevail, where a systematic and organized charity like this does not exist." This is a prevalent pattern in the East. All at once, the pace of commercial development seemed to outstrip the new cities' ability to cope with its consequences.[16]

Even smaller poor relief efforts, such as those of the Sons of Malta, the Ladies' Home Missionary Society of the First Methodist Church, and the City Mission of the Euclid Street Presbyterian Church, evidenced the concern of the 1850s for methodical benevolence to address the dislocations of the city. The Ladies' Home Missionary Society stated that it was called into existence "to rescue from degradation and crime a class of human beings hitherto beyond the pale of Christian effort in our city, but now brought under the influence of well directed and systematic Christian philanthropy."[17]

Euclid Street Presbyterian Church's City Mission organized a visitation program that combined a concern for systematic poor relief with insistent proselytizing. Visitors subjected potential recipients to scrutiny designed to see whether the needy evidenced preferred behaviors and values. Visitors were to find out how many in each family attended Sunday school or church as well as whether any were in want or in need of employment. Tracts were distributed, families were encouraged to attend church or Sunday school, and those who did not attend church were offered free seats if they were unable to pay pew rents.[18]

In moving toward more explicit criteria for dispensing aid, Protestants honed benevolence as an instrument for achieving particular purposes in the public culture. The chief value the more discriminating giving was designed to serve was purposeful work. This was a market-oriented approach suited to the commercial economy. Individuals were not seen as part of an organic society marked by inevitable poverty and dependence. Rather, they were part of a dynamic society where worth was assessed according to one's ability and willingness to contribute to the society and economy. Aid became more grudging and conditional than it had been when Rouse provided it, since donors concerned themselves with whether each recipient was "deserving."[19]

The shift toward more discriminating and systematic giving had the result of diminishing women's role and enhancing the role of men and the city government, providing an indication of the contours of power and authority in the city's public culture. The Society for the Relief of the Poor, soon known as the Relief Association, was formed in 1850 with Rebecca Rouse and her husband Benjamin Rouse as agents. The new association may have had the benefit of the MWDS's Rebecca Rouse, but it represented a decidedly different approach to poor relief, one which reflected a significant move into the public arena. The society was run by men, with women relegated to a Committee on Entertainments. Funding was on a larger basis than had been available for the MWDS. Where the earlier society had raised much of its money with door-to-door solicitations, the Relief Association depended on large subscriptions from male benefactors who formed a "committee of twenty."[20]

As women lost power, men gained it. What had been a promising opening for women to extend their influence in the public culture through informal, patient setting of a tone of concern for others succumbed to the desire to "manage" the problem of poverty. Public officials increased their involvement in poor relief in the aftermath of the collapse of the MWDS. The immediate rationale was the same as sparked more systematic relief, that there were insufficient resources to meet the needs of the poor. The Relief Association was uncomfortable with the responsibility of being the major source of poor relief in Cleveland. A notice for a meeting of the association in 1852 reported that the question of whether poor relief would "continue to be done by this and other voluntary Associations, or by a well arranged Municipal Plan" would probably be discussed. Later that month, the association's position was stated clearly: poor relief was an appropriate and necessary city responsibility. When done by the city the "expense and burden of it fall upon all alike, in proportion to their property and means, like any other city expenditure, instead of being drawn from such as, while they are ever ready, should never in justice be *required* to do more than their due share of what is a common and public duty."[21]

The result of these calls for city involvement was a pattern of cooperation between Protestant benevolent projects and the city government. This is a telling moment, both for benevolence and for the public culture. The city had long funded a poorhouse and outdoor relief. Cleveland's poor relief efforts culminated in 1855 with the opening of the City Infirmary, built at a cost of $20,000.[22] But the city's efforts had always been modest and undependable. It was the city's Protestants who provided dependable benevolence. All this changed in the 1850s. The pattern that dominated the city's "pre-commercial" public culture and delegated to religion the concern for the poor, now shifted. Dealing with the poor became public business, and managing the poor toward certain ends that benefited the commercial economy became part of the public culture.

Benevolence directed toward children repeated many of the patterns of benevolence on behalf of the poor. Efforts to serve the interests of the commercial economy and its public culture became pronounced by the 1850s. Concerns stemming from their dual identities as both Christians and boosters guided benevolent efforts dealing with children as much as they did with benevolence for the poor. Benevolence aimed at children also paralleled the trend evident in poor relief in the shift to more systematic and institutional approaches and toward cooperation between the city government and private, religiously based societies. If anything, supporters of voluntary benevolent projects seemed to regard their work with children as even more crucial than their general poor relief. Aimed as they were at forming the characters of youth, benevolent projects directed toward children intended to shape the future public culture as much as the current one.

Worries about neglected and vagrant children crested in the 1850s, much as did the concern about the growing numbers of poor. Nascent industrial development left many new city dwellers, children and adults alike, without an economic function, carving out a precarious existence on the margins of city life. For children there was the added factor of lack of supervision, often because parents were overworked. Those involved in benevolence worried that failure to incorporate children as productive members of the city, or at least to neutralize their disruptive potential, could undercut the attempt to create a thriving commercial and manufacturing city. Destitute and neglected children, the *Leader* informed its readers, faced the daily temptation to lie, cheat, and steal: "Every hour in the city is a prison which is sealing such young offenders to a life of infamy and disgrace." The paper found "knee beggars" the most annoying of the city's ill-disciplined children. "These urchins, always unwashed and uncombed, open your door, and pop down on their knees, commencing a whining supplication for a loaf of bread, or for something else as the case may be." The *Daily True Democrat* summed up the worries:

> Our cities are nests of corruption for boys without parents, or with parents who cannot control them. Here in Cleveland they may be seen daily.
>
> But nothing is done for them; and all they know of society, of religion of God, is through the fangs of the law, or the abuse of the people. Society pays dearly for its neglect, and as years roll on, and our population increases, it will pay dearer yet.[23]

In the 1850s came the moments when the city set the pattern of public culture's response to "disruptive" children. The city's first benevolent projects aimed especially at children were all organized as institutions—Catholic and Protestant orphan asylums in 1851 and 1852, the Ragged School in 1853, and the public House of Correction in 1857. These drew from what seemed to be an inexhaustible supply of children deemed in need of care.[24]

The cooperation of private, voluntary, and Protestant efforts with the local government was even firmer in children's benevolence projects than in poor relief efforts. The Cleveland Orphan Asylum exemplifies a persistent pattern of cooperation between city officials and an explicitly Protestant benevolent project. Organized in a meeting at the First Presbyterian Church, it was a cooperative endeavor of the members of many Protestant churches. The local government became involved in the Cleveland Orphan Asylum in 1855, when the asylum solicited and received city funds of $150 a year because it took in children from the City Infirmary. The city also agreed to pay $150 that year for the support of a teacher. Not content with such supplemental aid, the asylum called on the local government to do still more, since private donations were not sufficient to sustain the project. The annual report published in March of 1861 argued that "an institution like an Orphan Asylum, which is an integral part of every Christian city, dare not rely for its maintenance on alms asked monthly, or yearly, of many whose sympathies are exhausted by minor enterprises." Once again, the informal, personal, benevolence conducted by women fell before the magnitude of the commercial economy's dislocations.[25]

The city's involvement in the Ragged School was even more substantial. The Ragged School was the project of a single Protestant church. It was organized in 1853 by Rev. Dillon Prosser and other Methodists, primarily from First Methodist Church. The Ladies' Home Missionary Society of that church supervised the school and provided money for it. The Ragged School was a day school that aimed to attract the unchurched, unsupervised children of the city. As the superintendent described it in 1858, the school "is made up of children that are too poor to attend public schools, or too degraded to submit to their rules."[26]

The school began as a private, voluntary, religious project, and ended as a publicly controlled but privately operated institution known as the Industrial School. The impetus for the shift came in 1855 when the city government appointed a committee to investigate the problem of vagrant, neglected, and disruptive children. The committee reported that the city harbored between two hundred and three hundred children between the ages of six and fifteen who were idle or begging, and who, if not already of vicious habits, soon would be. "What they most need is the extension of a friendly hand to guide and direct them," the committee concluded. Other cities had established successful industrial schools to educate and train children, concluded the committee, and it recommended the same for Cleveland. The *Plain Dealer* agreed, arguing that city funds spent for an industrial school would be the ounce of prevention that would be better than the pound of cure then being provided by the courts and prisons.[27]

The result was that in 1857 the Ragged School was adopted by the city. The city council assumed control of the school, renamed it the Industrial School, and supported its work out of general city funds. The city paid the salary of the superintendent and three teachers. One year, the city council made up the difference between the school's expenses and the income it got from private contributions. At other times, the city took responsibility for major improvements or expenses—building an addition, painting, fixing up a basement, or providing for wood and coal. In an address in 1858, John A. Foote, a state as well as a local leader, found city government support appropriate, since the school had a public purpose: "It is changing scholars from dangerous into industrious citizens."[28] The Ragged School could now take its place as a contributing member of the public culture.

The two Catholic orphan asylums remained private, church-related institutions throughout the antebellum years, and there is no evidence that the city gave any support to them. That the Protestant but not the Catholic institutions received aid is yet another indication of the cooperation between the city government and Protestants, a relationship verging on a *de facto* establishment. When they enlisted local public authorities in support of their projects, Protestants gained a conduit for public influence. Even more, when public authorities embraced their efforts and their values, Protestants achieved public legitimation for their benevolent projects as well as a prominent role in shaping the formation of the public culture.

The close alliance between the city's benevolence projects and the city, similar to the accommodation between Protestants and business, was cemented by shared membership in an interlocking religious and cultural community. The officers of benevolent societies were not only predominantly Protestant, they were also part of a network of Cleveland's business, political, educational, and moral reform leaders. Of the 88 male benevolent society officers who served from 1837 to 1860, 17 (19.3 percent) were officers of businesses, 23 (26.1 percent) were government office-holders, 27 (30.7 percent) were political party candidates, 26 (29.6 percent) were officers of moral reform societies, and 26 (29.6 percent) were educational administrators or board members, or teachers in schools (Table 5.1). The male benevolent society officers were especially active in banks, public education, Cleveland government, and temperance. Politically, they were most likely found in the Whig or Republican parties, although a few were Democrats.

Table 5.1   Office-Holding in Benevolent
and Temperance Organizations for Officers of
Business Organizations

| | OFFICERS IN BENEVOLENT AND TEMPERANCE MORAL REFORM ORGANIZATIONS, 1837 . . 60 | | | |
| | Benevolence (N=88) | | Temperance (N=88) | |
	N	%	N	%
BUSINESS OFFICERS, 1837 . . 60				
Any Business (N=172)	17	9.8	24	14.0
Banks (N=72)	17	23.6	19	26.4
Board of Trade (N=16)	-	-	-	-
Railroad (N=18)	2	11.1	-	-
Other Business (N=109)	6	5.5	11	10.1

Sources and Notes: See Appendix.

The activities of the women who were benevolent society officers were not as extensive as was true for the men, but they were active within the sphere in which they were confined, benevolence and moral reform. A few of the women were found in lists of temperance society officers, and there was some crisscrossing of officers among the individual benevolent societies.[29]

The dependence of benevolence on those who had money beyond what was needed for basic necessities further solidified the links between benevolence and the well-connected. Wealthy men and businessmen were commonly mentioned targets for requesting donations. Contributions in goods and services from the city's railroads, omnibus lines, business colleges, and merchants helped sustain many of the larger benevolent projects. After one benefit concert the *Plain Dealer* concluded that "all the good looking and benevolent people of the city were there, besides a number of others"; it was "one of the largest and most fashionable looking audiences we have seen in some time past."[30]

Rebecca and Benjamin Rouse, the pillars of antebellum Cleveland benevolence, fit perfectly the profile of benevolent activists connected to the city's leadership elite. Rebecca Cromwell was born in Salem, Massachusetts, in 1799. A history of Cleveland's charity described her childhood as one spent in affluence and liberal education. In 1817 she married Benjamin Rouse, a young man in the business circles of Boston. She and Benjamin Rouse moved to New York in 1825, where, under the lead of the noted reformer and abolitionist Arthur Tappan, she became active in charitable work. Rebecca and Benjamin Rouse moved to Cleveland in 1830 as agents of the American Sabbath School Union. In Cleveland, Rebecca Rouse and her husband were founding members of First Baptist (1833) and Erie Street Baptist (1852) Churches.[31]

Rebecca Rouse cut a wide swathe through Cleveland benevolence. She was the only president of the Martha Washington and Dorcas Society (from 1844–1850) and she was on the Board of Managers of the Protestant Orphan Asylum (1860). She was the first president of the Female Baptist Sewing Society, an officer of the Female Reform Society (1843) and the Cleveland Ladies' Temperance Union (1850, 1853), and she served on a committee for the Society for the Relief of the Poor (1851). During the Civil War she was President of Cleveland's Soldiers' Aid Society.[32]

Like Rebecca Rouse, Benjamin Rouse had a New England upbringing. Born in Boston in 1795, he was orphaned at age six and raised by relatives. As an adolescent, he attended William Ellery Channing's church in Boston and was a member of the church's choir. Rouse was drafted in 1812 but found military life uncongenial. He later reported that he disliked the obscene stories and profane language of the barracks. Rouse made his way to New York in 1817, where he became a successful builder until he accepted the

Sabbath School Union's offer in 1830. Rouse organized Presbyterian, Episcopal, and Methodist Sunday Schools in Cleveland, an indication that in these fluid early years Protestants opted for unity and evangelizing over keeping denominational boundaries intact. Rouse served as an officer of both First and Second Baptist Churches.[33]

Rouse's benevolent and moral reform activities rivalled his wife's. He was an officer of the Western Seamen's Friend Society (1848, 1850, 1853, 1857), the Protestant Orphan Asylum (1853, 1860), the Cleveland Relief Association (1852), the Ladies' Temperance Union (1850), and the Cleveland Bible Society (1857).

Rouse's prominence went well beyond religion and benevolence. He continued his business career in Cleveland, most noticeably with "Rouse's Block" on a corner of Public Square, described by a later historian as Cleveland's finest office building. Rouse also served as a director of the Society for Savings Bank (1857, 1860). Rouse was a trustee of Cleveland township (1844) and treasurer of the Free Soil Party (1849). He was a nominee of the Democratic Party for a minor city office in 1844, and a nominee of the Free Soil Party for a seat on the city's council in 1849. Finally, Rouse was the first president of the New England Society, a group formed in 1855 to preserve the traditions and memories of the settlers from New England.[34]

Judging from the activities of the Rouses and the other benevolent society officers, benevolence in Cleveland on the eve of the Civil War was one of the natural social functions of being part of the city's leadership elite and a mainstay of the public culture. Protestant projects blended easily into public projects, and both carried with them religiously based values conducive to commercial development and the developing public culture. As William Pease and Jane Pease remark about Charleston and Boston, "Whether as part of patriarchal slavery, noblesse oblige, Calvinist stewardship, or capitalist success, self-conscious benevolence legitimized wealth and privileged position.[35]

By enlisting the cooperation of public authorities for religiously based benevolent projects, the city's Protestants commanded a significant force for influencing public culture. This set the stage for the infusion of Protestant influence into the public culture since the benevolent projects promoted a cluster of behaviors, values, and institutions shaped by the religious and social concerns of the interconnected elite of Protestants and city leaders.

Benevolent projects aimed to spread two sets of values, those of Protestantism and those having to do with the discipline appropriate for a commercial economy. Many of the benevolent projects doubled as proselytizing efforts. One way to influence society's values and institutions would be to convert a sizable proportion of the population, and benevolence could be an instrument in this.

There was a markedly proselytizing tone to almost all charitable efforts, reflecting James A. Thome's description of true Christianity as a union of piety and philanthropy. Thomas Starkey, minister of Trinity Episcopal Church, in calling for a well-arranged and systematic plan of charity, saw such a project as both "a ministry of mercy to men's bodies" and "a ministry of reconciliation to men's souls." Many of the voluntary societies established with some statement of a benevolent purpose were instead primarily vehicles for evangelizing and moral reform. The Western Seamen's Friend Society focused on evangelizing and sustaining its Bethel Church in Cleveland, although it also served as a mutual aid organization for seamen. The Female Moral Reform Society promoted moral uplift, in addition to aiding women in trouble. The Martha Washington and Dorcas Society, the Cleveland Orphan Asylum, the Ragged School, and the Euclid Street Presbyterian Church's City Mission all had a healthy measure of proselytizing attached to them. The City Mission, for example, intended its aid to be temporary relief, with strings attached. The trustees resolved that "no continued and permanent relief shall be granted to any family from the Relief Fund that is not or will not become connected with some Protestant Church or Sabbath School or congregation and that in some cases where destitute families are found to be connected with some church or congregation such church will be requested to support and aid such families."[36] When benevolent reformers extended a helping hand with food, provisions, and concern, the likelihood was that the other hand held a Bible or tract.

Some observers complained that the culture-shaping impulse overwhelmed the provision of aid. The *Plain Dealer*, with its Democratic and presumably less Protestant audience, expressed doubts about the prevailing mixture of benevolence and evangelizing. Efforts to improve morals, educate minds, supply Bibles, and save souls were good in their place, the paper agreed, but

> It is hard to acquire knowledge on an empty stomach, or to read the Lord's Prayer without 'daily bread,' or to get religion without

pork and potatoes. The poor want something to eat, and where-
withal to be clothed. The superfluities of grace will do well as a
dessert, but are a poor substitute for the substantial necessaries of
life.[37]

The proselytizing aspects of benevolence aimed to guarantee, if
nothing else, that the public culture would not be Catholic. Anti-
Catholicism pervaded much of the city's benevolence. When the
MWDS reported in 1848 that 59 of the 82 families helped were
Catholic, it remarked: "We would not complain of the preponder-
ance of Catholics, if the church to which they belong manifested a
disposition to aid us in proportion to others." Recipients noticed
anti-Catholic aspects to benevolence. A letter to the *Plain Dealer* in
1852 complained that under the Relief Association and its agent,
Benjamin Rouse, "the funds for the poor are taking a selfish, sectar-
ian, close communion direction." The letter added that "the Deacon [Benjamin Rouse was a deacon of First Baptist Church] seems
to act much like the Priest and Levite who found the man half dead
between Jerusalem and Jericho, he passes him by the other side."[38]

Protestant intolerance marked much of the city's public benevolence as well, not surprisingly, given the Protestant representation
among city officials. A letter signed "Constitution" complained in
the *Plain Dealer* in 1853 that Catholics were being denied relief by
the City Infirmary. "Constitution" reminded the newspaper's readers that public funds, from members of every sect and denomination, financed the poorhouse. When an unfortunate and destitute
man knocked on the door it should be open to his relief if he is
found worthy, insisted "Constitution,"

> whether he be Jew or Gentile, Catholic or Protestant. But no! he
> is turned away, not because he is an imposter, for want and dis-
> tress stand confessed in every garb and feature, but because he is
> too honest to deny that he worships at an altar different from
> those public servants having temporary charge of the poor.

"Is this Christianity?" the letter asked. "God forbid."[39]

When the Ragged School was established in 1853 by the Rev.
Prosser and the members of the city's Methodist churches in an
area where immigrants lived, Catholics were understandably
alarmed. The city directory for 1857 recognized its religious overtones, listing it as the "Mission Church and Ragged School."

According to the later reminiscences of one of the organizers, Lucius F. Mellen, Catholics who lived nearby tried to drive the school out. Boys threw stones through the windows and the school had to get police protection. Finally, the women involved in supporting the school decided to offer a picnic lunch in the afternoon and invite neighborhood youths. The picnic was a great success, and after that relations between the school and its neighbors improved, recounted Mellen.[40]

Despite these efforts, relations between the Ragged School and Catholics were still strained three years later, as is evident in the controversy surrounding the death in 1856 of a young child, Barbara Forman. Her gravestone, like contemporary accounts, told the story from a Protestant perspective: "Little Barbara died from a whipping, a cruel punishment inflicted by a bigoted Teacher for her attendance upon the Ragged School."[41] The report was that she had been beaten with a thick cane while placed across a chair by a teacher at St. Mary's Catholic School. The Ragged School resolved to erect a monument to her memory, while on the other side of the religious divide, the *Leader* reported that a Catholic priest advised members of his congregation to contribute money for the release of the accused murderer.[42]

Beyond the more narrowly religious effort to shape a Protestant, or at least a non-Catholic culture, Protestant benevolence aimed to inculcate another set of values, which would lay the foundation for the new commercial city and its public culture. The benevolent projects created by the Protestant leadership elite were wedded to a vision of self-reliance and self-discipline within the framework of prevailing political, economic, and social arrangements. The governing principle was to fit individual recipients into useful slots in the developing commercial and industrial city.

Because they incorporated the values of the commercial culture, benevolent activities addressed the personal level rather than the societal. Voluntary poor relief organizations such as the Martha Washington and Dorcas Society saw their duty as aiding families and individuals in temporary distress.[43] The Relief Association and the MWDS attributed instances of poverty and suffering to illness, catastrophe, intemperance, or, in the cases of women, death of or abandonment by a husband. Existing economic arrangements, business fluctuations, or low wages were seldom blamed.

Since the diagnosis of the problem of suffering was individual circumstance or failure, the prescription offered by benevolent societies was personal moral reform and the pursuit of success through individual effort and self-discipline. The motto of the Industrial School newspaper incorporated an ethic thought suitable for ragged children moving into what the benevolently inclined assumed was an unalterable economic structure: "Labor Conquers; Education and Industry, Secure Wealth and Happiness." This was the rationale behind the Industrial School's program of brush-making for the boys and sewing for the girls. The Ladies' Home Missionary Society of First Baptist Church evaluated its efforts along similar lines. In its third annual report, presented in 1857, the Society reported having found homes for 18 indigent individuals. Some who had been cared for "are now filling positions of trust in stores and business houses, to the entire satisfaction of their benefactors."[44]

In the Orphan Asylum, according to its reports, ill-disciplined and neglected children would be given what their upbringing lacked: proper nurture compounded of a healthy environment, persuasion, example, precept, and carefully formed habits. Cleveland's children's institutions would put their stamp on the soft wax of their charges' characters by regimentation, discipline, and training in useful skills, followed by placement in a respectable family or apprenticeship in a trade. The expectation was that the children who entered the institutions would be transformed into useful and worthy citizens who could take their places in the new commercial city.[45]

In stressing self-restraint and self-reliance, Protestant benevolence became one instrument for creating a new public culture appropriate for a commercial, and later, an industrial, economy. The regimens of the Protestant Orphan Asylum, the City Infirmary, and the Industrial School were models for a society to come. They were part of a cultural innovation by which an older, face-to-face, personal, organic, public culture made way for a public culture based on individual responsibility and self-discipline.[46]

Benevolent projects that offered broader prescriptions or which undermined or challenged prevailing assumptions of the emerging public culture had difficulty establishing themselves. Cleveland's benevolent community always acted safely within the confines of existing political, economic, and social arrangements. A salient example is the response to a women's labor organization, the Female Protective Union. The Union was organized in late 1850 by sewing women unhappy with their long hours, low wages, and payment in orders which merchants refused to accept at face value. Many were widows with large families.[47]

Initially, the plight of the sewing women attracted the attention of benevolent, Protestant Clevelanders. A meeting to consider the condition of the sewing women was chaired by Samuel Aiken, minister of First Presbyterian Church. The meeting appointed a committee to draft a report on the women and their cooperative store. Rebecca Rouse served on a committee to arrange a fund-raising entertainment for the Union. So long as they were seen to be individualistic, disciplined workers, they replicated the shape of the public culture and garnered Protestant support.[48]

But the Female Protective Union refused to accept the dependent status of the usual recipient of aid. The Union appealed to philanthropic citizens for help in establishing a cooperative store where they could market their goods for themselves: "we ask not for charity, but for a loan of sufficient capital to commence an establishment, where we shall receive from our labor a more adequate reward. . . . " The Female Cooperative Union Store opened May 1, 1851, "with a small capital contributed and loaned by the friends of the cause." The store gave more or less constant employment to 50 of the approximately 400 sewing women in Cleveland. The prices were usually higher than those paid by the sewing proprietors and in all instances the pay was in cash.[49]

One Union supporter, in a letter to the *Daily True Democrat*, summarized a broad conception of benevolence that included the Female Protective Union. According to "One Who Will Help":

> True benevolence does not always consist in giving, for in many instances it fosters idleness and vice. Employment and fair wages to those that will work, not only secures them a livelihood, but develops and strengthens habits of industry and thrift. This is what the sewing women ask, and I have very much mistaken the character of our citizen[s], if their appeal shall prove in vain.[50]

The argument is still couched in familiar moral terms—idleness, vice, industry, and thrift—but there is an unfamiliar twist. Employment and fair wages, not Protestant piety and self-discipline, are identified as the proper elements of benevolence. These, though, were not the values of the public culture Protestants were creating.

The Female Protective Union and its cooperative store were clearly outside the arena of Protestant benevolence. There is no evidence that the support of figures such as Aiken and Rouse lasted beyond the first months of the Union's work. The suffering of individual sewing women engendered concern which did not survive the realization that the seamstresses were pushing for structural changes in economic life. The benevolent community that initially responded with enthusiasm was closely associated with the sewing proprietors, other businessmen, and city leaders who would be most threatened by a realignment of economic power.[51]

In the end, the Female Protective Union and its store were short-lived and it was Morse's conception of benevolence that carried the day. Six months after the establishment of the store a committee reported that it suffered "many discouragements." Except for a flurry of activity in November and December 1851, the Union and its store vanished as quickly as they had appeared.[52] In this moment when Protestants responded to the suffering of sewing women, the outlines of the public culture came to view: piety and self-discipline, rather than employment and fair wages, defined the new society's public culture.

Although benevolence directed to the poor and children, with its emphasis on Protestantism, individualism, and self-discipline was sometimes narrow-minded and grudging, at its best it perpetuated a sense of communal and personal responsibility that blunted some of the harsher edges of an economic development otherwise fueled by a desire for personal gain heedless of the consequences for others. With benevolence, the city's Protestants did not simply accommodate to commercial development—they succeeded in establishing their own, independent, religiously generated values as a counterweight to the imperatives of economic development.

Elements of the benevolent work incorporated values into the public culture that impeded, and at times deflected, the culture's tendency to pursue maximum individual advantage in a market, commercial economy. While the dominant ideology of benevolent institutions was one conducive to the values of the commercial economy, other elements testified to the importance Protestants gave to the family as a counterweight to some of the harsher tendencies of the marketplace. The regimens of the children's institutions reflected uneasiness about the destructive aspects of the new economy on community and family ties. The solution, as in many of the poor relief projects, was to recreate a family atmosphere. The Protestant Orphan Asylum and the Ragged School were designed to see that children received all the education and training the family usually provided. The Orphan Asylum considered itself "not a mere place of sojourn for a month or a year, but a Christian home." The Asylum was a surrogate parent, in fact as well as in intent, because it required that parents relinquish control over their offspring to the institution.[53]

The Orphan Asylum did not have the resources to serve as a Christian home for all who needed it. Whenever possible, children were placed in families or work. Children in the Asylum were available for apprenticeship, adoption, and indenture. It was the Board's policy to give the children to those who would treat them well, and who would educate them in a responsible and religious manner. The Asylum hoped "to provide them with good homes, in respectable families."[54]

The Church Home for the Sick and Friendless of Trinity Episcopal Church, intended for aged women, also sought to create a family atmosphere. The Trinity Church Home would be, true to its name, a home modeled along the lines of a church. As Trinity Episcopal Church's rector, James A. Bolles, imagined it, the institution would be "such a Home as God designed his Church to be—a shelter, a rest, a refuge, a sanctuary in Christ from all the tribulations of the outward world." Bolles' description of the Home gathered up all the images of sheltering, mothering, and childhood which Horace Bushnell, and later Henry Ward Beecher, made so potent a part of mid-century American Protestantism. Trinity's institution would be

> a Home for the friendless in which the church, as a faithful mother, shall apply her nursing care, and revive the affections and associations of childhood and youth; and in which the warning and inviting voice of the Great Father of us all shall be heard, teaching, guiding, instructing, rescuing, and saving, His lost and perishing children.[55]

The work of benevolent activists thus had two quite different results in the public culture. To a large extent, benevolent projects animated by Protestant impulses inculcated values congruent with the religious and social interests of the well-connected leadership elite. At the same time, benevolence set some mild restraints on economic development. Service became part of the ethos of commercial development, which promoted a sense of moral responsibility among the city's leaders for those less fortunate.

To a great extent, the role played by Protestants in shaping the culture through benevolence was quiet, indirect, and informal. It was not the heavy-handedness suggested by the term "social control." Benevolence was marked, rather, by the optimism and confidence with which Protestants assumed the virtue of their approach to aiding the needy and shaping the society. But interpreting benevolence as social control does at least recognize that charity served a variety of personal and social motives and functions. Benevolence is best understood as one expression of what many Protestants determined to be the appropriate way to live as a Christian within a rapidly expanding commercial economy. The element of genuine caring and concern should not be dismissed. Yet the caring and concern existed in a social context that shaped the form in which they were expressed. For antebellum Protestants, concern and caring were inextricably linked to anxiety about having to live in a city with growing numbers of poor and to the booster's concern for molding individuals who would contribute to creating a thriving economy which would make Cleveland a winner in the city-building sweepstakes that were such an important part of the public culture.[56]

Women played a substantial part in charting the direction of benevolence. In benevolence, as in so many other areas of nineteenth-century American life, women were relegated to a separate sphere. Yet in this instance it was not entirely a private sphere, since the values promoted by private, religiously based voluntary projects became public values by virtue of the local government's cooperation with Protestant benevolent activities. Still, benevolent women can be described in Nancy Hewitt's phrase—they were ameliorists. Their work sprang from their domestic identities as mothers, wives, sisters, and grandmothers. In doing this they settled for the semblance but not the substance of power.[57] Charity conducted by women helped bridge the gap between class distinctions. In Lori Ginzberg's judgment, charity "mediated the most blatant harshness and dislocation of nineteenth-century capitalism and urbanization." In this way, benevolent associations became mediating institutions where the values of the sphere allotted to women entered the public culture. If, by the early 1850s, the mediation came to rest in the hands of men, something of the concern for embracing and nurturing each individual remained to mitigate the regimen of training for commercial employment. The benevolent work of Cleveland's Protestant women kept alive a sense of responsibility for all members of society. This preserved a kernel of the small-community sense of an interdependent society that persisted despite the force of the social atomism of the laissez-faire commercial economy. This is an instance where the impera-tives of economic development gave way before Protestant religious ideals. Through benevolence, Cleveland's interconnected elite made a place for moral and social concerns within the reign-ing ideology of commercial capitalism.[58]

In both economic development and benevolence Protestants had a relative degree of influence they would not be able to match in temperance, politics, or community rituals. Conducting busi-ness and benevolence were both accepted, seemingly "natural," functions of the city's leadership elite. Other groups did not com-mand the resources or, in the case of benevolence, the time, to challenge the virtual Protestant monopoly in these two areas. Con-sequently, Protestants fashioned an ideology of moral and material progress that set the framework for the public culture. To be a Christian in antebellum Cleveland meant to be active in benevo-lence which aided the less fortunate without challenging the direc-tion of economic development. This must be counted as one of the Protestant community's signal "successes" in the public culture. Protestants had defined appropriate attitudes for individuals who were part of that culture and they had enlisted public authorities to support their vision of a prosperous, well-disciplined, hard-work-ing, and Protestant community.[59]

Chapter 6

Temperance:
The Cold Water Army
Tastes Defeat

Of all the activities Protestants mounted to establish and institutionalize their values in the public culture, temperance seemed the most likely to succeed. Temperance commitments unified Protestants, so they did not have to deal with the kinds of divisions and ambivalence they faced in the economic realm over questions such as keeping the Sabbath. Temperance activity involved more Protestants and generated more enthusiasm than any other activity. Protestants from every denomination joined the effort, and the dozens of voluntary groups cooperated in the common cause. The unity was marred only by a rift between Washingtonians, seen as an upstart, lower-class group, and the more established organizations.[1]

Temperance drew forth the efforts of both men and women as did no other cause. As we have seen, business, politics, and community rituals were dominated by men while women took the initiative in benevolence—until the 1850s when men seized control. Only in temperance did women and men continue working side by side throughout the antebellum years, even though, true to the gender divisions enshrined in the cult of true womanhood, women worked in separate temperance organizations that were often auxiliaries of male groups.

The temperance movement seemed primed for success in other ways, too. In the temperance crusade, the Protestants' strategic palette was used to the fullest. They drew on every formal or informal, public or private tactic they could find. They approached individuals to sign pledges, but they also lobbied the state to pass a law. They embraced both moral persuasion and legal coercion, employing whichever seemed most promising at the moment. Voluntary societies played a central role in their temperance activity, but temperance advocates also relied on a variety of other devices to convince and cajole—public lectures, holiday observances, and dramas and entertainments, including street theater. In using their full palette of strategies, Cleveland Protestants threw every color they had at the canvas of public culture; surely some of their efforts would stick, or, even better, dominate the painting.

Yet, despite their focused, intense involvement, their relative unity, and their strategic resourcefulness, they fell short. Thousands signed pledges, and temperance became a moral standard for Protestants, but temperance principles failed to become the norm for the public culture. Their power never became authoritative. In the contest to dominate the public culture, Protestant temperance efforts faced concerted opposition. To a much greater degree than in economic development and benevolence, Protestants had to share power in the public culture's decision about temperance. Other groups, primarily the Irish, the Germans, and the religiously indifferent, opposed their efforts and circumscribed their power. On this issue, where their prospects for success seemed so favorable, and where their activity was the most concerted and varied, they fell short. The public culture, always subject to multiple pressures as it formed, took a different direction than the one they proposed.

The temperance crusade began with the solid and enthusiastic support of the city's Protestants. For many Cleveland Protestants, temperance was the key to the future. They embraced the ideology of moral and material progress, hoping their city would win the city-building sweepstakes and become the City of the West. The presence of liquor and grog shops loomed as a major obstacle to the hope that Cleveland would become the "Emerald City of the Lakes," since these establishments brought sin, social disorder, poverty, and crime. Intoxicating drink and the "grog shops" that served it came to represent all that stood in the way of commercial progress and the millennium.[2]

Protestants faced an uphill battle. Liquor sellers and drinkers had a head start in the battle over temperance in antebellum Cleveland. The city's first "public house," Lorenzo Carter's cabin, where a traveller could get a meal, a bed, and a drink of New England rum, appeared in 1797. The village's first whiskey distillery started production in 1800, 16 years before the first church was organized.[3] If the founding of the first church and the first bank in the same year can be taken as symbolic of the cooperative relationship between the religious community and the promoters of economic development, the establishment of the first distillery long before the first church is an indication of the obstacles Protestants encountered in curtailing the flow of liquor.

Visitors passing through Cleveland in the 1830s sent home reports of the flourishing liquor trade in the new town on the shores of Lake Erie. An early settler who came from Rochester in 1831, while admitting that the village presented "the pleasantest sight that you ever saw," was appalled that although the four churches barely struggled along with less than a half dozen members each, "there are between fifteen and twenty grog-shops, and they all live!"[4]

The sellers of liquor did not go unchallenged. Sustained efforts by dozens of voluntary organizations sought to loosen their grip on the public culture. Except for the Father Mathew Temperance Society, a Catholic group active in the 1850s, temperance in Cleveland had a Protestant aura. A conservative estimate would be that 75 percent or more of the temperance leaders were Protestant church members (Tables 3.2, 3.3, and 3.5). Not only did the temperance officials join churches, they were leaders in the churches. Even more temperance society officials showed up in lists of church officers than in the less complete lists of church-joiners. Approximately two-thirds of the temperance officers were located on lists of those who served as Protestant church officers in the years from 1836 to 1860 (Table 3.2).[5]

Not unexpectedly, since so many of the temperance officials were also church members and officers, temperance societies functioned in harmony with the city's Protestant churches. Temperance organizations met in the city's churches, especially in the 1840s. Thirty-three of the 49 temperance meetings and addresses listed in newspapers in the 1840s were held in Protestant churches. Many of the characteristic features of the temperance societies were modeled on church activities. Officers of the societies gave temperance speeches much as ministers gave sermons, they enlisted pledges of abstinence just as churches gathered converts, and they sent out temperance speakers the way churches sent out missionaries. Their meetings resembled nothing so much as church services, even to the extent of including confessions of intemperance and vows of sobriety. The timing of temperance voluntary society growth is an indirect indication of the connection between the city's Protestant churches and temperance. The golden age of the voluntary societies began just after the revival of 1840 brought enthusiasm and converts to the churches.[6]

Temperance activity united the city's Protestants across denominational lines, forming them into something close to an evangelical united front. Ministers spoke at temperance meetings held in other ministers' churches, and ministers from many denominations joined the efforts of the same temperance organizations. Nothing shows the uniting effect of temperance more than a series of coordinated temperance lectures held in 15 churches during the summer and fall of 1858. Most of the Cleveland Protestant ministers who served any appreciable time in the city, with the exception of those from the Episcopal churches, spoke to the city's temperance societies or allowed their churches to be used for temperance meetings. In addition, the wives of the ministers of major Presbyterian and Episcopal churches served on a committee of lectures for the Ladies' Temperance Union.[7]

The most striking indication of the Protestant tenor of the temperance crusade was the failure of the main body of temperance organizations to ally themselves with the Catholic Father Mathew Temperance Society or the diocese's strongly pro-temperance bishop, Amadeus Rappe. Catholic efforts were noticed or applauded on only a few occasions. In general, Catholic and Protestant temperance work proceeded independently. The meetings of umbrella temperance organizations did not incorporate the Father Mathew Temperance Society, nor did temperance societies meet in the city's Catholic churches, and Catholic priests were not included in temperance lecture series. In general, temperance in Cleveland was the work of Protestants.[8]

The only substantial rift in the temperance campaign in these years stemmed from friction between Washingtonians and the more traditional, Protestant church-based temperance organizations. Washingtonians formed independent of formal or informal church sponsorship. Rather than aim their attention at the already sober and respectable, Washingtonians addressed the drunkard. In comparison with other temperance activists, historians have found, they were less likely to be church members and socially prominent, and more likely to be artisans. Washingtonians in Cleveland fit this profile, especially in their concern that more attention should be paid to rescuing the drunkard. They thus put more stress on mutual aid and self-help and less on temperance as a means of shaping the public culture's attitude toward drinking.[9]

The city's Protestant churches were initially hospitable to the Washingtonians. Newspaper notices indicate that Presbyterian, Baptist, and Methodist churches all hosted Washingtonian meetings in the early 1840s. By the mid-1840s the enthusiasm of the churches and some of Cleveland's original temperance advocates for the Washingtonians had cooled. The President of the Cuyahoga County Temperance Association, John Foote, explained in a letter to the *Plain Dealer* that when temperance work began "it was emphatically in the hands of the moral and religious portion of the community." Other classes were comparatively unaffected, and the reformation of the drunkard was not expected, Foote noted. With the Washingtonian movement, thousands were "reclaimed," but they seemed to consider themselves "honorably discharged" with no further need to help the movement beyond their own abstinence. Foote appealed to the new Washingtonian temperance converts for continued service beyond personal reclamation. In this testy claiming of temperance turf, Foote expressed the resentment of the well-connected temperance elite that other groups did not willingly follow their lead.[10]

These tensions between the Washingtonians and others did not seriously hamper the temperance effort. A number of individuals bridged whatever gulf there might have been between the Washingtonians and the other temperance societies. John Foote himself had participated in both an old-line temperance organization, the Cleveland City Temperance Society, and a Washingtonian society. Such involvement was not unusual. Because of people such as Foote, the various temperance voluntary societies led a generally united, Protestant campaign to rid the city of alcohol.[11]

For purposes of assessing their influence in the public culture, the other salient characteristic of those involved in temperance, much like those active in benevolence, was that they were prominent in a broad range of business, political, and social activities. The men were especially visible as political party candidates, local government officials, and officers of businesses, benevolent associations, and schools. For example, almost a third (28, or 31.8 percent) of the 88 male officers of temperance organizations were found in the lists of political party candidates in the years from 1837 to 1860, and a similar percentage populated the lists of government officeholders. Temperance officers joined the business world, too. Nineteen (21.6 percent) could be located on lists of bank officers. Given the difficulty of matching names, it is likely that well over half of the temperance society officers made their mark in politics or government, and almost as many in banking.[12]

As was true for the women active in benevolence, women temperance leaders were difficult to link with what might have been their other activities because of incomplete reporting of names. Three of the 15 women temperance officials, though, were found in lists of benevolent society officers.

What these statistical interconnections meant in practice is evident in the work of John A. Foote, the premier example of the well-connected temperance leader. Foote was born in New Haven, Connecticut, in 1803. His father, Samuel A. Foote, had been governor of Connecticut and a U.S. Senator. A Yale graduate, the junior Foote arrived in Cleveland in 1833. Foote's temperance work was extensive. He served the Cleveland City Temperance Society as President (1831 and 1841) and as an officer (1834, 1836, and 1837). He was also a trustee of the Marine Temperance Society (1850, 1857, 1860), a delegate for the Washingtonian Total Abstinence Society (1844), and an officer in the Young Men's Total Abstinence Society (1837).[13]

Foote was also prominent in benevolent work. He served as a trustee for the Industrial School (1860) and was a long-time trustee of the Western Seamen's Friend Society (1837, 1853, 1857). He was a trustee of Ohio's Boy's Industrial School (from 1854–75) and was one of three people appointed by Governor Salmon P. Chase to investigate the feasibility of establishing a state reform farm. Foote spoke at the first and second annual meetings of the Children's Aid Society. His was more than token support—he adopted a child from the society's institution, the Cleveland Industrial School.

Foote's prominence in politics and other activities kept pace with his temperance and benevolent work. He served in both houses of the Ohio legislature and on Cleveland's City Council (1839, 1840). He was a vice-president of the Cuyahoga County Anti-Slavery Society (1837) and a director of the Cuyahoga County Sabbath Society (1844, 1860). He served on committees for the Cleveland Anti-Gambling Society (1845), the Fourth of July celebration (1841), and an Anti-Mexican War meeting (1848). In business affairs, Foote was a trustee of the Cleveland, Sandusky and Toledo Railroad (1850) and of a major bank, the Society for Savings (1857, 1860).

Foote was part of the Protestant community, as well. He joined
First Presbyterian Church in 1834. He left twice for other churches,
in the schisms of 1837 and 1844 (Chapter 2), only to return each
time. He was an elder of the church in 1845, and was still a member in 1860.

Through his law partners in Andrews, Foote, and Hoyt, Foote
had an even greater reach into the city's public life. One partner,
Sherlock J. Andrews, was a Superior Court Judge, a U.S. Congress-
man, Common Council President, founder and first President of
the Cleveland Bar Association, and a bank president in the years
before the Civil War. Andrews maintained pews in both First Presbyterian and Trinity Episcopal Churches, and he was prominent in
antislavery work and the Protestant Orphan Asylum.

Foote's other partner, James M. Hoyt, lagged only slightly
behind the other two in public involvement. He was President of
the YMCA and active in Bible and temperance work. Hoyt
enhanced the ecumenical tone of Andrews, Foote, and Hoyt. He
joined First Baptist Church in 1836 and served it as a trustee and
deacon. For 25 years he was the President of the Ohio Baptist State
Convention, and for many years he was President of the American
Baptist Home Missionary Society.[14]

Foote and the other male officers of temperance groups were a
well-connected leadership elite that was predominantly Protestant.
As is evident from the extent of their activity, they constituted a
vibrant, functioning elite, not a group suffering from status decline
as earlier historical treatments of antebellum temperance have suggested. Foote and other temperance activists had a large stake in
the city's life and were positioned to spread their ideas and values
into the public culture.[15]

The well-connected Protestant cohort of temperance women
and men of which Foote was a part shaped the general outlines of
the temperance crusade. Their assumptions and arguments, their
reliance on voluntary societies, their use of the strategies of both
moral persuasion and legal coercion, and their successes and failures in implanting their ideals in the public culture, can all be seen
as flowing from their social identity as a Protestant elite.

This Protestant leadership elite assumed that religion's role
was to permeate all aspects of life. The boundaries between public
and private were fluid. This was evident in the public and private
support of benevolent institutions and even more prominent in

the temperance crusade. Indeed, antebellum Protestants would have barely understood the modern distinction of public and private. Their temperance activity underscores the argument that their efforts should not be understood as a case of bringing private morality into public life. Rather, their religion generated moral ideals which they assumed were normative for the public life of the city and the nation as much as for individuals.

For Protestants, there was no such thing as strictly private behavior. Private acts reflected on both the individual and the church. Immoral conduct endangered the church, since it called into question the link between professed belief and living a moral life. Protestants were concerned to establish the churches as the guardians of society's morality and to present individual members as models for conduct for all in the community. As Donald Mathews puts it, "Evangelicals believed that actions of church members represented the seriousness and devotion of the entire fellowship, so when one Christian relaxed his struggle with the world, he brought disgrace upon all his fellows."[16]

First Presbyterian Church, Ohio City, summarized the concern for the stigma that might be attached to religion because of the malfeasance of its adherents when it dealt with the case of a member who was guilty of intemperance and theft, "and thereby has inflicted a deep wound on this church and the cause of Christ generally . . . "[17]

For Protestants the stakes involved in maintaining moral conduct were high, and so their arguments for temperance often evinced a demanding and harsh tone. Protestants claimed that personal morality was the key to present and future prospects of the individual, the community, and the nation. Sherman Canfield of Second Presbyterian Church expressed a common view in saying that he saw "in the character and conduct of the redeemed while on their way to the Eternal City" an indication of the likelihood of future salvation. Canfield also noted a "correspondence between the moral character of men and the felicity or infelicity of their terrestrial state." For society as a whole, Canfield suggested, adopting a moral standard such as temperance as a norm promised a host of pleasant results, including prosperity for the country and happiness for mankind.[18]

The death of Elisha Sterling brought home to Cleveland's Protestants the powerful challenge liquor offered to their efforts to lead moral lives and create a moral city. It also struck at the heart of their efforts to set the moral norms for the public culture, since Sterling was one of them. Sterling was the president of the Cuyahoga County Steam Furnace Company, the first of Cleveland's manufacturers, and he had been a founder and member of the vestry of St. Paul's Episcopal Church.

In 1859, passersby found Sterling lying unconscious on Bank Street. He died shortly after. The cause of his death was unclear, but it soon became known that he had spent the night in a card game at a "Mr. Sherman's." Sherman said that Sterling had fallen down some stairs, but five physicians concluded that more than a fall was involved. The coroner's jury determined that a fractured skull caused Sterling's death, and that the circumstances pointed to criminal violence. The widely believed explanation held that Sterling had gotten into a drunken altercation over gambling debts. The probable circumstances made Sterling's death especially painful for the city's Protestants in view of his prominence in St. Paul's Episcopal Church.[19]

Cleveland's ministers jumped at the opportunity for moralizing provided by Sterling's death. According to the *Leader*, all Cleveland churches presented well-attended discourses on Sterling's murder. R. B. Claxton of St. Paul's Episcopal Church, Sterling's own minister, was as harsh as any. "Drunkenness drags a man down to the level of a brute," was his judgment.[20] Rev. James Eells of Euclid Street Presbyterian Church drew even deeper implications from the death: "The death of one man by violence in the midst of degrading vices is only an index which points to evils more dreadful." Eells drew a lurid picture of life in Cleveland. People who went quietly to their homes every evening knew nothing of the iniquity which abounded in Cleveland. There were the low and filthy dens, he cautioned, but the real places of temptation were the elegant saloons which could be visited without disgrace.[21]

The comments on the death of Elisha Sterling epitomized the arguments of the temperance reformers throughout the antebellum years: temperance was demanded by God while intemperance could only bring individual suffering and social misery. Intemperance and all it represented—lack of self-restraint, destruction of free will, blighted families, social disorder—had no place in the growing commercial city. John Foote provided a convenient summary in 1843 when he argued that "our cause is literally the means in the hands of a gracious God of administering to the wants of the needy—of restoring reason to the maniac—domestic happiness to

the family circle—of diminishing crime, pauperism, and death—
and of preparing the soul for the high and holy duties and privileges of religion." The Cuyahoga County Temperance Society
expected the adoption of temperance principles to amount to a
second American Revolution. It resolved in 1844 "that the political
revolution of 1776 gave the nation liberty and that the temperance
revolution of this day will perpetuate it."[22]

Temperance societies constantly pushed the connection
between intemperance and the scourges of crime and poverty. The
Cleveland City Temperance Society claimed in 1847 that it was "a
fact fully established, beyond all dispute," that three-fourths of all
pauperism and crime in the city was the result of the sale of intoxicating drinks, and so three-fourths of the taxes paid for the poor,
police, and jails were the direct outgrowth of alcohol. Temperance
voluntary societies delighted in counting the number of inmates in
the jails and the poorhouse whose presence could be attributed to
intemperance.[23]

There was an undercurrent of nativism attached to the scan-
dalous stories of the death and suffering brought by intemperance.
The implication, if not the direct point, of many of the tales was
often that the inebriate was German or Irish, and probably
Catholic. Even Catholics, like the Cleveland Diocese's bishop,
Amadeus Rappe, made some of the same connections. The French-
born Rappe saw the Irish as impoverished, improvident, and igno-
rant. He wrote to the Pope that their drinking habits "produced
quarrels, public battles, the breakup of families, divorce, profana-
tion of the Sabbath." These assumptions and arguments, which
combined hopes for the city's future, worries about suffering, insistence on the moral duty to be sober, and nativism fueled the temperance crusade.[24]

As for the strategy which would eradicate the menace of liquor
and the grog shop, Protestants called on all the devices at their disposal—moral exhortation, church discipline, voluntary society activity, and political agitation. In practice, they did not draw a firm line
between moral persuasion and legal coercion. They worked with a
dogged persistence, using whatever strategy seemed most promising
at the moment. They were insistent on being a significant force in
the formation of the public culture's attitude toward liquor.

Seeing that their own Protestant community observed temperance principles represented one strategy. Within their own
churches, Protestants developed and promoted the moral standards

they would take out into society through resolutions, confessions of faith, affirmations in church manuals, church discipline, and the pronouncements of ministers. Churches were deeply concerned with monitoring the conduct of their members. Being a Christian implied a certain kind of life. Private conduct that failed to exhibit the characteristics expected of the Christian deserved censure, and, as Elisha Sterling's death showed, endangered the Protestants' ability to be the culture's moral guardian. If members strayed, they were visited, admonished, and, if necessary, disciplined.[25]

Out in the public arena, things became more complex. Here the strategy of choice was the use of the voluntary society. Like the well-connected Protestants themselves, voluntary societies integrated private and public spheres. The societies lay at the intersection between church and public life and served as the vehicles for Protestants to express their conviction that religious ideals applied to all aspects of life.

Voluntary societies were the bulwark of both the moral and legal crusade against the evils of intemperance. They rallied the committed, convinced the fallen, gathered pledges of abstinence, and provided mutual support for their members. While all these activities lie comfortably in the private sphere, other work by the societies took them into public life. Voluntary societies were the base from which temperance advocates fought against the issuing of licenses for liquor-selling and in favor of stricter regulation of alcohol sales. The societies circulated petitions on public issues, including licensing, and they took it as their task to monitor the enforcement of licensing and regulation in the first half of the 1840s. The Young Men's Washingtonian Total Abstinence Society, for example, offered its help procuring evidence and securing convictions against temperance law violators. As they reminded, prodded, and cajoled public officials, the voluntary societies were brought directly into the political arena. The Cuyahoga County Temperance Society, for instance, declared it would not support the Prosecuting Attorney for election in 1845 unless he pledged to support the existing law.[26]

While voluntary societies were the primary vehicle of the temperance effort, the resourceful activists who led the effort to promote temperance as a central element of the public culture continually searched for other avenues through which to promote their cause. The doubts Protestants had about the theater and

other amusements did not stop temperance reformers from turning entertainments to their advantage. Clevelanders, were they so
inclined, could hear Mr. Dobbin, "the teetotal nightingale" from
Utica, sing his temperance songs. Or they could attend "Dr. Clark's
Temperance Dramatic Company" in its drama of "The Reformed
Drunkard," or see T. S. Arthur's "The Broken Merchant" sponsored
by the New York Temperance Association. First Methodist Church
offered its own contribution, a "Temperance Musical Entertainment," in 1845, and the Young People's Washingtonian Total
Abstinence Society presented the "Trial of King Alcohol for Murder" in 1846.[27]

The temperance dramas and entertainments were simply an
adaptation of an already popular form to serve a temperance cause,
and they seem to have brought little if any opposition, either from
churchgoers who had earlier distrusted theater or from liquor sellers. The same cannot be said for temperance's other venture into
popular entertainment—street theater. Two actors, known as Dean
and McDowell, entertained and outraged Clevelanders for over a
month in the fall of 1845 with their outdoor temperance plays.
Wherever they found a liquor-selling establishment, Dean and
McDowell would mount a dray or a dry goods box set up in front
of it, "call around them a crowd, and score the rum dealers in language always severe and often abusive." While in town, Dean and
McDowell staged several performances of skits such as "The Teeto-
taler and the Grog-Seller" in front of all the public houses. Needless
to say, the outdoor temperance dramas did not go unnoticed by
the liquor sellers. Workers from the houses disrupted the meetings
with eggs, bells, and tin horns.[28]

Other forays into public life met with more acceptance. Temperance groups recognized a golden opportunity for their cause in
holiday celebrations such as the Fourth of July. By identifying temperance with patriotism, they added legitimacy to their cause and
symbolically incorporated temperance into those qualities which
made for an American. The *Herald* approved of the call of temperance organizations for a sober Fourth: "This 'Spirit of 76' needs no
stimulus from the intoxicating grape—for it was born when grape-
shot rattled." Temperance groups from Cleveland and neighboring
areas of Cuyahoga County marched in the Fourth of July processions then often held dinners or picnics afterward. In 1843 the
marchers, referred to as the Cuyahoga Cold Water Army by the
Herald, numbered 2,000. Whether it was using voluntary societies,

entertainments, or holiday observances, Protestants were remark-ably resourceful in their use of strategies for promoting the temper-ance cause.[29]

The messages promoted through these various channels took two chief forms—moral persuasion and legal coercion. It has been an accepted part of the historical treatment of temperance to find a shift in strategy from moral persuasion centered in voluntary orga-nizations, which is held to have characterized the 1830s and 1840s, to legal coercion, symbolized by the passage of the Maine Laws, which is seen as the hallmark of the 1850s.[30] Temperance activity in Cleveland made no such dramatic shift. National tem-perance organizations may have shifted their focus from moral persuasion to legal coercion, but, at the local level, the two strate-gies proceeded simultaneously.

Moral persuasion in all its guises—the cajoling of church members, the solicitation of pledges, the formation of voluntary societies, and temperance parades—marked the temperance effort from the beginning. New voluntary societies were always being formed and re-formed, new campaigns begun, new horror stories about the evils of intemperance told, and new converts signed to temperance pledges. Legal coercion, likewise, persisted from the 1830s to the Civil War as a strategy for imprinting temperance principles on the developing public culture. The question of whether liquor-selling establishments should be licensed or regu-lated persisted throughout these years. As Ian Tyrrell has observed, legal remedies were pursued not as a last resort by those whose efforts at moral persuasion were unsuccessful, but were part of a temperance strategy adopted by settlers familiar with the New Eng-land tradition of community regulation of moral behavior. While temperance advocates may have believed that true goodness could only spring from a converted heart, they were not content to wait until all hearts were changed. In the interim, they invoked the legal system and political pressure to make the unconverted behave. Protestants, in short, used whatever means seemed poten-tially effective in order to stamp their temperance imprint on the public culture.[31]

There was an ebb and flow to the relation between the strate-gies of oral persuasion and legal coercion. At times the focus was on the pledge signings and mutual support of the voluntary associ-ations. At other times lobbying for prohibition or regulation came to the fore. The two aspects of the temperance movement were often—but not always—inversely related in terms of vigor and momentum. When licensing and regulation were most effective, the pledge signings and organizational growth of voluntary societies quieted. When legal enforcement lagged, pledge signings and other moral persuasion efforts generally spurted. The one constant was pressure: whatever the primary method of the moment, Protestants mounted a concerted effort to spread temperance principles and practices. An account of these efforts provides the most extensive evidence available of the multiple strategies by which Protestants sought to influence the public culture.

Four distinct phases marked the ebb and flow between moral persuasion and legal coercion in the public arena. During the first phase, in the decade following the city's incorporation in 1836, legal efforts flourished, then ended in disappointment, while pledge signings and the work of voluntary associations proliferated. The license question—whether the city should allow the selling of liquor by granting licenses—dominated the legal side of Cleveland's temperance agitation in these years. A public meeting chaired by Benjamin Rouse resolved that the most appalling cause of the evil of intemperance was the existing license system. Rouse argued that the licensing system "gives respectability and sanction, as well as protects with the strong arm of the law, a practice that is multiplying drunkards, paupers, criminals, while it inflicts anguish on thousands of unfortunate families. . . . " The Cleveland Presbytery joined the campaign against the license law on the same grounds: "it protects the agents of drunkenness."[32]

The city had been granted the exclusive power to license the sale of liquor in the Act of Incorporation which the Ohio General Assembly passed in creating Cleveland in 1836. Objections to the city's use of its licensing power were raised soon after. Meetings of the "Friends of Temperance of Cleveland and Ohio Cities" in the summer of 1837, first at the Bethel Church and then at the First Baptist Church, prepared an appeal to "enlist this entire community against the enormous evil of licensed groggeries, and procure the same to be circulated into every family in Cleveland." Despite receiving petitions with thousands of signatures, the Common Council left the licensing system intact. The *Herald* asked "Why do not the city council pay some regard to the opinions, interest and welfare of so large and respectable a number of their fellow citizens?"[33]

The debates over whether the city should license taverns were rendered moot in 1839 when the General Assembly took the licensing power out of the city's hands, placing it with the county Court of Common Pleas. This served as a reminder that temperance battles fought in the city had to be waged with one eye on the state and whatever other jurisdictions it designated to exercise authority over liquor selling.[34]

Having failed to prevent the issuing of licenses, temperance advocates could still defend their fallback legal position, regulation. Primarily, this meant overseeing liquor-selling establishments and limiting the quantities in which liquor could be sold. Cleveland's 1836 incorporation law gave the city the power to prevent the unlicensed sale of liquor and to regulate all places where liquor was sold in quantities of less than a quart. An amendment to the charter passed by the General Assembly in 1839 gave the city the further power to suppress all houses of public entertainment where intoxicating liquor was sold. The Common Council used its power in 1840 to prohibit the sale of liquor in quantities of less than a quart, which had the effect of halting the sale of liquor by the drink.[35]

Concurrent with the licensing defeats and the limited progress in regulation, pledge signings and voluntary society activity, which had been minimal in the 1830s, gained momentum in the early 1840s. The first half of the 1840s was the golden age of the moral persuasion side of the temperance effort. Voluntary societies multiplied. The city had only one temperance organization in 1837. Five years later a temperance reformer had a choice among County, City, Marine, Ladies', black, Catholic, and Washingtonian societies, among others. Thousands signed the pledges offered by these temperance organizations.[36]

All these voluntary societies managed to combine their efforts in umbrella groups, the Cleveland City Temperance Society (1833) and the Cuyahoga County Temperance Society (1841), which were as close as Cleveland's Protestants would come to forming an evangelical united front. The county society declared that it was "designed to unite the friends of the cause in more efficient, extended, and permanent efforts for the suppression, of intemperance." In a show of temperance unity, the call for the organizational meeting of the Society, to take place at First Presbyterian Church in Cleveland, included the signatures of the presidents of the Marine Total Abstinence Society, the Young Men's Total Abstinence Society, the Washingtonian Total Abstinence Society, and the Cleveland City Temperance Society. The society coordinated the efforts of the local town organizations and linked them to national temperance efforts.[37]

In the early 1840s, during the first phase of the temperance campaign, the goals of the city's voluntary temperance organizations became more defined, coinciding with similar developments among other temperance organizations in the northeast and midwest. Before 1840, a new society was likely to be a "temperance society." After that, it was more likely to be a "total abstinence" society. Thus the Marine Temperance Society, begun in 1834, was reorganized as the Marine Total Abstinence Society in 1840 and the Cuyahoga County Temperance Society, founded in 1841, was reorganized as the Cuyahoga County Total Abstinence Society in 1845. The Washingtonian societies of the 1840s usually included "total abstinence" in their name. Even those few societies that took the name "temperance" were committed, after 1840, to the principle of total abstinence.[38]

This first phase of the temperance campaign was also the high tide of what might be termed "the cultural war against intemperance." These were the years when temperance dramas and recitals competed with the city's more conventional entertainments and when the temperance street theater of Dean and McDowell flourished. These same years marked the concerted effort to incorporate temperance activity into the city's Fourth of July activities.[39]

In addition to the thousands of pledge signings, the temperance movement could take comfort in some other victories in the early 1840s. The number of "grog-shops" was reduced, hotels adopted temperance principles, and pressure from temperance advocates convinced the county court to refuse licenses when evidence warranted it. The Cleveland City Temperance Society took pride in the fact that liquor-selling establishments were closing. When the city was founded in 1836, there were 99 places where intoxicating drinks could be sold, while in 1843 there were only eight.[40]

All in all, the 1840s were heady years for temperance advocates. A "Committee of Safety," meeting in the spring of 1841 to report on the progress of the temperance cause, contended that the number of people in jails greatly diminished, public sentiment constantly became more favorable, and large numbers signed pledges. In 1841 the *Herald*, noting that 2,000 had joined the "Cold Water Army" and that nearly as many practiced total abstinence, was "gratified that our youthful city is not falling in the rear of older and more populous places in the Temperance Reform." J. Maplebeck of the Marine Total Abstinence Society reported that Dean and McDowell, the stagers of the temperance street dramas, "produced such a revolution as has never been witnessed." Converts signed several hundred pledges, a number of "rum holes" were shut, and some "rum taverns" changed into temperance houses.[41]

The sheer exuberance of this first phase sets it apart from later ones. The triumph of temperance principles seemed near. Temperance activities blossomed as public meetings, church resolutions, petitions, pledge signings, and entertainments all promoted the cause. Temperance activists immersed themselves in the intricacies of the public debate. Not content to stay on the high moral ground of denouncing drinking as a sin, they plunged into the minutia of licensing and regulation.

During the second phase of the ebb and flow between the strategies of moral persuasion and legal coercion, from the mid-1840s to 1851, the euphoria of the early years of the decade dissipated. The temperance movement enjoyed some progress on the legal front but ended the decade with a number of setbacks. Moral persuasion activities, too, were a disappointment to temperance leaders since the movement lost some of the momentum built during the early 1840s. During these years, the likelihood that temperance principles would be incorporated into the public culture began to recede, despite the best efforts of Cleveland's Protestants.

The state set the stage for new activity on the license issue in 1845 when it gave townships the power to decide whether licensed taverns or groceries should exist. In 1847 the township, an area including, but larger than, the city, voted 901 to 752 that no new licenses would be issued. The same law prohibited liquor sales of less than one quart. The city's temperance reformers pressured public officials to make sure the law was enforced. Public officers were deserving of support only when they enforced the law, warned the Cleveland City Temperance Society in 1847. The Society's "Special Committee of ONE HUNDRED" was the most visible effort to let city officials know their enforcement effort would be watched.[42]

For reasons that are unclear, two years after the no-license vote of the township in 1847 came a reversal. The city, this time without the rest of the township, voted 498 to 64 in favor of granting licenses to tavern keepers.[43] The moral persuasion side of the temperance crusade stagnated in these years, too. The voluntary societies were relatively quiescent. The 1845 city directory listed five temperance societies, with about 4,000 members. Four of the five, including the Cleveland City Temperance Society and the Washingtonian and Independent Washingtonian Societies, were listed as "idle." Of the societies listed in the directory, only the Young People's Washingtonian Total Abstinence Society, with 400–500 members, flourished. Some of the other voluntary societies also escaped the doldrums. In 1846 the Marine Total Abstinence Society counted 160 members, and reported that 1,500 or "about four fathoms of names," had signed the pledge since its founding. In 1849 the Society claimed 3,000 pledges. The majority of those who commented on the temperance situation in the late 1840s had a sense that both moral persuasion and legal coercion had fallen short.[44]

The third phase of the ebb and flow between the strategies of moral persuasion and legal coercion, from the early to the mid-1850s, brought an upswing in the fortunes of the temperance movement. Once again, the lure of exercising influence over the formation of the public culture animated Cleveland's Protestants. Two new developments in 1851—Maine's passage of a temperance law and the adoption of a new state Constitution—shifted the focus to the legal arena. The Maine Law heartened temperance reformers everywhere and became the model for efforts in other states to prohibit liquor traffic. Now Clevelanders had a chance to recover from the loss of the 1849 vote in the city by gaining a victory at the state level.

First Presbyterian Church's Samuel Aiken supported the Maine Law in a sermon, and the city's temperance organizations petitioned the state legislature for a similar law for Ohio. New umbrella organizations, like the Cuyahoga County Temperance Alliance and the City Temperance Alliance, worked for the law. A petition of 600 signatures "procured through the exertions of a lady who, with her children, was robbed of a husband and father by means of the accursed traffic" was presented to the Common Council asking for a Maine Law. Another petition added 1,661 names to the list.[45]

Thirteen states passed Maine Laws in the early 1850s, but Ohio was not one of them. Ever resourceful, temperance advocates found another vehicle for their cause, the revision of the state constitution. They worked to attach a provision ending licensing to the new document. Not wanting to endanger the passage of the constitution by including a temperance article, the state legislature placed the licensing issue on the ballot to be voted on separately at the time of the vote on the new constitution. The provision was defeated in the state and lost narrowly in the city of Cleveland, 672 to 579. As a result, licensing remained.[46]

The political fights of the early 1850s involving the Maine Law and the state constitution directed the attention of voluntary society reformers beyond the local arena to state politics. In 1852, the Cuyahoga County Total Abstinence Society supported the effort to elect as state representatives only those who would support a Maine Law for Ohio. The North Ohio Methodist Conference, which represented the Methodist churches on the west side of the Cuyahoga, resolved in 1851 and 1855 to support only candidates committed to passing temperance legislation. The Cuyahoga County Temperance Alliance carried political involvement one step further by endorsing a specific candidate, John A. Foote, for the U.S. Senate because he was a supporter of the Maine Law.[47]

A few successes on the local level partially compensated for the Maine Law and state constitution defeats. As a byproduct of the adoption of the new state constitution, the city adopted a new incorporation statute which reinforced Cleveland's power to supervise liquor selling. The city was given the power "to regulate taverns, and other houses for public entertainment, and to regulate or prohibit ale and porter shops and houses, and places for significant or habitual resort for tippling and intemperance." In 1853 the city stopped Sunday sales and prohibited liquor sales at bars and hotels.[48]

A new voluntary society, the Carson League, played a substantial role in the campaign to enforce the new laws, a clear indication that though voluntary societies may have been private organizations, their activities involved politics in the public sphere. Named after similar local organizations in other cities, the League mobilized in 1854 to aid in enforcing the law prohibiting Sunday sales by searching out violators. Late in 1854 the League reported that 73 prosecutions had begun since November 1. Thirty-one ended with fines and payment of court costs or discontinuation of liquor selling. After prosecutions began, a number of liquor dealers as well as three hotels ceased sales. The Carson League lasted less than a year, and so, by all indications, did the enforcement effort. City authorities, according to the *Leader*, did not enforce the Sunday closing law, with the result that "rowdyism and drunkenness on the Sabbath day have fearfully increased."[49]

With so much effort directed toward the political arena in the early 1850s, the moral persuasion arm of the temperance crusade was relatively dormant. Reports of pledge signings, always a prime indicator of the strength of moral persuasion, failed to match the heady levels of the early 1840s. Women's groups were the exceptions, perhaps because their access to the political side of temperance was limited, so their efforts were concentrated on moral persuasion. Two weeks after being organized in 1850, the Cleveland Ladies' Temperance Union numbered 700 members. By January 1853, it had enrolled 1,400."[50]

In this third phase of the ebb and flow between moral persuasion and legal coercion, temperance campaigners recaptured some of the momentum of the first phase a decade earlier. They extended the temperance campaign even further into the public arena by involving it in state Constitutional politics, elections, and law enforcement. During these years, they invoked the formal instruments of power—laws, regulations, and law enforcement—in their quest for influence in the developing public culture.

The middle and late 1850s, the fourth phase of the antebellum temperance effort in Cleveland, was a fallow period for temperance strategists relying on legal coercion, while those engaged in efforts of moral persuasion continued their labors at a steady pace. The prohibition forces never regained their momentum after the defeat of Ohio's version of the Maine Law and the failure to incorporate a no-license provision in the state constitution. Even the Sunday prohibition ordinance, one of the few legal victories of the decade, proved ineffectual, despite a unanimously adopted City Council resolution in 1859 directing the city marshal to enforce it. At a meeting held in Perry Park on Public Square, Rev. William H. Brewster of Wesleyan Methodist Church deemed it "a piece of ineffable impudence" for the saloons to be open on Sunday, when all other businesses were closed. The "saloon keepers had no right to disregard the moral and religious right of the community," Brewster argued.[51]

On the moral persuasion front, a new network of societies, the Sons of Temperance, and their women's auxiliaries, the Daughters of Samaria, were founded. The other temperance organizations continued their pledge signings. In the late 1850s, the Marine Total Abstinence Association was reporting 7,000 "enrolled and pledged."[52]

The ebb and flow between the strategies of legal coercion and moral persuasion in the years from 1836 to 1860 suggests that historical accounts that find a decisive shift from moral persuasion to legal coercion in the antebellum years need to be reexamined. In Cleveland there was oscillation between the two strategies, rather than a one-time, decisive shift from one to the other. To some extent, moral persuasion activity grew when laws were lax and a push was needed to promote moral conduct or new laws. Moral persuasion lagged when laws were strictest and efforts to convince not as necessary. The same symbiotic relation between legal and moral strategies is evident from the legal side. Prohibitive and regulatory legislation generally followed moral persuasion efforts, yet the political activity the legislation called for seemingly diverted the focus of the temperance movement away from the moral persuasion side of the crusade. Throughout, however, efforts at moral persuasion and legal coercion coexisted. Protestant temperance activists, ever resourceful, used whatever avenue seemed open— formal or informal, public or private. When they saw a political opening, as with the Maine Law or the state constitution, they pushed for legal coercion. Meanwhile, they probed on the moral persuasion front, seizing on opportunities, like temperance street theater or particularly gruesome examples of the pernicious effects of alcohol, such as Elisha Sterling's death, to hammer home their message. Eternal vigilance and activity on both fronts was the watchword if they were to be successful in the contest to wrest control of the developing public culture form their opponents.

For all their resourcefulness, persistence, and attention to the details of legislation and enforcement, Protestants failed to translate their ideals into law. The defeat of Ohio's Maine Law and the city vote to keep licensing stood out as clear indications that their efforts fell short. They undoubtedly placed temperance firmly in the ethos of the upper- and upper-middle classes of the Protestant churches, but their impact on the broader public culture lagged behind. The work of voluntary societies had established a firm basis for success in the 1840s. It appeared that the Protestants' values would be adopted by the society at large. By the late-1840s, though, the developing public culture told a different tale: lax enforcement of laws, a flourishing liquor trade, and sizeable segments of the public tolerated liquor. Under these circumstances, it is clear that Protestant intentions notwithstanding, temperance failed to become the dominant value of the public culture, although it firmly established itself as a central part of the culture of middle- and upper-class Protestants of British descent.

The crux of the problem temperance advocates faced was that they represented only a particular slice of the city's population. The persuasive and coercive powers of the elite who guided temperance efforts were constantly tested by groups with different ideas about what interests and values should hold sway in the public culture.

The temperance campaign met with resistance in many forms. Many of the city's German- and Irish-born were not persuaded that abstinence was a central element of a virtuous life. Circumventing the prohibition against liquor-selling on Sunday became a weekly ritual for some of the city's Germans. The *Plain Dealer* reported that they moved their picnics and outings to a grove in nearby Brooklyn township, where no laws restricted Sunday sales. Two thousand took advantage of the spot one Sunday in 1857, drinking 42 kegs of beer, the paper reported.[53]

A less subtle form of resistance, anti-temperance violence, also hindered the reformers' efforts. Dean and McDowell, the dramatists of the street, had to put up with harassment, often by the employees of the establishments they harassed. Yet, they were able to present their dramas despite rotten eggs, horns, bells, and other distractions. Another temperance advocate was not so fortunate. In 1845, several "slaves of alcohol" attacked Rev. Gardner Dean while he lectured. They knocked over the barrel he stood on, breaking his arm and "injuring him internally." The assailants were jailed.[54]

The direct opposition of the liquor sellers was another, more formidable force in resisting temperance reform. They had a number of arguments at their disposal. First, liquor licenses provided significant city revenue. In 1847, in the months just before the vote on whether the city should prohibit the granting of licenses, one letter to the *Plain Dealer* contended that the question seemed to be, should the city "derive sufficient revenue from license, to extinguish the city debt within a short time, and thereby relieve to some extent, their other taxes." Liquor sellers could also argue that brewing was an important economic activity in the city. In 1845 the three city breweries employed 13 workers and made 177,000 gallons of beer and ale with an estimated value of $17,000. Attaching the booster sentiment to the pro-liquor position was unusual, although one letter to the editor, in addition to complimenting the city's pure air and clean, broad streets, included as one of Cleveland's attractions a "grand western saloon."[55]

Flouting and evading license laws, quart laws, and Sunday prohibition laws was another form of resistance open to liquor sellers.
Evading the law promoted ingenuity. One liquor dealer put a
"Drug Store" sign out front. A common ploy to circumvent the
prohibition against drinking liquor on the premises where it was
sold was to sell drinks in small vials, and have customers go to
another saloon to drink them. Even more venturesome were two of
the principal bars of the city. Liquor was not sold, but crackers
could be bought for 6-1/4 cents apiece, accompanied, without
charge, by something to wash them down.[56]

Liquor sellers fought back in the courts when enforcement of
the licensing laws stiffened. In November 1854, 85 of the city's
principal liquor retailers were arrested for violating the new liquor
law on Sunday closing. The sellers "will make a formidable fight"
said the *Leader*. They employed six lawyers to defend them, and
were confident of victory, the paper reported. What happened after
the arrests is unclear. Later newspapers did not publicize mass convictions, suggesting that these cases may have followed the pattern
of other cases, with some sellers agreeing to close, some being
fined, some promising not to sell on Sunday, and some, undoubtedly, continuing to sell liquor as before. The same day as the arrests
of the 85 liquor dealers, the *Plain Dealer* reported the formation of
an anti-Carson League by liquor retailers. By November, the League
had a war chest of $500.[57]

Political opposition was as difficult to contend with as the defi-
ance of liquor sellers. Temperance reformers, despite their efforts to
present themselves as the moral voice of the community, could not
escape the maelstrom of party politics. Elections that hinged on
fidelity to temperance could have a comic element. Harvey Rice
later recalled that when he campaigned for Congress against John
Foote in 1851, "though I had voted for the most stringent temperance measures, yet it got to be noised around that Mr. Foote was
the better temperance man, because he did not allow his wife to
put brandy in her mince pies, and pickles too. The result was that
Mr. Foote got elected."[58]

The temperance issue in politics seldom had such a benign
aspect. More often, it crystallized intense partisan maneuvering
between Democrats and their chief rivals, first the Whigs and then
the Republicans. Temperance reformers may have regarded themselves as the moral and respectable part of the population, but
their political influence was generally channelled into only some

of the parties, the Whigs and later the Republicans or Free Soilers.[59]

Democrats saw hidden motives lurking behind the fight over liquor regulation. They claimed that the fight to pass a law in Ohio comparable to the Maine Law was an effort by the Free Soilers to undermine them. The *Plain Dealer*, a Democratic Party paper, suspected that the agitation for enforcement of the Sunday liquor law was a Republican ploy to rally supporters. The Republicans "always claim that their party contains all the religious, moral, intelligent and temperate elements of society and that consequently their Democratic neighbors and fellow citizens are a set of blackguards and the dregs of society." Yet the Republicans never had a yearning to enforce the liquor laws until election time, the paper noted. Not only were Republicans hypocritical, charged the *Plain Dealer*, they were two-faced. In the spring 1859 election, they told saloon-keepers the Democratic mayoral candidate would close them down, then told temperance people he was a drinking man. The Republicans carried the election with an anti-liquor campaign, but once in office did not enforce the liquor laws, said the paper.[60]

Many of the city's German and Irish resisted temperance laws. In 1847 Germans met to oppose the license law soon to be voted on. In early 1857, 3,000 Germans petitioned City Council for a modification of the Sunday and election-day prohibition ordinances. They asked that the $50 fine for giving beer or ale away in one's own house be repealed, and they also wanted sales allowed in boarding houses and hotels. Every Democrat on the council voted in favor of the amendment, which nevertheless lost by a large majority.[61]

The problems temperance reformers confronted in trying to impose their temperance commitment on the public highlights a perpetual dilemma of moral reform—the problem of a politically influential portion of the population, even a majority, trying to enforce moral and social standards not shared by another significant part of the population. Diverse pressures and powers shaped the culture of Cleveland. Protestants were just one pressure point, albeit an especially powerful one, contesting over a process in which many others participated. What the temperance activists saw as a clear-cut and self-evident moral standard was to others one bone of contention in the bitter rivalry of political parties, ethnic groups, and religions in the antebellum city. Temperance matters became enmeshed in a variety of religious and ethnic battles—between Democrats and their political opponents, including Whigs, Free Soilers, and Republicans; between Catholics and

Lutherans who were more comfortable with drinking and other Protestants who weren't; and between Germans, Irish, and "native citizens." The temperance advocates could sometimes pass restrictive legislation, and they could elect sympathetic candidates, but they could not stop many of their German, Irish, and non-believing neighbors from making beer and alcohol integral and accepted parts of their lives.

The temperance reformers were only one of many interests and powers in the city vying for influence on this issue in the public culture. In the pluralist environment of the antebellum city, victories were hard-earned, fleeting, and often unenforceable. This self-appointed moral and respectable element of the community found that it could not translate its own personal moral standards into public policy. Despite their efforts, groggeries and drinking remained a permanent feature of Cleveland's public culture.[62]

While Protestants as a group tasted defeat, the situation is more ambiguous for the women active in the crusade. A number of historians have found in the movement the beginnings of ideas of sisterhood, which led to later campaigns for women's rights. In their temperance campaigns women grasped for direct coercive, formal, institutional, and legal power in the form of local and state laws which would be enforced. To some extent, women also asserted their authority over the conduct of men, who were the target of most temperance activity. That they fell short meant that most of their influence on issues of temperance, like most of their efforts in other arenas of the public culture, would have to rely on indirect, informal, and persuasive approaches. Protestants would find these methods, customarily assigned to the woman's sphere, their most dependable avenue for public influence. The extent to which these measures could move Protestants deep within public life through petition drives and lobbying the state legislature suggests that neither women nor Protestants were relegated to the private sphere in their efforts to participate in the process of forming the public culture. Their work affected what laws were passed and enforced, a clearly "public" impact. To this extent, women, in Nancy Hewitt's phrase, stood "at the junction" of the public and private spheres. Both women and men found that a creative use of the informal instruments of power available to them, particularly the voluntary society, provided access to the public life of the city.[63]

Temperance activity, then, took women beyond the woman's sphere. It took them directly into public life, unlike benevolence which limited them to quasi-public involvement through voluntary societies that received public money. In the work of the Cold Water Army, women emerged into partisan political activity. Protestant women used temperance to press at the boundaries of the cult of true womanhood because to be the ones responsible for moral education and character formation in an antebellum city seemed to them to require public, political efforts to promote abstinence.

Temperance reformers observing the groggeries or the Germans on the nearby Brooklyn township hills drinking beer on the Fourth of July must have been disappointed. The temperance campaign should have found Protestants at the height of their culture-shaping power. As a community, they had been virtually united in their commitment to temperance. The issue was acknowledged to be well within their sphere. Furthermore, promoting temperance was not beset with the complications that hampered their other attempts to shape the city. Benevolent efforts, by rewarding proper conduct with aid or by encouraging proper attitudes through institutions, influenced recipients only indirectly. Antislavery agitation was enmeshed with complex political, sectional, and constitutional issues. The task of addressing the problems of wealth, business, and technology was hindered by their own ambiguous reaction to economic development. Temperance had few of these drawbacks because Protestants could tap the widely shared assumption that morality flowed directly from religion. The message of temperance had the potential to change people's behavior directly and immediately. Temperance was entangled in many of the crosscurrents of city and state politics, but not nearly so much as antislavery with its capacity to disrupt existing political alignments and national unity.

These favorable circumstances set the stage for some substantial successes for the city's temperance reformers in the quarter century after the city's incorporation. Clevelanders signed temperance pledges, the Common Council passed license laws, and abstinence became the standard for the respectable and moral element of the population. That theater owners were staging plays with temperance themes and that they made a point of calling attention to the respectability of their audience is testimony to the influence of the Protestant temperance campaign to influence the public culture.[64]

Despite all these favorable circumstances and successes, the twenty-five year temperance campaign came up short. If power and influence in the public culture can be measured partly by the extent to which a group is able to translate its ideals into enforceable legislation and widely shared attitudes, it must be concluded that in regard to temperance the power of Cleveland's Protestants was limited.

In the temperance campaigns of the "Cold Water Army," Protestants failed to ensconce themselves as the public culture's moral guardians and definers of proper conduct whose ideals were translated into law and widely shared social attitudes. Instead, they were one of many contestants for the role of conscience of the city, and they had to contend with others whose consciences sent them a different message. The Germans who spent Sunday on the Brooklyn hills drinking beer reminded Protestants that there were other claimants to the city's public culture.

Chapter 7

Cowardly Castles?:
Protestant Involvement in
Antislavery Debates

In none of their other public activities did Protestants face so much opposition as they did when they entered the debate about slavery. When they involved themselves in temperance campaigns and benevolence, their work was taken to be a natural outgrowth of their religious beliefs, but when they took positions on slavery they were charged with intruding where they did not belong. Even their comments on economic development were more welcome than their antislavery activity, perhaps because Protestants reinforced economic values promoted by the city's boosters and because there was not yet a significant labor movement to object to their message.[1]

When they sought to enter the antislavery debates, Protestants embroiled themselves in a contentious environment, one in which others questioned their motives, their competence, and the legitimacy of their participation. The perception that they supported a particular, partisan view, rather than embodying any widely shared moral sentiment of the kind which characterized their benevolent work, also hemmed them in. In this area of the formation of culture in antebellum Cleveland, Protestants had to wage a concerted campaign to convince others they should even participate.

The constraints imposed by the Founding Fathers' ambiguous resolution of the question of how church and state were to be related made establishing a substantial foothold in the world of public issues arduous. Religion was to guide and nurture the republic while at the same time avoiding any direct, formal links with the state. These expectations cut both ways. They furnished

ammunition to those suspicious of extensive Protestant involvement in the culture, while also providing a rationale for activity in
the name of religion. The fragile consensus that governed religion's
role, then, provided the wedge for Protestant involvement in public affairs. It was also fodder for opponents who feared that religion
brought intolerance and threatened liberty.[2]

In their antislavery work, Cleveland Protestants pushed at the
constraints imposed by the society's understanding of religion's
"place." To do otherwise would be to forgo efforts to influence a
crucial issue with broad implications for the values that would
dominate the public culture. For Cleveland Protestants, as for their
counterparts across the nation, it was axiomatic that religion lay at
the heart of any prosperous, well-ordered society. The city's ministers, churches, and church members assumed that religion furnished appropriate truths and guidelines as applicable to public
issues as to any other human endeavor. The force of these ideas
pushed Protestants out into the public arena. The preamble to the
constitution of the Euclid Street Presbyterian Church summed up
this view:

> Whereas morality is essential to a free Government and is the
> foundation of civil liberty and social happiness, and since gen-
> uine morality is the legitimate result of the Christian religion
> and is best promoted by the preaching of the Gospel: and, espe-
> cially, since the preaching of the Gospel is one of the means
> which God has appointed for the salvation of His creatures, it
> becomes the duty of all who love their country to lend their aid
> in supporting the institutions of Religion and in maintaining the
> public and state administration of truth; and since this object is
> better accomplished by the united and systematic exertions of
> well organized societies, than by the occasional efforts of indi-
> viduals, we, the subscribers, do form ourselves into a society and
> agree to be governed by the following *Constitution*:. . . .

In this understanding, forming a church becomes a public act, and
the church serves as an essential foundation for the polity.

The state, just as much as the church, served a religious purpose, as far as Cleveland's Protestants were concerned. As Sherman
S. Canfield, minister of Second Presbyterian Church remarked, "Its
aim is to protect, to encourage, and to prompt in 'doing justly, lov-
ing mercy, and walking humbly with God,' and its end is fulfilled

when the Nation's collective Mind—enlightened and pure—has become a Temple of Liberty dedicated to the Father of Lights."[3]

The city's Protestants assumed that religion ought to play an especially important role in defining the identity and values of the American republic. They shared the general evangelical conviction that the United States played a central role in God's plan for the world. Canfield argued that "God seems to have designed to render our country free and prosperous through the institutions of Christianity; and thus a medium of blessings to the world." He saw religion at work in the very foundations of the country, since "the theory of American freedom was derived from the word of God."[4]

The only Protestant dissenters to the sanctioning of religious involvement in public matters were Seymour W. Adams and Gideon Perry. When Adams took over the pulpit of First Baptist Church in 1846, he insisted that the prime job of the minister was to watch over souls. The minister was not a political advisor: "He is not called to figure in the strife of politics, nor should any seek to draw him into that arena." Perry, who at the time was associate rector at Trinity Episcopal Church, was, as usual, a dissident fly in the Protestant ointment. He distrusted what he called "pulpit politics," because it degraded religion. "The holy influence of religion should never be lent to political strife." Perry advised his fellow ministers to preach peace, love, and good will, and not to sow dissension in the community. The *Plain Dealer*, a Democratic Party organ, commended his remarks to "Avery, Bittenger, Smith and Co.," three politically active ministers identified with antislavery.[5]

In accepting a sphere for religion separate from the public realm, Adams and Perry expressed a minority opinion. For most Cleveland ministers, involvement in public debates was a logical extension of religious concerns made all the more important by the belief that religion was the proper foundation for both personal morality and a virtuous and prosperous republic.

Although themselves firmly persuaded of the necessity of public activity, Protestant ministers, churches, church members, and voluntary societies had to be careful in light of the constraints imposed by society's expectations about appropriate religious involvement in affairs of state. They moved gingerly and obliquely, conscious that to do otherwise might threaten the ambiguous compromise which guided the relationship between church and state.

Protestants were careful about the political issues they addressed and the rhetoric they used. They chose issues that could be presented as logical extensions of their acknowledged role of superintending morals, such as temperance, moral reform, antislavery, and war. This hindered their efforts little, since most issues could be couched in moral terms. As long as they could relate their positions on public issues to moral concerns, they could engage in debates from which notions of separation of church and state might have barred them.[6]

Protestant public rhetoric, too, reflected the knowledge that religious efforts to deal with public issues attracted critical scrutiny. Cleveland's Protestants relied on what historian Sandra Sizer refers to as "the political uses of apolitical rhetoric," framing their public pronouncements in moral terms where their acknowledged expertise provided cover. The more they could present themselves as upholding widely shared moral principles, the greater their chances of being allowed to remain in the public arena. Protestants often framed their arguments in terms of sin and Biblical injunctions. First Baptist Church, for example, after debating about the "propriety or utility of bringing the subject within the church for its action," decided to oppose slavery, a system "that deeply involves the Spiritual, Moral & physical welfare and happiness of millions of our fellow creatures." The church concluded that "American slavery is repugnant to the principles and precepts of the Gospel & is therefore wrong in Principle & wicked in all its legitimate tendencies."[7]

While addressing some issues could be justified by arguing that moral questions were raised, involvement in electoral and legislative politics was especially problematic. Ministers were particularly vulnerable to complaints. No Cleveland Protestant minister held elective political office. Clergy participation in electoral and legislative politics was episodic, growing out of particular issues at specific times, rather than the permanent and institutional role which could be pursued through political parties.[8]

Churches, too, were largely divorced from the political process where most public issues were debated. Churches and political parties were separate, independent groups that did not enter into the patterns of cooperation which marked the relation of churches to railroads, banks, and benevolent and moral reform societies. Political parties were not formed in churches nor did they meet in churches as temperance and benevolence societies did. Similarly, church officers did not meet in political party offices, and political parties did not offer services to churches or church groups in the form of rides or provisions, both of which characterized the relationship between churches and businesses.

Church members were not subject to the same strictures as ministers and churches when they entered the political arena. One indication of the presence of church members in electoral and legislative politics was that a substantial number of political party candidates and government officeholders were church joiners. Roughly a quarter of those who were political party candidates (23.7 percent) or government officeholders (25.2 percent) from 1836 to 1860 were located on lists of antebellum church joiners. Had complete lists of church joiners been available, and if name matching were not so problematic, as many as half of the political party candidates and government officeholders might be found to have been Protestant church members (Tables 3.2 and 3.3.). With so many members in decision-making positions, Protestants could unobtrusively permeate electoral and legislative politics.[9]

Besides temperance, the moral and public issue that most agitated Cleveland Protestants was slavery. Cleveland's churches, ministers, and church members took stronger antislavery positions than did their regional or national associations, stemming in part from their New England heritage and the influence of the perfectionist, evangelical religion which extended through the Burned-Over District of New York to the Western Reserve.

Officers of antislavery societies were members of Protestant churches. Seven of the 11 officers of antislavery organizations were traced to lists of church joiners—six of these joined First Presbyterian Church. Like members of temperance and benevolent groups, these antislavery activists were heavily involved in the city's social life, particularly in government and politics, and so constituted part of the city's leadership elite.[10]

Because they were less explicitly religious, voluntary societies enjoyed a freedom that ministers and churches lacked. The major political organizations that interested Protestants, the antislavery societies, had close links to the city's churches. The Cuyahoga County Anti-Slavery Society was organized at First Presbyterian Church, and met in Cleveland at the First Presbyterian, Wesleyan Methodist and A.M.E. Churches.[11]

There was universal agreement among leading Protestants in Cleveland that slavery was a sin and lacked scriptural support. Beyond that broad agreement lurked large areas of bitter disagreement between what may be labelled "moderate" and "strong" antislavery churches and ministers. Strong antislavery churches were quicker to label slavery the "darkest social evil of our country," as Sherman Canfield of Second Presbyterian Church did. They identified with the abolitionist cause and usually with its tactics. Strong antislavery advocates insisted that their denominations not extend fellowship to slaveholders.[12]

Moderate antislavery churches and ministers, who most likely represented the majority of Clevelanders, generally shared a distaste for slavery, but worried that contention over the issue needlessly disrupted church unity. Some moderate antislavery ministers, such as Samuel Aiken of First Presbyterian Church, feared that the agitation of antislavery activists threatened respect for the law and the constitution, and made compromise and maintaining the union more difficult. The most celebrated instance of Aiken's moderate position on slavery came around 1850 when a fugitive slave took refuge in his church. A posse seized the fugitive and dragged him out of the sanctuary while Aiken hid behind a pillar. Aiken's actions were of a piece with his paeans to railroads— Aiken cast his lot with existing social arrangements. For partisans of strong antislavery principles, Aiken's refusal to intervene marked him as someone unwilling to act on his beliefs and fed the desire to set up churches dedicated to a stronger antislavery stance.[13]

In their antislavery pronouncements, many ministers moved in a direction they had avoided in responding to economic development or in their benevolent and temperance work. They questioned some of society's fundamental understandings and institutional arrangements. They adopted a higher law argument which led them to judge slavery, one of their society's central institutions, in light of their religious ideals and then impelled them to disobey society's laws when they were in conflict with God's.

William H. Brewster of Wesleyan Methodist Church promoted the higher law doctrine in a speech against the Fugitive Slave Law. The authority of God is supreme—that was Brewster's starting point. Civil authority and government have only derivative authority: "The great end of civil government is to protect all men in the enjoyment of those rights conferred by the Creator." The Bible enjoined obedience to civil authority, Brewster acknowledged, but he added a crucial qualification: "when that authority is exercised for proper and legitimate ends, and within due bounds." When civil authority claimed what belonged to God, its claim must be rejected. Such an overreaching by civil authority had occurred in the passage of the Fugitive Slave Law, said Brewster.[14]

Cleveland ministers working with this higher law standard lent their support to a number of antislavery efforts that challenged civil and criminal laws. Many of Cleveland's Protestant ministers and congregations offered their support to those charged with freeing a fugitive slave captured by slave hunters in what became known as the Oberlin-Wellington rescue case. While the accused were jailed in Cleveland, local Protestants rallied to their cause. When an Oberlin Sunday School came to visit, Cleveland's Plymouth Congregational Church Sunday School met them at the station with a band and banners and escorted them to the jail. Ministers James A. Thome of First Presbyterian Church, Ohio City, and James C. White of Plymouth Congregational Church preached in their support.[15]

After John Brown was hanged in 1859 for leading his ill-fated slave rebellion, Wesleyan Methodist Church called for a meeting and the tolling of bells "on the occasion of the sacrifice to the Moloch of slavery by the killing of the body of John Brown by the Commonwealth of Virginia." Rev. J. C. White of Plymouth Congregational Church told a gathering that "John Brown was a man of God and had gone home." Later histories of Congregationalism in Cleveland report that Congregational churches observed the day of Brown's death as a day of humiliation, fasting, and prayer.[16]

Despite Protestant efforts to legitimate their antislavery activity by casting their arguments in moral terms, their active involvement in the public debate, their support for a higher law, their disregard of the Fugitive Slave Law, and their wholehearted endorsement of John Brown's raid brought heated opposition. Instead of offering apolitical, general moral guidance about the sin of slavery, critics asserted, Protestants served identifiable partisan interests. The *Plain Dealer* printed the most forceful denunciations of clerical involvement in antislavery. The paper had an axe to grind. It supported the Democratic Party and feared that the antislavery movement threatened the unity of the nation, while the views of the leading Protestant clergy tended to mesh with those of the more strongly antislavery groups, the Whig, Liberty, Free Soil, and Republican parties. As the sectional controversy heated up, so did the stridency of the *Plain Dealer*'s attacks on the antislavery parties and their clerical allies.

As much as they presented themselves as apolitical and motivated strictly by moral concerns, churches promoted specific, partisan political positions, according to one article. Protected in their
"Cowardly Castles," the article charged, ministers could deliver partisan political sermons. The *Plain Dealer* challenged the ministers to
submit to the rough and tumble of politics: "Pulpits are often to
clergymen what the shell is to a tortoise—an ornament and a shield.
Out of it they sometimes cut very clumsy and funny figures."[17] The
talents and inspiration of ministers, the *Plain Dealer* added, were not
necessarily appropriate to judging contemporary political issues:
"the general relation by the Savior eighteen hundred years ago, did
not determine what construction ought to be given to any particular clause of the constitution of the United States." The newspaper
asked "why do our clergymen, who are well sustained and paid to
preach and practice the doctrines of the Bible, jump out of its teachings and turn political crusaders! Why do they meddle with matters
foreign to their profession—of which they know nothing—and
upon which nobody wants their opinion"?[18]

The *Plain Dealer* argued that politics in the pulpit short-cir-
cuited the democratic process and the sovereignty of the people.
When J. Hyatt Smith, minister of Second Baptist Church, spoke at
his church to more than 1,000 people about the Kansas-Nebraska
controversy, he claimed that in all matters, spiritual as well as temporal, the "pulpit had the floor." That claim could not be accepted
by the *Plain Dealer*, for in its view the pulpit had to give way to the
higher claims of the press and the people. If it did not, concluded
the paper, the country might as well throw away the ballot box. In
setting up democratic procedures and the sovereignty of the people as social authorities with precedence over the views of ministers and religious ideals, the paper undercut the Protestant bid for
power in the public culture.[19]

The specter of religious intolerance also fed the worries of the
Plain Dealer. The paper charged that Christian involvement in politics was a step backward into an undesirable past: "It took nearly
two hundred years to secure the rights of conscience to the people
of the New England states from the clutches of persecuted and per-
secuting Intolerance." Churches had to be watched since "they all
hunger and thirst after temporal power, as much as they do for
righteousness or any other good things."[20]

Underlying the objections of the *Plain Dealer* was the expectation that religion should play a circumscribed role in public life.

Religion's chief concerns should be saving individual souls and offering general moral guidelines to the polity, rather than becoming directly and significantly involved in politics and other "worldly affairs." The *Plain Dealer* marshalled Biblical support for its view. From Luke 22:17 came the oft-quoted "Render unto Cesar [sic], the things which are Cesar's [sic] and unto God the things which are God's." As far as the paper was concerned, religion's resources were being misused: "We should like to know if the *legitimate* work of the Gospel has all been done?" asked the paper. "Are there no more souls to save? . . . Is there no crime in our streets that demands rebuke—no poverty to be alleviated—no ignorance to be removed[?] Have we all arrived at social, moral, and religious perfection?" As far as the *Plain Dealer* was concerned, Protestant ministers had violated society's expectations for clergy, and they had presented an obviously partisan message that could not be camouflaged by apolitical rhetoric about the sin of slavery.[21]

Although they established a continuing, although tenuous, presence in the public debates about slavery, it is hard to assess Protestant antislavery activity as anything but a hindrance in terms of their efforts to shape the city's public culture. The *Plain Dealer's* image for Protestant ministers active in politics—that they indicted society from the safe vantage point of their "Cowardly Castles"— aptly summarized a popular view. Pulpits and churches were castles in the sense that Protestants were protected when they spoke in moral terms. They had a large degree of freedom in addressing public issues such as slavery because they were often seen to be expressing widely shared moral sentiments. Yet when Protestants ventured too far out of their castles or departed too much from their role of upholding morality, segments of the population for which the *Plain Dealer* spoke clamored to have them retreat, and charged them with being self-serving, uninformed, unrealistic, politically partisan, and potentially coercive. Protestants could speak from the castle of religious ideals, yet they were hampered by expectations that religion and public issues belonged to separate realms.

More than in any of their other attempts to influence the public culture, in addressing public issues Protestants were constrained by society's expectations about religion's proper role. When they tried to define issues in terms of religious ideals, others counterpoised more "worldly" and "practical" considerations. When they invoked the authority of Scripture, others countered with the authority of the ballot box. Even when ministers, members, churches, and voluntary societies moved cautiously, or chose their issues or rhetoric with care, opponents challenged their presence in the political realm.

Involvement in antislavery debates ultimately proved a drawback in terms of the Protestants' influence in the public culture in other ways as well. Arriving at a position on slavery involved Protestants in an explosive debate that divided churches and church members into moderate and passionate antislavery camps. Some congregations, First Presbyterian Church in particular, split as a result (Chapter 3). The bitterness and hostility slavery discussions engendered cracked the facade of Protestant unity, which made shaping the public culture that much more difficult. Cooperation on other issues was more difficult with the slavery issue festering beneath the surface. Further, the conflicts within churches, denominations, and the Protestant community generally over slavery muted the effectiveness of the churches' antislavery witness. In the paramount moral issue of the day, the Protestant tradition did not yield clear, unambiguous guidelines to which all Cleveland churches could rally.

In their effort to shape the public culture of the city, antislavery proved to be a diversion. The more they worked to overcome objections to their presence, and the more involved they became in the slavery issue, the less time and energy they had to focus their attention on developments in the city. Antislavery activity deflected the interest of Cleveland Protestant churches away from urban concerns and toward national issues and controversies. As they oriented themselves to national political and antislavery efforts, Protestants dissipated their potential impact on Cleveland.

There was reason why Protestant antislavery activity failed to have a decisive impact on the culture being shaped in these years. In their antislavery activity, many Protestant ministers adopted a stance not taken when they addressed the issues of poverty and society's economic arrangements—they invoked religious ideals to challenge the powers that be. It helped that the powers that be on this issue were far away, in Washington and the South. That they did not take the same opportunity to challenge their own community's values and institutional arrangements suggests the extent to which they were enmeshed in those arrangements and establishes the limits of their willingness to invoke their religious ideals to judge and challenge the reigning values of the city's public culture.

There is an irony in this. Protestants fashioned their most thoroughgoing application of religious ideals to public questions when they dealt with slavery, an issue over which they had minimal influence. Closer to home, where they occupied positions of power and influence, they accommodated their religious ideals to their society's existing arrangements, all but forgetting that such a thing as a higher law existed. Or, rather than forgetting the higher law, perhaps it could be said that they convinced themselves that the higher law coincided with their vision of moral and material progress, so they did not need to call into question the economic or social values and institutions that constituted their city's public culture.

This suggests once again the importance of the social characteristics of the city's Protestants. As the city's leadership elite, they had a large stake in perpetuating the city's existing fundamental values and economic and social arrangements. Indeed, they helped create those values and arrangements. They could afford to offer a fundamental critique of slavery, an institution far removed from their immediate setting, but they were far too captivated by the prospect of being part of "the Emerald City of the Lakes" to turn a critical eye on their own environment by applying the higher law to the values and institutions being formed in the public culture of their own city. This was the mote in their eye—they diverted their attention and their critical moral judgment from the city's public culture in just the years when the central values and structures of the commercial and industrial society were being forged.

Chapter 8

Rituals of Community Life

As with their political activity, the efforts of Cleveland's Protestants to stamp their imprint on the rituals of community life brought reminders of the limits of their influence. Unlike their relative success in turning business, benevolence, and temperance into avenues for establishing their influence in the public culture, Protestants encountered substantial resistance when they tried to establish their preeminence in community rituals such as Fourth of July ceremonies, civic celebrations, and holiday observances.

Community rituals share some of the characteristics of all rituals. Through rituals people affirm what is meaningful to them by engaging in a carefully structured use of particularly evocative symbols, images, words, and actions. Individuals find in such rituals keys to their own identity as well as a link to a transcendent source of meaning, whether sacred or secular. Community rituals have some additional functions. They crystallize the community's sense of itself. Community rituals involve collective affirmations of the beliefs, values, behaviors, institutions, and historical events deemed important, legitimate, and primary. Performing community rituals is one of the ways the public culture is constructed. Through these rituals the public culture is given meaning by particular groups, for particular purposes. As Susan Davis writes in *Parades and Power*, a community ritual such as a parade serves a variety of social functions: "Parades are public dramas of social relations, and in them performers define who can be a social actor and what subjects and ideas are available for communication and consideration." Community rituals are at once "modes of propaganda, recreation, local celebration, and national commemoration."[1]

In serving these various functions, community rituals contributed to forming the public culture. As Davis notes, they "influenced perceptions and ideas" in the public realm, which was "contested terrain, shifting and continually being redefined." They helped the society define meaningful events in its past, they indicated which groups enjoyed the society's sanction of legitimacy, and they modelled appropriate conduct.[2]

Community rituals took a variety of forms in antebellum America. Some are obvious, such as July 4th observances, Thanksgiving celebrations, ceremonies marking the arrival of a railroad, or dedications of public school buildings. Others do not fall so clearly into traditional patterns, but they nevertheless fit the definition of ritual, being highly structured occasions when the community and the individuals in it search for, or affirm, meaning in highly stylized ways. Keeping the Sabbath, for example, involves setting aside a sacred time when the community acknowledges allegiance to God. Public lectures and debates often served ritual functions, too, since speakers and debaters often discussed the new findings of science and their implications for religion in front of audiences who had come in order to take part in a search for answers to such troubling, fundamental questions. In addition, public entertainments often served the purposes of community ritual in the early nineteenth century. Exhibitions of mesmerism and spiritualism, much like the Christian sacraments, offered to their audiences an understanding of transcendent reality and a dramatic illustration of how one might have access to that reality. In all these instances, participants attempted to establish their values, attitudes, beliefs, and institutions as the ones deserving a place in the city's public culture.

Participation in collective rituals offered Cleveland's Protestants a prime opportunity to establish and maintain their prestige and authority in a crucial area of the culture. Just as much as in economic development, temperance, or politics, they aimed to incorporate practical and symbolic affirmations of religion's centrality in the city's rituals. Their destiny was tied to the effort. In placing religion at the heart of the community's rituals, they were making a place for themselves as well. If the public culture acknowledged its obedience and faithfulness to God, it would implicitly recognize the leadership role of God's followers on earth.

Their task proved formidable. Protestants vied with many others—Roman Catholics, the religiously indifferent, those following the imperatives of economic development—to control the rituals that would guide individuals and the community in their search for meaning and self-definition and would allow Protestants to furnish the meaning-giving component of community life.

Community rituals where Protestants sought to establish a decisive, visible role in the culture ranged from public holidays and civic ceremonies to school dedications, celebrations of the completions of railroads, and scientific lectures and exhibitions. Placing Protestantism at the heart of public holidays and civic celebrations loomed most important. When the city government included Protestants in public holidays and civic ceremonies, this in effect granted Protestants official status and recognized the centrality of religion as the meaning-giving component of community life. Public ceremonies and holidays crystallize a community's collective identity. They inevitably draw on sacred or quasi-sacred motifs such as the use of sacred space and time and the reliance on actions and observances freighted with symbolic and transcendent meanings for the community.[3]

For Protestants, by far the most important "holiday" which needed attention was the Sabbath. Although not a holiday in the customary sense of being a particular day of the year set aside to mark a specific event, the Sabbath was for Protestants a weekly "holiday" denoting a sacred time when obligations to God were acknowledged as primary. The attempt to establish Sabbath observance as a community ritual was thus a crucial element in the Protestants' battle for control of the values of the new commercial society's public culture, since to honor the Sabbath was to acknowledge the priority of religious concerns.

The Sabbath's place in the new city was precarious, threatened by Protestant ambivalence, economic imperatives, and the indifference of a large segment of the population. The accommodation between the Biblical injunction to observe the Sabbath and the overpowering imperatives of economic development has already been discussed (Chapter 3). Considering the Sabbath as a community ritual adds another dimension to that account. The Sabbath crusade was not just an assertion of religion's primacy over mammon. Even more significantly, it marked a claim that religion, specifically Protestantism, should reign over the entire public culture. By setting aside a day devoted to religious observance, the community would be acknowledging that its life, like the days of the week, pivoted around a religious center.

Observing the Sabbath, according to the uniform testimony of Cleveland's Protestant ministers, represented an acknowledgment of God's governance of the world and was a necessity for any individual or society seeking security or prosperity. "The Sabbath," said

Rev. Stephen Peet of First Presbyterian Church in the *Boatman's Magazine*, was *"indispensable* to the existence and preservation both of religion and sound morals. . . . Where there is no Sabbath, the gospel is not preached, the Bible is not read, no attention [is] paid to religion and no means of moral improvement are used." Levi Tucker, minister of First Baptist Church, extolled the Sabbath and tied its observance to the national destiny: "the blessed Sabbath, the polar star of hope, the anchor of our nation's ship, the day of rest and worship, the dawn of heaven itself." No country was ever blessed where God's holy day was desecrated, he warned. Without Sabbath observance, "this world would at once become one vast 'theatre of mischief and of misery; an immense den of thieves and robbers; a sink of moral pollution; a scene of impiety, injustice, rapine and devastation'. . . . "[4]

For the community to adopt the Sabbath, support from the city government was necessary. Although it was theoretically possible that Sabbath observance could be adopted universally without coercion, as a practical matter Sabbath legislation and law enforcement were necessary. Like temperance advocates, Sabbath reformers were moderately successful in enlisting the support of local authorities. The city invoked its general powers against disturbances to protect Sabbath worship from being disrupted. In the 1840s, the city made it illegal for any person "to play marbles, pitch quoits, or engage in any other game or sport, or cause any other disturbance within the city of Cleveland, on the Sabbath day, commonly called Sunday." The city also passed a law that provided that "any person, who by rude and indecent behavior, or by making noise within or near the place of worship, disturbed the order and solemnity of the meeting," would be subject to a fine not to exceed $100. Yet no laws were passed prohibiting travel or the operation of businesses on Sunday, the essential legislation which would have given the Sabbath legal protection and would have marked its observance as a civic commitment.[5]

Since Cleveland Protestants looked to Sabbath observance as a barometer of religion's standing in the city, the 1850s must have been a time of disappointment for them. Concern for Sabbath observance persisted through the 1850s—but without the prominence, activity, and organization of the 1840s. The Cuyahoga County Sabbath Society and the Cleveland Sabbath Union largely sank from view in the 1850s, replaced by an occasional *ad hoc* meeting of those concerned with Sabbath observance.[6]

Much of the worry over desecration of the Sabbath, which in the 1840s had centered on the railroads and steamboats (Chapter 3), shifted in the 1850s to concerns about immigrants. Episcopal Bishop McIlvaine worried that the masses coming from Europe would endanger the Sabbath. A *Plain Dealer* editorial in 1850 also took note of the implications for Sabbath observance of the city's increasingly pluralistic population. Not all groups observed Sunday the same way, the paper noted. Germans enjoyed it as a day of amusement, and Jews treated it as a half-holiday and half-business day. It seemed to the *Plain Dealer* that "the general rule should be with all good neighbors and citizens, to so order their pursuits and inclinations as not to infringe upon the liberty of others. The pious have a right to a quiet observance of the day, while those of freer sentiments should not be molested, if they do not disturb others."[7]

Much like the temperance cause, which had given way in the 1850s to the difficulties of convincing a heterogeneous population to abstain from drink, so, too, did Sabbath efforts fall back in the 1850s due to the Protestants' inability to persuade the diverse population of the rapidly growing city, and their own ambivalence about keeping the Sabbath given their interest in promoting the city's commercial economy. In their temperance reform work they had staked out territory where religion's resources were strongest. Temperance reform could be framed entirely in moral terms, and morality was recognized throughout the 1840s and 1850s as one of the appropriate functions of religion. Temperance also appealed to an audience that extended beyond the church-going community. Anyone who could be moved by tales of blighted lives and suffering families was a potential adherent. Finally, the business community was an ally. Intemperance caused accidents, disrupted businesses, and made workers less efficient and dependable.

The Sabbath cause lacked most of these advantages. Keeping the Sabbath was less an issue of practical morality than one of symbolic dedication to Biblical injunctions. Consequently, its appeal tended to be limited to those already securely within the Protestant fold. The social implications of Sabbath-breaking seemed less immediate and less threatening than the poverty and disorder temperance reformers pointed to. Sabbath observers could not broaden their appeal, as temperance advocates could, with tragic stories of loss and suffering featuring widows and abandoned, starving children. Furthermore, instead of having the business community as an ally, Sabbath activists encountered resistance. Arguments that a

Sabbath day of rest was due workers failed to strike a responsive chord in the city's commercial elite, many of whom found it profitable to maintain seven-day operations.[8]

The Protestant commitment to Sabbath observance was attenuated by qualifications and accommodations, in marked contrast to the unity forged in the temperance campaign. To some extent, keeping the Sabbath fell victim to Protestant priority setting. This was typified by the decision to allow members to satisfy the criteria for Sabbath observance by sitting in their pews, thus avoiding being personally engaged in business, while their companies and their workers conducted business as usual (Chapter 4). Given such an accommodation to economic self-interest, Protestants could not approach the Sabbath issue in the same wholehearted manner they brought to temperance.

Undermined from within and ignored and resisted from without, efforts at keeping the Sabbath reminded Protestants that their efforts to control civic ritual and public culture faced formidable opposition. The failure of Sabbath observance to take hold deprived Protestants of a visible, weekly holiday that would have served as a continual reminder that the dominant loyalty of the culture was to God and that, by extension, Protestantism lay at the heart of the culture. But Protestants were nothing if not persistent, and they endeavored to incorporate religious motifs into many of the city's other widely observed holidays and celebrations. Fourth of July celebrations presented a golden opportunity for the Protestants' program of infusing the culture with religion. Celebrating the Fourth of July invoked a sacred time of national origins. Attaching Protestantism to the occasion would establish Protestant centrality in the collective historical memory of Americans by linking Protestants with the formative event of the nation's history and the central symbol of the republic, the flag. Protestants could then stand comfortably at the center of not only the city's but also the nation's public culture. Unlike the situation with the Sabbath, there was no ambivalence within the Protestant ideology or community about what constituted an appropriate Fourth of July observance: The nation's birthday celebration should be centered around Protestant churches, with Protestant ministers and church members playing a major role.[9]

As an initial step in cementing the connection between Protestantism and the nation's history and identity, Protestant churches offered common services on the Fourth of July. The honor of hosting the observance rotated among the major Protestant churches in the mid-1830s. After that, individual churches tended to host the ceremonies year after year: First Baptist Church in the late 1830s, First Methodist Church in the early 1840s, Second Presbyterian Church in the late 1840s. The services welded the religious to the political—they customarily featured an orator of the day and a reading of the Declaration.[10]

In the 1830s and 1840s the Protestant effort to orchestrate Fourth of July observances in such a way as to establish their primacy in the public culture appeared successful. Protestant religious services and Sunday School processions dominated Fourth of July festivities. A procession that ended at one of the city's Protestant churches usually provided the focal point for the day's activities. Customarily included in the processions were church members, Sunday School students, and, beginning in the early 1840s, temperance groups. Like all groups, temperance leaders "used processions to invent and present favorable images of themselves and their programs." According to Susan Davis in *Parades and Power*, their participation "opposed the usual patterns of urban festivity by constructing orderly and rational meanings for street ceremonies." Temperance participation in Fourth of July parades also brought women directly into the public sphere, where they could trumpet the virtues that should guide the public culture.[11]

For the July 4, 1843, celebration, for example, Baptist, Wesleyan Methodist, and Congregational church members formed a procession that joined First Methodist Church members at First Presbyterian Church. The celebrants marched to a grove, where a picnic and religious and patriotic discourses rounded out the occasion. James M. Hoyt, an officer of First Baptist Church, spoke to a throng including 1,900 Sabbath School scholars, proclaiming "This is the Sabbath day of Freedom!" Hoyt asked his audience to walk in the ways of their fathers, and to "instil [sic] into these infant minds the celestial precepts of the Prince of Peace." If that were done, said Hoyt, we could feel assured they will hand down "the inheritance which was the spirit of Pilgrim toil and revolutionary blood." Hoyt's paradigm for the nation's collective historical memory firmly linked Protestants and the country's founders in a way that laid claim not just to the past but also to the present and future, since it devolved on his listeners to take responsibility for perpetuating the work begun by the Pilgrims and revolutionaries.[12]

The course of Protestant participation in Fourth of July observance, paralleled the Sabbath fight. Cleveland Protestant churches led the Fourth of July observances through the 1840s. After that, their influence declined. What had been a unified civic occasion pervaded by Protestantism gave way in the 1850s to an urban free-for-all.

In the 1850s Protestants still had an important role in Fourth of July ceremonies, but no longer the central role. Clergy marched in the main procession and gave the benedictions at the ceremonies. But the procession no longer ended at a church; it ended on Public Square. The clergy and their Sunday School scholars and church members no longer led the march; rather, they joined military and fire companies, carpenters, butchers, teamsters, and bands. What had been a procession could now be characterized as a parade. Railroads and the city's boosters joined in promoting the day, helping to transform the Fourth of July from a Protestant-centered religious celebration of a small community into an extravaganza where a regional commercial center promoted its standing by offering activities and amusements for all. Churches were crowded on the Fourth of July, but so were railroads, steamboats, circuses, balloon ascensions, and fireworks displays. Even churches succumbed to the new mode of celebrating the Fourth of July in the 1850s. The Bethel Church used the holiday to raise funds by offering 50 cent excursions on steamboats. Some of the Protestants' activities elbowed their way into the celebrations when temperance and antislavery groups marched, but they had to compete with myriad other attractions.[13]

The growth of the city contributed in a number of ways to reducing the hold of the Protestant churches on Fourth of July celebrations. No single church could hold all those interested in attending the exercises as they had done in the early years; Public Square was larger. No single church could even hold the entire Protestant community. So individual churches conducted their separate services, then the church members joined the rest of the city's residents as part of the general parade and the crowd for the other events and amusements of the day.

Urban growth also brought German and Irish residents who required a different Fourth of July. Native Protestant clergy and their Sunday School scholars had to open their procession to the Hibernian Guards of the Irish and the Brass Bands of the Germans. These new participants undoubtedly preferred to end their march at Public Square and then head to the picnic grounds, rather than conclude with a Protestant church's religious exercises.

The Protestant linking of revolutionaries and Pilgrims failed to draw in the new German and Irish immigrants, who needed a different collective historical memory—one which would stress the search for freedom and opportunity, or perhaps the contributions of newcomers to building the canals and railroads on which the progress of the city depended. The community no longer was homogeneous enough to support a ritual based on a historical account of Pilgrims and revolutionaries that gave Protestants pride of place.

Another public holiday, Thanksgiving, retained its Protestant religious identity throughout the antebellum years. Thanksgiving celebrated the role of religion in the founding of the nation and in the forging of specifically American values. In observing Thanksgiving, said the *Herald*, Americans celebrated "an event that stamped the impress of Civil and Religious Liberty upon every crag and mountain top of the then wild waste from Ocean to Ocean." Although this sentiment rather arbitrarily ignored the denial of liberty to Native Americans, African Americans, and women, not to mention the two hundred year struggle of the dissenting sects and the followers of the Enlightenment to secure religious liberty, it staked out a claim for Protestants to be included in the very definition of what it meant to be an American. At Thanksgiving, the city and the nation gave thanks to God for their blessings, both civil and religious. Thanksgiving would be a time when particularly religious concerns dominated. Businesses stopped on Thanksgiving, a clear bowing to concerns other than economic imperatives. Since the governor officially proclaimed the holiday, the state acknowledged religion's place in the society's history and identity, and by extension, Protestantism's centrality in the public culture.[14]

Days of fasting, humiliation, and prayer were other public holidays with definite religious overtones. The rituals reminded Cleveland Protestants of their New England religious traditions, and they helped to knit the community together in acknowledgment of God's power and the polity's obedience to it. In 1841, when President John Tyler called for a day of fasting and prayer after the death of President William Henry Harrison, all the churches of the city held services to mark the occasion. Ministers Samuel Aiken of First Presbyterian Church, Levi Tucker of First Baptist Church, and Peter McLaughlin of St. Mary's Catholic Church, among others, delivered sermons commemorating Harrison's death. The *Herald* reported that "the national fast was yesterday observed in a manner becoming a Christian people."[15]

Eight years later President Zachary Taylor called for a day of fasting and prayer against cholera. The *Daily True Democrat* thought there was "something grand in the thought of a whole nation bowing before the living God in prayer." Participation may not have been as widespread as Protestants would have wanted. Benjamin Rouse, an active member of First Baptist Church and the spouse of benevolent activist Rebecca Rouse, complained that churches failed to respond to Taylor's call:

> All must acknowledge as a nation we have been exalted to heaven in point of civil and religious liberty, (*excepting the three millions of slaves*) and under the benign influences of a wise government, prosperity beyond the history of any other nation has made what we are a happy people. But how unmindful we have been. How few returns of gratitude have we made to the Giver of all our mercies. Do we not richly deserve the just judgment of an offended God?

In this support for the ritual of the fast, Rouse preserved the dual meaning of the idea that the nation was under God. It was not just that America was under God's protection—it was also under God's judgment. Obedience must be shown. How becoming it would be for a great, a prosperous, a happy nation like America to bow down and humble itself before God, wrote Rouse.[16]

After the late 1840s, calls for fasts virtually disappeared. Perhaps, as more non-Protestants and non-believers moved into the city, the old Protestant fasting tradition lost its audience. Perhaps Protestants themselves placed less faith in fasting and prayer when confronted with moments of social and political trauma. The voluntary society seemed to be a more appropriate way for dealing with intemperance, slavery, or poverty in the late 1840s and the 1850s. This particular community ritual no longer seemed as intellectually convincing nor as emotionally compelling as it had in an earlier day.[17]

With the exception of Thanksgiving, Protestants failed to establish their influence over the holidays Clevelanders celebrated. Although they had lost their ability to speak for the entire population, apparent in the erosion of their influence over Fourth of July observances, Protestants still exercised decisive influence among the city's leadership elite when it came to another crucial set of community rituals, official civic celebrations. Ceremonies welcoming visiting officials, marking milestones in the city's development, or dedicating public school buildings, were conducted by city officials with whom Protestants kept close ties. Only Protestant ministers were included in the contingent of clergy for major civic ceremonies such as those held to mark the completion of the Cleveland, Columbus, and Cincinnati Railroad in 1851 (see Chapter 3) or to welcome the Hungarian revolutionary Louis Kossuth.[18]

The welcome Kossuth received in 1852 exhibited the alliance of Protestants and civic officials that characterized many official civic ceremonies. Mayor Case and Judge Samuel Starkweather greeted Kossuth, and Rev. Samuel Aiken of First Presbyterian Church officially welcomed him on behalf of Cleveland's clergy. Aiken lauded Kossuth as a friend of humanity and an advocate of civil and religious liberty, and he invoked God's blessing for the Hungarian: "May the God of Heaven direct & prosper you, and yet make you the honored instrument of overturning despotism, and in establishing upon its ruins constitutional liberty, not only in Hungary but throughout the world." Rev. E. H. Nevin of Plymouth Congregational Church saluted Kossuth as a representative of freedom and expressed his optimism that Kossuth would succeed in accomplishing the great work God had committed to him. The children of the Sabbath Schools of First and Second Presbyterian Churches called on Kossuth at Weddell House and presented him with $80 they had raised. Black citizens of Cleveland met separately at Wesleyan Methodist Church to praise Kossuth and give him aid.[19]

What Cleveland Catholics made of all this is not apparent from local newspapers, even the Democratic *Plain Dealer*. The *Daily True Democrat* (despite its name, it opposed the Democratic Party) wrote that Catholic journals opposed Kossuth, fearing that his success would ensure the overthrow of the Pope. Whether or not they worried about the threat to the Pope, Cleveland Catholics could take little comfort in the symbolic joining together of the city's political leaders and Protestant clergy in welcoming an anti-Catholic revolutionary.[20]

The favor of public officials also gave Protestants a featured role in public school dedications and commencements. One of the triumphs of antebellum Protestantism toward infusing their values into the public culture was their close identification with education, including public education. School dedications, moments symbolizing the community's commitment to its young and their future, featured a strong Protestant presence. Ministers presided and spoke at many, if not most, of the school dedications in the antebellum years. Protestants participated at the other end of the schooling process, too, by having churches host public school commencements and public examinations at the end of the school year. In these moments of participation and cooperation with the public schools, Protestants embedded themselves at the heart of the city's educational efforts.[21]

School dedications by ministers and commencement exercises in churches knit public education and Protestantism together. Whatever opposition there might have been from Roman Catholics, Jews, or the religiously indifferent, Protestants could rest assured that when it came to education, a public institution accepted Protestants as the providers of moral and character formation for the next generation. This was a powerful role, and a potent wedge for shaping the public culture. The results might not be apparent for a generation, but the seeds would have been sown.

In less official public occasions, Protestants could not hope to achieve formal recognition and legitimation as moral guides for the community, but they could establish a substantial presence that might deter rivals for influence in the public culture. Public entertainments and lectures do not seem likely candidates for being considered community rituals, but in the early nineteenth century they regularly gathered groups together, then enticed them with discoveries promising access to new realities and significant powers. These lectures and entertainments served educational purposes in a society with limited access to books and magazines and none of the mass media available in the twentieth century. As a major intellectual presence in the city, Protestants found it necessary to respond to these public entertainments in order to safeguard their meaning-giving role in the public culture.

The chief challenge came from science. Public lectures focused Clevelanders' attention on the potential conflict between religion and scientific findings, especially in natural history and geology. Any possible conflict, however, quickly gave way to an accommodation between the two in which Protestants befriended science as a useful ally in the search for the order of God's universe. Cleveland's ministers minimized tension between science and religion by appropriating the natural theology developed by William Paley in England and elaborated by Samuel Tyler, Benjamin Silliman, and Edward Hitchcock in America. Conveniently enough for them, they concluded that the study of nature led ineluctably to evidence of God's creation and intentions. Religion, in essence, absorbed science.[22]

Samuel St. John, the leading voice of science in Cleveland, delivered a series of six lectures at First Baptist Church on "the harmony between Geology and Revelation." St. John reached a large audience. The newspaper reported three days later that he spoke "before the largest audience we have ever seen assembled in our city." In these and other public lectures through the 1840s and 1850s, St. John argued that "there is evident progress from period to period of the geological history, but for the successive and higher developments of life there is no assignable source and original but the Deity."[23]

Through public lectures, St. John mediated science and religion. Protestants who attended partook of a ritual: They were offered new knowledge while being assured that their existing faith still described reality, and they gathered with others to hear this message in the structured environment of a public lecture. These public lectures epitomized the alliance of Protestantism and science. Filled with the confidence that science supplemented the claims of religion, churches and religious groups welcomed science lectures, and Second Presbyterian Church hosted the American Association for the Advancement of Science's national meeting in 1853.[24]

This befriending of science by religion is less dramatic than popular images of a warfare between science and religion. This is an instance of the significance of the more subtle, undramatic exercise of influence by Protestants. Whatever potential science had for suggesting alternative paradigms for understanding reality was sidetracked. In addition, religion enlisted science in its cause, creating an alliance which produced a powerful and culturally convincing account of reality which would dominate the public culture of the next half century in Cleveland and the rest of the nation.

The most unsettling public entertainments as far as Protestants were concerned were those promoting the "sciences" of spiritualism and mesmerism. The entertainments and public lectures offered by spiritualists and mesmerists entailed a potent mix of evangelical Protestantism, rationalism, spirit worship, and scientific experiment. Spiritualism and mesmerism capitalized on the most immediately accessible and extraordinary of the century's scientific developments, electricity. It lent itself to public demonstrations, such as the lectures of Chauncey and Heman Burr in 1849. In announcing the lectures, the *Plain Dealer* warned: "Go tonight, but take the precaution to keep as far from Burr as possible, or he will 'Biologize' you, and cause you to perform all sorts of silly tricks." The paper pointedly described the demonstration in religious terms. By passing electricity through volunteers, the Burrs "can produce compunctions of conscience, induce confessions, and penitence, and finally, make their subjects rejoice in forgiveness. Their services are much needed in this community of sinners. They can turn water into wine, make wizzards [sic] of men and witches of women, turn Aaron's rod into a serpent, and, for aught we know, can enact 'Moses in the bull rushes.'" The *Plain Dealer* described electricity as Christ-like, remarking that its chief effects were ensuring "equilibrium of the body, making the blind to see, the deaf to hear, and the lame to walk." Seen in these terms, electricity's influence was likened to revelation, revivalists, and sacraments—inducing conviction of sin, prompting repentance, turning water into wine, and performing miracles. There were even reports that the Burrs had cured three people of blindness.[25]

Spiritualism and mesmerism were seen by many as a scientific form of religion. Spiritualism provided physical, scientific evidence to support religious beliefs when it was able to contact the dead and relay messages back to the living. It claimed to base beliefs on demonstrable proof rather than a leap of faith. One no longer had to believe; it was now possible to know. This represented a potentially formidable challenge to Protestants.[26]

These potential contributions to intellectual and religious understanding were often barely perceptible in the theatrical exhibitions through which most Clevelanders learned of spiritualism and mesmerism. The performances of a group such as the Davenport Boys, who sat in the dark, blindfolded and with hands tied, while spirits played their musical instruments, were especially suspect. The newspapers printed letters calling the Davenport Boys hoaxes, but continued to report on their performances. One group of cynics "came away saying if they were humbugged, it was most cleverly and scientifically done." Even if they were doubters, audiences found the lure of mysterious and unexplainable powers and realities difficult to resist.[27]

The Cleveland *Herald* summed up much of the skepticism toward mesmerism and spiritualism as popular entertainment. Commenting on a report of a man in England who could break

headstrong horses and make them able to understand his conversation by mesmerizing them, the *Herald* commented that "this is
new as to the horses, but asses have been mesmerized here for
some time."[28]

A two-week public debate in 1855 between a spiritualist and a
Christian provided Clevelanders with a ritualized contest for their
support, as well as, implicitly, a contest for control of a significant
element of the public culture—its intellectual framework. Joel
Tiffany, a local resident, presented the case for spiritualism. Tiffany's
spiritualism was a form of pantheistic religion that embraced elements of transcendentalism, nineteenth-century evangelicalism,
anti-clericalism, and a touch of fortune-telling. For Tiffany, the
Divine Father was everywhere present. To this mixture of Christian
and transcendental motifs, Tiffany added the idea of universal salvation popular with nineteenth-century revivalists. God's plan,
according to Tiffany, was to work out the salvation of every human
being. Spirits were the evidence through which human beings were
to be made aware of God.[29]

Tiffany's approach was starkly Protestant, verging on a doctrine of authority similar to that of the Quakers. Since God was
omnipresent, the knowledge of God would come directly. No
mediator, such as a church or minister, was necessary to help
receive or interpret the message. Not only did this disparage
Catholicism, it threatened the Protestant clergy, who would be left
without a role if knowledge of God arrived directly to the
believer.[30]

In response to Tiffany, Asa Mahan upheld the claims of Christianity. Mahan had been the first president of Oberlin College and
had come to Cleveland to head the Cleveland Institute, which was
to be modeled after Oberlin. He criticized Tiffany's spiritualism
because it had abandoned Christianity. Mahan insisted that belief
must rest on the Bible and its accounts of the interposition of a creative power. Not to be outdone by Tiffany's new ideas, Mahan also
incorporated mesmerism into his theology. He agreed with Tiffany
on the existence of a force, but could not accept that it was guided
and controlled by spirits. Spiritual phenomena, said Mahan, were
caused by electricity, magnetism, mesmerism, clairvoyance, and
the odic force. Mahan preferred the term animal magnetism for
this phenomenon, for he saw it as the medium of intelligent communication between minds and the means for believers to pene-
trate deep within the spiritual realm. It is testimony to the

persuasive power of the mesmerists that Mahan accommodated their findings so completely, even in lamenting their neglect of the Bible and the church.[31]

Most Cleveland ministers were more hostile to spiritualism than Mahan. Mahan's reconciliation of religion and spiritualism was not an easy path to take for those adhering to conventional notions of a personal God whose revelation was contained in the Bible and observed in the church. James A. Thome of the First Presbyterian Church, Ohio City, preached a sermon against spiritualism. Two clergy, Samuel Aiken of First Presbyterian Church and John Wheeler of Second Baptist Church, were among thirteen signers of a letter urging a repeat of a lecture critical of spiritualism. James C. White, minister of Plymouth Congregational Church, appealed to all "to trust, not in the blind fallacy of spiritualism, but in plain teachings of the Bible; not to give way to superstitious fears or idler fancies of an unknown future; and not to seek fellowship or favor with witches, diviners, ghostly oracles or spiritual mediums."[32]

The two-week long debate was a sensationalized public spectacle. It was also a carefully structured ritual encounter between traditional belief and new discoveries. The mix of science, religion, and entertainment evident in spiritualism and mesmerism enticed Cleveland's Protestants on a number of levels. Spiritualism and mesmerism provided an alternative source of instruction and entertainment replete with rappings, magic, mystery, and speaking with the dead. By introducing audiences to electricity and magnetism and by incorporating these new findings of science, spiritualists appeared to be in the vanguard of intellectual change. They offered a vision of wonder and meaning that competed with the one provided by Protestantism. Like the Protestant churches, they spoke to the issues of God and human nature, death and the soul, and success and earthly reward. They claimed to induce moral conduct, arouse the conscience, and perform miracles. That the traditional belief met the newcomer part way in Mahan's embrace of the odic force, for example, is indicative of the Protestant approach in many areas of the community's life. Here, as elsewhere, Cleveland's Protestants displayed an immense capacity to maintain their influence in the public culture by being able to bend, accommodate, and absorb.[33]

If economic development and benevolence may be considered

the areas where Protestants enjoyed relative success in stamping their imprint on the public culture, community crusades like temperance and antislavery must be judged as areas where Protestants settled for much less than they would have liked. Similarly, trying to incorporate Protestantism into the city's ritual life was a lesson in limits.

As Susan Davis remarks in *Parades and Power*, "As a stage for public culture, the city offered a field of space and practice useful for framing and disseminating ideas, shaping powers and opinions, but as human construction, this stage did not yield all residents equal time, space, and power to perform." Protestants managed to dominate that space for a time with their participation in Fourth of July parades, their prominence in particular civic occasions, their dominance of school dedications and commencements, and as catalysts for bringing new intellectual ideas to Cleveland. However, other residents crowded the space on the public culture's stage. Protestants failed to establish Sabbath keeping as normative, saw their role in Fourth of July ceremonies diminish, enjoyed decreasing support for days of fasting, accommodated to the findings of science, and watched many of their members attracted by spiritualism.[34]

Two factors account for much of the trouble Protestants experienced. One is that the imperatives of economic development and the ambiguous, conflicted response to those imperatives by Protestants, crippled the Sabbath effort (Chapter 4). A second factor, equally important as an contributor to the Protestant inability to dominate the ritual life of the community, is pluralism. In community rituals, as in temperance, Protestants in the 1850s faced the fact that they could no longer define their culture unilaterally. Other voices—with German and Irish accents, no less—demanded their place on the city's stage. While many still gathered in churches and the picnic grounds to conclude Fourth of July services with political and religious discourses, other members of the community headed for the balloon rides and the beer gardens, moving away from the Protestant vision of public culture both practically and symbolically.

PART THREE

A Measure of Success

Chapter 9

A Substantial but Eroding Presence

Filled with the confidence that religion applied to all aspects of life, Protestants in Cleveland resolved to be the molders of their city, and with the help of Protestants elsewhere, shapers of the nation. Michel Foucault's insistence on "the constructed character of social life"—that values, attitudes, and social arrangements are not natural and inevitable but are rather the result of human activity and intention—is appropriate in this regard. The Protestant leadership elite was aware of itself as a distinctive group with a specific vision of society, and its members consciously pursued strategies calculated to mold the public culture to that vision.

The Protestants' strategy relied on participation, cooperation, and accommodation, not antagonism and conflict. They accommodated to some challenges, such as those represented by the commercial economy. In their temperance work, the crux of their campaign was to dissuade and convert, although they pursued coercive legal remedies, as well. They absorbed one of their rivals for influence by incorporating natural history and geology into their theology, thus producing a mutually reinforcing description of the nature of the world. Protestants avoided a war with science by embracing it. With spiritualists they channeled their energies into distancing themselves from a potentially appealing rival. With these strategies they did not conquer the culture, they insinuated themselves into it.

Voluntary societies served as the primary instrument for carrying out these strategies. The voluntary society was a private organization with a public impact. It bridged public and private, virtually obliterating the line between the two. For women, the voluntary society offered a socially approved vehicle that could have substantial public influence, thus circumventing some of the constraints of the cult of true womanhood. Neither women nor Protestants could be kept in the private sphere. The Protestants' conviction that the public culture must reflect religious ideals, combined with the activity of voluntary societies, erased any clear line the rest of society might have wanted to draw between private and public or between men's and women's spheres.

Protestants pursued these strategies with a resourcefulness that belies any image of a religion limited to private life or relegated to the spheres of morals and ethos. The relatively unformed state of the just-founded, expanding city gave the public culture an openness and fluidity that invited participation. The culture's understandings, symbols, ideas, practices, assumptions, institutions, and collective historical memories were constantly being discussed, reevaluated, revised, and transformed. The multitude of arenas available to those interested in shaping the public culture—business, politics, benevolence, temperance, antislavery, community rituals—and the variety of strategies at the Protestants' disposal, offered boundless opportunities for efforts to establish influence.

Protestants kept the public culture percolating. If temperance voluntary societies lagged, they tried temperance entertainments. If the state refused to adopt a Maine Law, then the city could be approached to tighten licensing. On issues in other areas, too, their creativity, resourcefulness, and persistence guaranteed that they would surely find a wedge for influence, even if it were not as large as they preferred. Although the Sabbath campaign against railroads and steamboats came up short, that did not prevent Protestants from stamping their imprint on railroads, which they embraced as one of God's instruments for bringing the millennium.

Protestants harnessed their strategic resourcefulness to a specific vision of what the public culture of an antebellum city should be. More than any other influence, the vision reflected their embrace of the emerging commercial city where they made their home. From its first days Cleveland fired the hopes of boosters, Protestants included. The Bridge War of 1837, just one year after the city's incorporation, featuring rival cities' "armies," one led by a minister, was a fitting beginning to Cleveland's history as an organized city and to the Protestants' role in it. Cleveland grew as the result of the efforts of speculators and traders hoping that their city would be "the City of the West." This booster mentality, transmuted later into the more sophisticated notion of moral and material progress, served as the matrix for the Protestant attempt to exert power over the culture of the city.[1]

The Protestants' religious and economic interests did not always mesh. Protestants found certain of the economy's imperatives threatening to their pre-existing religious ideals. Railroad and steamboat operators, for example, resisted efforts to bring transportation to a halt on the Sabbath. That, to them, would not only be uneconomical, but would doom the city's chances to become the commercial hub of the Great Lakes. On other issues, too, economic development clashed with Protestant values. The headlong pursuit of wealth and economic and urban growth by entrepreneurs and boosters threatened community cohesion and loosened traditional moral constraints. A flourishing seaport community, after all, depended on the grog shop to ease the plight of weary seamen. Thus Protestants were defining their beliefs and values in contests within their community even as they moved outside their churches to engage in the contest over the values, attitudes, and institutions that would shape the developing public culture.

Protestants brought substantial resources and strategic flexibility to the task of forming the culture. Being a well-connected leadership elite allowed Protestants to avail themselves of the direct instruments of influence available to those in power. Protestants were so deeply embedded in the civic life of the town that there was no need to conquer the city—they were the city. At the least, they occupied key positions where many decisions were made. All they needed to do in order to spread their religious ideals was to tap the resources at their disposal since they could entice with official approval or favor. In such a situation, there was no need to wage a battle or a war for influence. What was called for was a deft orchestration of influence to respond to opportunities or challenges.

Protestants could exercise more informal and indirect power by using their positions of influence in churches, voluntary associations, politics, and businesses to create incentives and punishments that would encourage the conduct and values they thought necessary for the newly emerging society. For example, they used their political offices to have public funds appropriated for privately controlled, voluntary benevolent organizations such as the Protestant Orphan Asylum. They also made loans available to those of appropriately "Christian" character such as John D. Rockefeller, and they supported fines and imprisonment for violators of temperance laws and withheld privileges from the children of the Industrial School who did not develop proper work habits.

Women, since they were two-thirds of the members of the churches, helped set much of the tone for Protestantism's characteristic strategies. Women brought with them a particular, socially prescribed means of exercising influence that relied on cooperation, not conflict. Protestants, both women and men, largely adopted this strategy, relying on the voluntary society to do the persuading and accommodating that would ensure their continual presence in the culture.

Church-state concerns, too, played a part in encouraging the strategy of cooperation rather than confrontation. Suggestions that they sought too direct or too formal a role in the city's culture could be answered by compromise and low-key persuasion. Even those able to invoke direct, formal authority by virtue of their official positions in business or politics might have been reluctant to confront the society's fears about religion intruding too directly.

The vision created for the evolving culture by this well-connected elite working primarily through informal means and voluntary societies reflected their religious commitments as well as their social characteristics. Perfectionist and millennarian beliefs led Protestants to see the hand of the Almighty directing the development of new factories and railroads, even when they threatened the Sabbath. Protestants thus acquiesced in the perpetuation of the booster mentality, already apparent when Rev. Pickands led the charge of the West Siders in the Bridge War. Protestants assured themselves that moral and material progress were inseparable, and so they sanctified commercial development and blessed existing economic arrangements as the inevitable working out of the divine plan.

Their former religious ideals were not completely lost in this embrace of the commercial culture. Concern for building a Christian community proved a counterweight to support for untrammelled economic development. Worries about the breakdown of social cohesion and the loss of shared values clouded the hopes some had for the nascent commercial society. Still, if these religious ideals were not totally lost, they were certainly muted. When Cleveland's well-connected, Protestant leadership elite resolved the tensions in their religious commitments in order to anoint the newly emerging commercial economy, they produced a vision of moral and material progress tempered only by the necessity of benevolence. In sermons extolling railroads as instruments of divine progress, their endorsement of an antebellum version of the Protestant ethic, their collaborative relationship with businesses, and their lack of support for workers, Protestants established a pattern of cooperation with the powers-that-be in the commercial city. In almost all cases where Protestants were forced to set priorities, the attractions of economic development crowded out pre-existing religious ideals: the railroad was invested with millennial hopes, but to fulfill those hopes it had to run on the Sabbath. Having forged a cozy relationship with the commercial economy, Protestants failed to invoke a higher law which might have cast the dominant institutions of their own culture into question. They abnegated their responsibility to apply transcendent ideas in judging their own city by convincing themselves that they were already on the way to reaching those ideals. God and the railroad became their twin lodestars.

Protestants had, in effect, struck a bargain. In return for bestowing their imprimatur on commercial development, the leaders of that development would incorporate a commitment to benevolence and service that accepted responsibility for those in the community who did not fully share in the bounty. Although this sense of responsibility was somewhat grudging and did nothing to share power with those being aided, it did curb the commercial economy's otherwise stark individualism which tended to subsume any sense of obligation to others under a scramble for personal advance.

Neither Protestants nor economic development "won"; rather, through a process of accommodation, a mutually acceptable arrangement was arrived at. Protestants were not merely apologists for the new society; they were its co-creators. Although economic development received their highest priority, Protestants did not abandon their religious ideals. As part of their tacit agreement with the culture, they had ensured that religious ideals, chiefly the notion of benevolence, would be incorporated into the developing ethos of the public culture. This was to be their principal victory in the contest over the values, attitudes, and institutions of the public culture.

How successful, in the end, were the Protestants' efforts to shape the public culture? Measuring the success of a religious group in achieving social influence is a delicate task. This book's analysis of the power and influence of Cleveland Protestants has called attention to formal and informal means of influence, moral persuasion and legal coercion, social status, and community commitments, decisions, and symbols, all in order to provide a wide-ranging set of indices by which to measure success. In addition, special attention has been paid to particular "moments" and "patterns" which indicate the shape and direction of the culture in formation during these years.

By using such a wide variety of measures, by applying these measures to various aspects of the city's life (economic, political, cultural, intellectual), and by measuring success in the process of public culture formation, this approach seeks to counter the fragmentation and specialization that have become the unfortunate legacies of social history. Protestants conceived of the whole society as their preserve. Using "measures" and the concept of "public culture" is, in terms of historiography, a step in the same direction.

When these measures of success are applied to the activities of Cleveland's Protestants from 1836 to 1856, it must be concluded that they achieved "a measure of success"—a substantial presence and influential impact, but something less than dominance. Through persistent and creative strategies and the promotion of their vision of moral and material progress, Cleveland's Protestants succeeded in establishing a substantial public presence for religion in the commercial city. What Rev. James Pickands started when he led the West Siders in the Bridge War in 1837 culminated in 1851 when Rev. Samuel Aiken welcomed the railroad which linked Cleveland, Columbus, and Cincinnati. In the intervening years, Protestants established considerable influence over the emerging values, attitudes, behaviors, and institutions—the public culture—of the expanding, commercial city.

By 1860, though, the prospect that Cleveland Protestants would dominate the public culture receded. Their displacement from the center of civic rituals such as the Fourth of July parades symbolized a situation apparent in their temperance and political efforts as well. For all their prominence, others—Irish and German Catholics, and non-believers especially—forced their way onto the public stage. Added to this were other factors that diminished the Protestants' ability to act as a united front. Divisions among Protestants over class issues such as pew rents and political issues such as slavery, and tensions in their thought as they sought to reconcile Sabbath-keeping with the imperatives of the commercial economy in which they played such a prominent role, hindered Protestant efforts. By 1860, Cleveland's Protestants found themselves to be a substantial but eroding presence in the expanding commercial city's public culture.

Amid the welter of particular successes and failures that characterized Protestant efforts to project their power into the public culture, the Protestants' principal accomplishment was to establish a pattern of cooperation that involved extensive participation in a variety of areas of the public culture, from business to benevolence to civic ceremonies. This established for Protestants a pervasive presence in Cleveland's public life. When city officials appropriated money for Protestant benevolent societies and when public schools held their commencements in church buildings, Protestants cemented an alliance that secured them a substantial place in the culture.

There were also specific moments that testified to Protestant influence. When the city officially celebrated the arrival of the Cleveland, Columbus and Cincinnati Railroad at First Presbyterian Church, with the church's minister, Samuel Aiken, as a featured speaker, the mantle of official approval settled on Protestants. There were many other such moments—Rev. Pickands leading the charge of West Siders across the bridge in 1837, the central Protestant role in welcoming Kossuth, and the establishing of a variety of poor relief, children's, and educational institutions through combined voluntary association and city efforts in the late 1840s and early 1850s. In these patterns and moments, Protestants constructed for themselves a substantial role in the contest over the shape and direction of the culture.

Protestant influence over other moments and patterns of the process of the formation of the culture was more problematic. In the cause they cared about the most, temperance, Protestants found themselves unable to translate their ideals into legislation, much less enforceable law. Voluntary, persuasive efforts also met with mixed results. Even when they spoke with unanimity and mounted their most vigorous efforts, as in the temperance campaigns, Protestants achieved only modest successes. The Sabbath campaign, another of their attempts to have the culture commit itself to following Protestant ideals, ended with only a few victories. When First Presbyterian Church allowed one of its members to meet the requirement for Sabbath keeping by ensconcing himself in his pew on Sunday while his employees continued to work, the church accommodated its previously held religious ideals to a new ideal of commercial progress, and, in the process, undercut their own claims for Protestant dominance of the culture.

On the more amorphous level of social and individual decision making, which, by the accretion of countless decisions, eventually coalesces into widely shared values and attitudes, Protestants could boast of some success. They had at least established in the elite the model of being of service to others through benevolence. In doing this, they had preserved a valuable remnant of an earlier, more homogeneous society, the sense of responsibility and obligation toward others. This mitigated the harsher implications of the individualism on which the commercial society—and the public culture—rested. Protestant efforts succeeded in setting some of the norms for personal conduct, too. The respectable citizen was expected to adopt temperance, if not abstinence, as a practice, and to follow the other guidelines of the antebellum version of the Protestant ethic summarized by banker Truman P. Handy—honesty, industry, prudence, economy, liberality in the cause of religion, and kindness to the poor.

Success came less frequently in the 1850s. The Protestants' reduced role in the annual Fourth of July celebration epitomizes the erosion of the Protestant impact on the culture by the last antebellum decade. It repeats a pattern clear from the earlier discussions of the Protestants' potential for influence (Chapter 2), benevolence efforts (Chapter 5), and temperance campaigns (Chapter 6) of diminishing success in the 1850s. Protestant habits of mind and heart were not adopted by the city and so were not accepted as "natural" and inevitable parts of the culture. The vision Cleveland Protestants promoted for the city and the nation vied with the visions of others for control of the public culture, and Protestants frequently lost.

Protestant power was eroded from within by their internal disagreements, by the tensions in their religious commitments, and by their own interest in perpetuating the commercial economy. Another serious challenge to their presence in the culture was brought by the competing groups of an increasingly pluralistic city. What in 1836 had been a small, relatively homogeneous town peopled by settlers from New England had become by 1860 a diverse commercial city with sizeable numbers of German and Irish immigrants. Church membership statistics tell part of the story. In 1840 Protestants constituted 18 percent of the population. By 1850 that had declined to 10 percent, and by 1860, to 8 percent. While the membership of Protestant churches increased by a factor of ten in the years from 1836 to 1860, the city's population jumped by a factor of 40, from approximately 1,000 to 40,000. There had been only one Catholic church in 1836, with a claimed membership of 200. By 1860 there were eight Catholic churches, and they counted 8,000 as members. Catholic newcomers resisted the Protestants' morality, objected to their politics, and preferred their own way of celebrating holidays. The Protestant monopoly over the city's religious life eroded, and with it any chance that Protestants could spread their power and authority unimpeded (Tables 2.3, 2.4, and 2.5).[2]

In the quarter-century after the city's incorporation in 1836, Cleveland's Protestants had achieved a measure of success. They had carved out significant areas of power and influence in antebellum Cleveland's public life. By 1860, though, prospects for the future had dimmed. They were still a formidable force, but they were now only one of many claimants who vied to shape the public culture. Despite their social position, persistence, and resourcefulness, Protestants fell short of the decisive culture-shaping role they preferred. Their authority was extensive, but not controlling. They could translate some of their ideals into public policy and widely shared social attitudes, but during the 1850s, they repeatedly faced resistance and defeat.

The dimensions of the erosion are cast into relief by two contrasting images: in 1837, a Protestant minister, Rev. James Pickands, led West Siders in the Bridge War; in 1857, 2,000 Germans gathered on a local hillside and consumed 42 kegs of beer as their way of celebrating one Sabbath afternoon. If Protestants needed any reminders that their temperance and Sabbath efforts, along with their hopes to preside over the city's public life, had faltered, there it was. Pluralism and the economic imperatives of a burgeoning commercial economy dashed the hopes of Protestants to dominate the public life. For all their resources and resourcefulness, by 1860 Cleveland's Protestants had become just one of many groups vying for power over the values, symbols, and institutions of the culture of the increasingly important commercial and industrial city.

APPENDIX

SOURCES OF CHURCH, ORGANIZATION, AND CENSUS INFORMATION

Descriptions of the church affiliations, organizational activity, and social characteristics of Cleveland's Protestants were based on information gathered from church records, city directories, newspapers, city histories, and the manuscript census of 1850. The analysis of church financial contributions was drawn from reports collected by denominational supervisory bodies. Following is a detailed description of this quantitative information.[1]

Church Members, Officers, and Ministers

Forty Protestant churches—non-Catholic and non-German—were established before 1860 in Cleveland. Of these, 29 lasted for four years or more. Complete or substantial listings of those who joined were available for 14 of these churches. These were all for churches of major denominations. Substantial records were found for 2 of the 3 Baptist churches, 3 of the 5 Episcopal, 6 of the 10 Presbyterian and Congregational, and 3 of the 6 Methodist. In all, names of 13,096 church joiners were gathered. Based on a comparison of the membership totals of the churches for which records were available to the totals for those whose records were not, it is probable that one-half to two-thirds of all those who joined non-Catholic and non-German churches in Cleveland before the Civil War were accounted for.

Officers of Organizations

Names of political party candidates, city government office-holders, school administrators and teachers, and officers of business, benevolent, moral reform and fraternal organizations were gathered primarily from newspapers and the city directories of 1837, 1845, 1850, 1853, 1857, and 1860 (6,117 names).

Because the city directories were such a rich source, much of the analysis of organizational participation is structured around the years covered by the directories. When information was based primarily on the city directories, the dates are listed in the form "1837–60" to emphasize that the entries are based on an episodic, not a continuous, base. It should be noted that directories were published more regularly in the 1850s than earlier, so entries covering the years 1837–60 tend to over-represent the 1850s. Where a list of officials for an organization was only available for a non-directory year, it was included according to the following rule: dates from 1834–42 were changed to 1837, 1843–47 to 1845, 1848–51 to 1850, 1852–55 to 1853; 1856–58 to 1857, and 1859–60 to 1860. Such revised entries accounted for only 5-10 percent of the organizational listings.

Names of political party candidates and government office-holders found in newspapers, local histories, and directories, were often available year by year. They were divided into five-year periods for analysis, 1836–40, 1841–45, 1846–50, 1851–55, and 1856–60. When entries for political candidates and government officials were available year by year the dates are given as "1836-60," as a reminder that the information from which they were drawn was continuous.

Census of 1850

A random five-letter sample was taken from the Federal Manuscript Census of 1850: all those whose last names began with G, E, N, I, O, or who lived in a household headed by someone with a last name beginning with those letters (2,450 names). Most of the information from the census was transcribed, including real property-holding and occupation. Occupation was divided into five vertical and three sector categories based on a classification developed by Theodore Hershberg and Robert Dockhorn.[2] It was assumed that the head of household was the first entry listed. In most cases this person was the oldest male.

Record Linkage

The process by which records from independent sources describing the activities of one individual are brought together is referred to as record linkage. The criteria for record linkage were adapted from procedures developed by the Philadelphia Social History Project.[3] Record linkage for this study was done by hand. One entry was matched with another when the two totalled 13 points according to the following criteria:

First, last and middle names, considered separately

perfectly matched names	5
match within one or two letters	4
same initial	3
variant name (e.g. Elizabeth, Lizzie, Betsy)	3
possibly close match (e.g. Cave, Gave)	2
possibly close initial (e.g. I, T, J)	1

Year of record

within 0–5 years	3
within 6–10 years	2
within 11–15 years	1

Activity

same organization or church	3

Point count determined whether two entries would be matched, with only a few exceptions. Some records were matched with fewer than the required 13 points. These links included cases where there was matching information available in the records not considered in the point count (entries which referred to the same spouse, or which referred to the person with the same title, such as Dr.).

In other cases, two records were not linked even with a point count of 13 or higher. This happened in instances where the patterns of activity suggested that a father and son or a mother and daughter were involved. It also occurred in cases where there were two different individuals with similar names, which made it impossible to separate reliably the activities of the two.

Record linkage is an inexact process. Undoubtedly, records were linked, based on common names, initials, activities, and years, which did not in fact belong to the same person. The reverse situation was even more likely—records were not linked even though they were for the same person. A number of factors limited possible matches. The record linkage point count made matching similar records (a record of joining a church with a record of being an officer of the same church, for example), easier than matching different types (a church record and an organizational record). Names given with only first and middle initials along with a last name were hard to match. This was a particular problem with women's names, which were often given in this form. Added to these difficulties was the error introduced by the difficulty of deciphering the handwritten names in census records and many church membership lists.

In general, the record linkage criteria erred on the side of caution. In all likelihood the plausible links which were bypassed far outweighed the links which were improperly made. If all the entries which actually belonged to each individual had been brought together, it is likely that the connections between Protestants and the worlds of business, politics, and government would have been even greater.

Church Contributions

The analysis of the contributions of Cleveland churches to local, national, and international causes was based primarily on information given by the individual churches to their denominational supervisory bodies. Individual church records were more complete, but not enough were available to sustain an extended investigation.

The denominational records gave a fairly accurate picture of individual church contributions. In many cases, contributions as listed in individual church records virtually matched the totals as given by the denominational supervisory bodies.

More often, there were discrepancies between the local and denominational records due to inconsistent categories and reporting periods, failures by the local church to report certain types of contributions, and the burying of many contributions in a "miscellaneous" category. The one consistent bias of the denominational records was to underreport the amount spent on local contributions, often by burying the local spending in a "miscellaneous" category.

Since many of the contributions to local evangelical and benevolent projects were either ignored or included in the miscellaneous category, it might be that one-third to two-thirds of local contributions were either unreported or buried in loosely defined categories such as "miscellaneous." Taking the middle ground and assuming that one-half of all local contributions did not make it into the "local" category, the percentage attributed to local projects could be multiplied by two to get a broad estimate that is closer to the true figure than that given by the denominational records.

Categorizing the contributions reported in the denominational records into "local," "national" and "foreign" has its own difficulties. Most of the specific categories used in analyzing the contributions reflect the categories listed in denominational reports. Contributions listed as being for "Poor Relief" or "The Poor" were counted as "local." These contributions often included funds accumulated by individual churches to help their own members in time of need. Money which went toward relieving the poor on a national and international level would have been reported as home or foreign missions or as aid to specific projects such as New York's Five Points Mission.

Contributions which did not fall into common categories or which were listed as "miscellaneous" or "other" are included in the "Other" category. The most common specific entry which has been placed in "Other" was money given for ministerial education.

NOTES

CHAPTER 1.
REVEREND PICKANDS, THE BRIDGE WAR,
AND THE PUBLIC CULTURE

1. The Bridge War is described in David D. Van Tassel and John J. Grabowski, eds., *The Encyclopedia of Cleveland History* (Bloomington, Ind.: Indiana University Press, 1987), pp. 290–91; William R. Coates, *A History of Cuyahoga County and the City of Cleveland: Historical and Biographical* (Chicago: American Historical Society, 1924), 1: 71; Samuel P. Orth, *A History of Cleveland, Ohio* (Chicago and Cleveland: S. J. Clarke Publishing Co., 1910), 1: 64–65; James Harrison Kennedy, *A History of The City of Cleveland, Its Settlement, Rise and Progress, 1796–1896* (Cleveland: Imperial Press, 1896), pp. 296–300; U.S., Work Projects Administration, Ohio [Works Progress Administration in Ohio], *Annals of Cleveland* (Cleveland: Works Progress Administration, 1936–38), 1836: 132–33; Charles Whittlesey, *Early History of Cleveland, Ohio* (Cleveland: Fairbanks, Benedict and Co., 1867), p. 477; Harvey Rice, *Pioneers of the Western Reserve* (Boston: Lee and Shepard, 1883), pp. 129–31; Early Settlers' Association of Cuyahoga County, *Annals* (Cleveland: Mount and Carroll, 1880–1931), 3 (1895): 565–71.

After the battle, a Cleveland judge issued a court injunction prohibiting any further interference with the bridge. The courts eventually ruled that both bridges must be maintained. This restored Ohio City's link with Cleveland, but the threat of the new bridge to Ohio City's economic growth remained. The fears of the West Siders, in fact, proved prescient, since Cleveland steadily outpaced its rival on the other side of the Cuyahoga.

2. Max Weber, *The Protestant Ethic and the Spirit of Capitalism* (New York: Charles Scribner's Sons, pb., 1958). Thomas L. Haskell writes that "Discovering non-reductionist ways of relating consciousness to social structure and change is, in my view, the most pressing historiographical issue before us today." Haskell, "Convention and Hegemonic Interest in the Debate over Antislavery: A Reply to Davis and Ashworth," *American Historical Review* 92 (October 1987): 833.

Among the most suggestive recent contributions to the discussion of antebellum religion are Paul E. Johnson, *A Shopkeeper's Millennium: Society and Revivals in Rochester, New York, 1815–1837* (New York: Hill and Wang, 1978); Anthony F. C. Wallace, *Rockdale: The Growth of an American Village in the Early Industrial Revolution* (New York: Alfred A. Knopf, 1978); William H. Pease and Jane H. Pease, *The Web of Progress: Private Values and Public Styles in Boston and Charleston, 1828–1843* (New York: Oxford University Press, 1985); and Anne C. Loveland, *Southern Evangelicals and the Social Order, 1800–1860* (Baton Rouge, LA: Louisiana State University Press, 1980).

Johnson's *A Shopkeeper's Millennium* is the clearest and most successful attempt to address this issue as it pertains to antebellum Protestants. He argues that revivals were an instrument by which proto-industrialists fought a battle to subject farm boys and pre-industrial artisans to the discipline of modern work. Johnson portrays Rochester's Protestants as having clear, unambiguous ideals which led directly to specific actions, which in turn succeeded in enhancing their social influence. My study, by way of contrast, argues that the elite's ideals were ambiguous, their actions were multi-faceted and to some extent at cross purposes, and the consequences which resulted were often unanticipated.

When Johnson describes the relation of Protestants to their society, he is content to repeat Durkheim's formulation that there is a close relation between religious belief and social actions surrounded by conscience, moral authority, and internalized restraint. More precision is possible with the systematic use of the analytical device of public culture, with a direct focus on the question of the relation of ideals, self-interest, and social activity, and with more attention to the process by which Protestants established, nurtured, and exercised their power.

3. Thomas Bender, *New York Intellect: A History of the Intellectual Life of New York City, from 1750 to the Beginnings of Our Own Time* (Baltimore, MD: The Johns Hopkins University Press, 1987), pp. xvi, xviii. T. H. Breen, reviewing Donald D. Hall's *World of Wonder, Days of Judgment: Popular Religious Belief in Early New England* (New York: Knopf, 1989), quotes Hall in referring to culture as "creative conversations," "a broad spectrum of possibilities," which is open, contingent and sometimes anxious. Breen, "The Miracle of Print: Shaping Popular Religion in Seventeenth-Century New England," *Reviews in American History* 19 (June 1991): 166–70.

4. Thomas Bender, "Making History Whole Again," *New York Times Book Review*, Oct. 6, 1985, pp. 1, 42–43; Bender, "Wholes and Parts: The Need for Synthesis in American History," *Journal of American History* 73 (June 1986): 120–36. "A Round Table: Synthesis in American History," *Journal of American History* 74 (June 1987): 107–30, includes comments on Ben-

der's "Wholes and Parts" essay by Nell Irvin Painter, Richard Wightman Fox, and Roy Rosenzweig, along with Bender's response. George M. Thomas, *Revivalism and Cultural Change: Christianity, Nation Building, and the Market in the Nineteenth-Century United States* (Chicago: University of Chicago Press, 1989), p. 5, comments on the way a cultural order defines reality and guides and justifies action.

5. Alexis de Tocqueville, *Democracy in America* (New York: Random House, Vintage, 1945), 1: 323 was one of the first to describe religion as occupying a limited circle within which its influence was pervasive. The most recent survey which describes Protestants as insiders "occupying the most visible public space" and looking on themselves as proprietors of American life is in Mark A. Noll, *A History of Christianity in the United States and Canada* (Grand Rapids, MI: Eerdmans, 1992), pp. 191–92, 163–90, 219–44. Similar approaches are found in Sydney E. Ahlstrom, *A Religious History of the American People* (New Haven: Yale University Press, 1972), pp 422–28, 637–47; Timothy L. Smith, *Revivalism and Social Reform: American Protestantism on the Eve of the Civil War* (New York: Harper and Row, pb., 1965), p. 36; Martin E. Marty, *Righteous Empire: The Protestant Experience in America* (New York: Dial, pb., 1970), pp. 37, 103, 122; Robert T. Handy, *A Christian America: Protestant Hopes and Historical Realities* (New York: Oxford University Press, 1971), pp. 27–64; Ann Douglas, *The Feminization of American Culture* (New York: Avon, 1977), p. 49; John S. Gilkeson, Jr., *Middle-Class Providence, 1820–1940* (Princeton, NJ: Princeton University Press, 1986), p. 93; Curtis D. Johnson, *Islands of Holiness: Rural Religion in Upstate New York, 1790–1860* (Ithaca, NY: Cornell University Press, 1989), p. 29; Terry D. Bilhartz, *Urban Religion and the Second Great Awakening: Church and Society in Early National Baltimore* (Cranbury, NJ: Fairleigh Dickinson University Press, 1986), pp. 52–53, 117; and Jon Butler, *Awash in a Sea of Faith: Christianizing the American People* (Cambridge, MA: Harvard University Press, 1990), pp. 257–88. Nathan O. Hatch's *The Democratization of American Christianity* (New Haven, CT: Yale University Press, 1989). pp. 9–11, 17–46, 206–09, describes the influence of Christianity on egalitarianism and democratization in a study that focuses on national leaders and movements.

6. The formative influence of Protestantism is described in Martin E. Marty, *Righteous Empire: The Protestant Experience in America* (New York: Dial, 1970); Ahlstrom, *A Religious History of the American People*, pp. 403–90, 635–69; and Robert T. Handy, *A History of the Churches of the United States and Canada* (New York: Oxford University Press, 1979), pp. 162–96.

7. Clifford S. Griffen, *Their Brothers' Keepers: Moral Stewardship in the United States, 1800–1850* (Brunswick, NJ: Rutgers University Press, 1960) provides a history of the work of Protestant voluntary groups.

8. Thomas, *Revivalism and Cultural Change*, p. 2, stresses the intentionality of religious groups in describing "aggressive religious movements that articulate and attempt to establish a new social order by advancing a specific agenda."

CHAPTER 2. THE EMERALD CITY OF THE LAKES

1. The company had purchased the land from the state of Connecticut, which had received it as the result of settling a number of land claims when it joined the union. When it agreed in 1800 to join other states in ceding western land claims, Connecticut "reserved" ownership and political jurisdiction of 3-1/2 million acres. The "Western Reserve," as it was named, ran from the Pennsylvania border to a line 120 miles west, and ranged from the 41st parallel to Lake Erie and the borders of New York and Michigan. For the early settlement of the city see Robert Wheeler, "A Commercial Hamlet is Founded, 1796–1824," and "Commercial Village to Commercial City, 1825–1860," in David D. Van Tassel and John J. Grabowski, *Encyclopedia of Cleveland History* (Bloomington, IN: Indiana University Press, 1987), pp. xvii–xxix; William Ganson Rose, *Cleveland: The Making of a City* (Cleveland: World Publishing Co., 1950), pp. 19–27, 30; Michael J. Hynes, *History of the Diocese of Cleveland: Origin and Growth (1847–1953)* (Cleveland: Diocese of Cleveland, 1953), p. 13; Samuel P. Orth, *A History of Cleveland, Ohio* (Chicago and Cleveland: S.J. Clarke Publishing Co., 1910), 1: 40, 77–79, 93; Julius P. Bolivar MacCabe, *Directory: Cleveland and Ohio City, for the Years 1837–38* (Cleveland: Sanford and Lott, 1837), pp. 2–20; William R. Coates, *A History of Cuyahoga County and the City of Cleveland: Historical and Biographical* (Chicago: American Historical Society, 1924), 1: 17–28; Harlan Hatcher, *The Western Reserve: The Story of New Connecticut in Ohio* (Cleveland: World, 1966), pp. 3–39; Harriet Taylor Upton, *History of the Western Reserve* (Chicago: Lewis Publishing Co., 1910), 1: 7–15; James Harrison Kennedy, *A History of the City of Cleveland, Its Settlement, Rise and Progress, 1796–1896* (Cleveland: The Imperial Press, 1896), pp. 17–27; Charles Whittlesey, *Early History of Cleveland, Ohio* (Cleveland: Fairbanks, Benedict and Co., 1867), pp. 165–70. The essays from *The Encyclopedia of Cleveland History* have been collected in Carol Poh Miller and Robert Wheeler, *Cleveland: A Concise History, 1796–1990* (Bloomington, IN: Indiana University Press, 1990).

2. Cleveland *Herald*, Feb. 26, 1833, p. 3 in U.S., Work Projects Administration in Ohio [Works Progress Administration in Ohio], *Annals of Cleveland* (Cleveland: Works Progress Administration, 1936–38), 1833: 135; *H*, May 11, 1844, p. 3 in *Annals*, 1844: 433; *H*, May 11, 1844, p. 3 in *Annals*, 1844: 437; *H*, Jan. 5, 1833, p. 3 in *Annals*, 1833: 63; Cleveland *Daily True*

Democrat, Mar. 20, 1852, p. 3 in *Annals*, 1852: 66; Cleveland *Leader*, Aug. 21, 1859, p. 1 in *Annals*, 1859: 71; Cleveland *Plain Dealer*, Oct. 10, 1851, p. 2; Elijah Peet, *Peet's General Business Directory of the Cities of Cleveland and Ohio, for the Years 1845–6* (Cleveland: Sanford and Hayward, 1845), p. 22; *PD*, July 18, 1849, p. 2; Cleveland *Whig & Herald*, July 21, 1847, p. 1 in *Annals*, 1847: 63; *WH*, Sept. 1, 1847, p. 1 in *Annals*, 1847: 63. Two perceptive accounts of boosterism and city-building are William Cronon, *Nature's Metropolis: Chicago and the Great West* (New York: W. W. Norton, 1992), pp. 31–46; and Robert Dykstra, *The Cattle Towns: A Social History of the Kansas Cattle Trading Centers, 1867 to 1885* (New York: Alfred A. Knopf, 1968).

3. Peet, *Directory, 1845–6*, p. 22; I. N. Mason, ed., *Smead and Cowles' General Business Directory For the City of Cleveland* (Cleveland: Smead and Cowles, 1850), pp. 27–28; Rose, *Cleveland*, p. 91, gives the date as 1809. George W. Knepper, *Ohio and Its People* (Kent, OH: Kent State University Press, 1989), pp. 153–54; Harry N. Scheiber, *Ohio Canal Era: A Case Study of Government and the Economy, 1820–1861* (Athens, OH: Ohio University Press, 1969); Whittlesey, *Early History of Cleveland*, pp. 131–33; *Directory, 1845–6*, pp. 9, 22.

4. For an account of the development of the town that did turn into the "City of the West," see Cronon, *Nature's Metropolis*, pp. 55–58, 63–91.

5. Ohio City had been part of Brooklyn township, organized in 1818. Kennedy, *History of the City of Cleveland*, p. 266; MacCabe, *Directory, 1837*, p. 19; Orth, *History of Cleveland*, 1: 242–44; Allen R. Pred, *The Spatial Dynamics of Urban Industrial Growth, 1800–1914* (Cambridge, MA: M.I.T. Press, 1966), p. 47.

6. For accounts of the development of comparable antebellum cities see Cronon, *Nature's Metropolis*; Kathleen D. McCarthy, *Noblesse Oblige: Charity and Philanthropy in Chicago, 1849–1929* (Chicago: University of Chicago Press, 1982); and Kathleen Neils Conzen, *Immigrant Milwaukee: Accommodation and Community in a Frontier City* (Cambridge, MA: Harvard University Press, 1976), and David Gerber, *The Making of American Pluralism: Buffalo, New York, 1825–60* (Urbana, IL: University of Illinois Press, 1989). In 1860 Detroit (45,619) and Milwaukee (45,246) had virtually the same population as Cleveland. Chicago, with a population of 29,963 in 1950, had by 1860 outpaced the others (109,260). The large Eastern cities were well established urban centers by this time. In 1860, New York's population was 813,669, and Boston's was 133,563. Parallels with Chicago are striking in terms of dates of incorporation, economic development, and the emergence of a network of voluntary organizations as described by Joseph Lee Lukonic, "Evangelicals in the City: Evangelical Protestant Social

Concerns in Early Chicago, 1837–1860" (Ph.D. Dissertation, University of Wisconsin, 1979).

7. Comparing Catholic and Protestant church membership statistics is notoriously difficult. Protestant statistics represent those who have made an explicit commitment to the church, while Catholic statistics customarily include all those within a diocese with even nominal Catholic heritage or ties. MacCabe, *Directory: Cleveland and Ohio City, 1837–38*; George F. Houck, *A History of Catholicity in Northern Ohio and In the Diocese of Cleveland From 1749 to December 31, 1900* (Cleveland: J.B. Savage, 1903), vol. 1: 24, 31, 58, 79–80, 89, 90; Hynes, *History of the Diocese of Cleveland*, pp. 41–42, 53, 58, 70, 71; Thomas Kremm, "Cleveland and the First Lincoln Election: The Ethnic Response to Nativism," *Journal of Interdisciplinary History* 8 (Summer 1977): 80, estimates that 13,135 (30.3 percent) of the city's residents were Catholic, based on an extrapolation from baptismal records. He estimates the Irish population at 8970 (20.7 percent of total Cleveland population) and the German at 14,987 (34.5 percent) and concludes that 77 percent of the city's Irish and 37 percent of the Germans were Catholic.

8. Lloyd P. Gartner, *History of the Jews of Cleveland* (Cleveland: Western Reserve Historical Society and Jewish Theological Seminary of America, 1978), pp. 10, 12, 31, 50; Sidney Z. Vincent and Judah Rubenstein, *Merging Traditions: Jewish Life in Cleveland* (Cleveland: The Western Reserve Historical Society and the Jewish Community Federation of Cleveland, 1978), pp. 71, 73, 80.

CHAPTER 3. THE CONTESTS WITHIN THE CONTEST

1. *Plain Dealer*, Apr. 13, 1852, p. 2; *PD*, Dec. 12, 1850, p. 2; *PD*, Mar. 9, 1854, p. 3. See also *PD*, Oct. 12, 1847, p. 2; *PD*, May 28, 1850, p. 2; *PD*, Nov. 8, 1851, p. 3; and *PD*, Jan. 20, 1852, p. 3.

2. *PD*, Feb. 18, 1853, p. 2. See also *PD*, Apr. 17, 1854, p. 2.

3. *PD*, Apr. 17, 1854, p. 2; and *PD*, Apr. 21, 1854, p. 3; Cleveland *Daily True Democrat*, May 28, 1853, p. 3 in U.S., Work Projects Administration, Ohio [Works Progress Administration in Ohio], *Annals of Cleveland* (Cleveland: Works Progress Administration, 1936–38), 1853, p. 537.

4. *PD*, Feb. 23, 1853, p. 3. "Volney" had been the pen name of a French philosopher and historian, Constantin-François de Chasseboeuf (1757–1820). He had been a representative of the third estate of the Revolutionary government in France, and he later served as a senator after Napoleon's coup. Volney was in the United States from 1795 to 1798, when he left after incurring the ire of John Adams and being accused of

being a secret agent. Paul Edwards, ed., *Encyclopedia of Philosophy* (New York: The Macmillan Co. and the Free Press, 1967), 8: 260–61.

5. *PD*, Feb. 26, 1853, p. 2.

6. *PD*, Mar. 5, 1853, p. 3. For other accounts of the charges and apprehensions that money endangered religion, see Daniel T. Rodgers, *The Work Ethic in Industrial America, 1850–1920* (Chicago: University of Chicago Press, 1978, pb.), p. 103; John A. Andrew III, *Rebuilding the Christian Commonwealth: New England Congregationalists and Foreign Missions, 1800–1830* (Lexington, KY.: The University Press of Kentucky, 1976), p. 68; Lois Banner, "Religious Benevolence as Social Control: A Critique of an Interpretation," in *Religion in American History: Interpretive Essays*, edited by John M. Mulder and John F. Wilson (Englewood Cliffs, NJ: Prentice-Hall, 1978), p. 231; Anne C. Loveland, *Southern Evangelicals and the Social Order, 1800–1860* (Baton Rouge, LA: Louisiana State University Press, 1980), pp. 48, 95–96, 101–04; Martin E. Marty, *Righteous Empire: The Protestant Experience in America* (New York: Dial, pb., 1970), pp. 101–10; Clifford E. Clark, Jr., *Henry Ward Beecher: Spokesman for a Middle-Class America* (Urbana, IL: University of Illinois Press, 1978), pp. 113–14.

7. Trinity Episcopal Church, Record of the Proceedings of the Vestry of Trinity Church Cleveland Commencing Easter May 1839 [to 1864], Trinity Cathedral, Cleveland, Articles of Association & By Laws of Trinity Church, 1839; amendment Apr. 5, 1847; Third Baptist Church, Church Record Book, 1852–67, 1884, 1885, Western Reserve Historical Society, 1852–67, Nov. 16, 1859.

8. Cleveland *Leader*, Mar. 5, 1859, p. 3 in WPA, *Annals*, 1859, p. 57; Trinity, Vestry Record, pp. 167–70, July 3, 1854; Henry E. Bourne, *The Church of the Covenant: The First Hundred Years* (Cleveland: Church of the Covenant, 1945), p. 26; *PD*, Feb. 28, 1857, p. 3; *PD*, Jan. 7, 1857, p. 3; Second Presbyterian sold 172 of 202 in 1859. Euclid Street Presbyterian sold 173 of 174 (one was for clergy) in 1852. Trinity Episcopal reported in 1854 that 48 of its 120 pews were sold. *L*, Mar. 5, 1859, p. 3 in WPA, *Annals*, 1859, p. 57; Euclid Avenue Presbyterian Church, Society and Trustees Record, 1853–1906, Church of the Covenant, Cleveland, Nov. 30, 1852; Trinity E., Vestry Record, 1836–64, pp. 167–70, July 3, 1854.

9. Trinity E., Vestry Record, Aug. 25, 1834; First Baptist Church, Record, January 5, 1849–April 1, 1859, First Baptist Church, Shaker Heights, Ohio, Apr. 23, 1855; Trinity E., Vestry Record, Aug. 26, 1840. See also St. John's Episcopal Church, Vestry Books, 1836–63, Western Reserve Historical Society (type-written), Apr. 6, 1840, Apr. 14, 1838, Mar. 28, 1839; First Presbyterian Church, Church Record, 1849–1878, First Presbyterian

Church, Cleveland; First Baptist Church, Trustee Minutes, 1855–83, First Baptist Church, Shaker Heights, Ohio, 1855; First Methodist Episcopal Church, Incorporation, 1839, The Book of Records for the First Methodist Episcopal Church of Cleveland, 1839–45, First United Methodist Church, Cleveland, 1841, 1845; St. Paul's Episcopal Church, Parish Files, Archives, Episcopal Diocese of Ohio, Trinity Cathedral, Cleveland.

10. First Presbyterian Church, Trustees Minutes, 1855–1909, First Presbyterian Church, Cleveland. See also Michael J. McTighe, "Embattled Establishment: Protestants and Power in Cleveland, 1836–1860" (Ph.D. Dissertation, University of Chicago, 1983), Table 28, pp. 453–54.

11. First P., Trustee Minutes, 1855–1909, June 18, 1855, Nov. 6, 1855, Apr. 19, 1856; Euclid Street Presbyterian Church, Records of the Euclid Street Presbyterian Church and Society, 1853 to 1870, Church of the Covenant, Cleveland, Mar. 3, 1856, Mar. 2, 1857; Trinity E., Vestry Record, 1839–64, pp. 41–42, Aug. 23, 1843; First Congregational Church, Minutes of the Church Society, January 6, 1857 to June 1, 1885, Congregational Library, Boston, Report of Trustees, Jan. 1, 1857. When Trinity Episcopal Church had financial problems it requested even further assessments: Trinity E., Vestry Record, Sept. 11, 1852, p. 124.

The information about incomes is drawn from Stuart M. Blumin, *The Emergence of the Middle Class: Social Experience in the American City* (New York: Cambridge University Press, 1989), pp. 109–115; and Sean Wilentz, *Chants Democratic: New York City and the Rise of the American Working Class, 1788–1850* (New York: Oxford University Press, 1984).

12. First Presbyterian Church, Church Record, 1837–1849, First Presbyterian Church, Cleveland, July 2, 1847. The widow's name was Mrs. Clark.

13. First Baptist Society, Minutes, March 31, 1837 to Dec. 18, 1848, First Baptist Church, Shaker Heights, Ohio, July 1847.

14. *PD*, Jan. 20, 1852, p. 3.

15. Alexander Varian, *Pastoral Letter to the Parishioners of Grace Church* (Cleveland: Smead & Cowles, 1847), pp. 6, 7.

16. Varian, Sermon, Mar. 26, 1848, in Grace [Episcopal Church], *Past and Present of Grace Church* (Cleveland: Grace Episcopal Church, 1898), pp. 18–19; *PD*, Jan. 11, 1850, p. 2; Grace Church, *Past and Present*, pp. 21–22.

17. James A. Bolles, "Free Churches: A Valedictory Sermon Preached in Trinity Church, Cleveland, Ohio, July 3, 1859," in James A. Bolles, *Sermons* (Boston: Henry W. Dutton & Son, 1859), pp. 14, 18–19.

18. Bolles, "Free Churches," pp. 15, 21.

19. Bolles, "Free Churches," pp. 16, 18, 11, emphasis in original. [James A. Bolles], Rector, Trinity Episcopal Church, *Fourth Annual Report and Pastoral Letter* (Cleveland: Fairbanks, Benedict and Co., 1858), p. 10, emphasis in original.

20. Bolles, "Free Churches," p. 16.

21. Bolles, *Fourth Annual Report and Pastoral Letter*, p. 6. Trinity E., Vestry Record, 1836–64, June 11, 1859; June 12, 1859, vote 6–2, with Mather and Lester in favor; Bolles, "Free Churches," pp. 4–5; Trinity E., Vestry Record, June 6, 1859; James A. Bolles, *A Free Memorial Church Salutory Address* (n. p., n. d.), compiled in James A. Bolles, *Sermons*, p. 1. He later became minister of a free pew church in Brooklyn, N.Y. The criticism of Bolles and Varian echoed the words of Henry Ward Beecher: "No minister can preach an unadulterated gospel to a dying world thro' the portals of a worldly—or dishonest, or hypocritical, or commercial church." Quoted by Clark, *Beecher*, pp. 77–78.

22. First P., Record, 1820–37, Mar. 9, 1836. The resulting First Congregational Church foundered during the depression of 1837. Most of the members rejoined First Presbyterian.

23. The three free churches were Varian's Grace Episcopal Church (from 1844–50), Free Presbyterian [Plymouth Congregational] Church (1850–) and John Avery's First Congregational Church. For Avery, see *PD*, Dec. 20, 1851, p. 2.

24. First Baptist Church, *History of the First Baptist Church of Cleveland, Ohio: And an Account of the Celebration of its Semi-Centennial, February 16th–20th, 1883* (Cleveland: J.B. Savage, 1883), p. 26; Protestant Episcopal Church, Ohio Diocese, *Journal, 1835–60* (n. p., 1835–60), 1853, p. 70, report by Lewis Burton; Horace Benton, "Franklin Ave. M.E. Church, 1870–1895," Western Reserve Historical Society, Hope-Wesley United Methodist Church Papers, 1895, p. 8.

25. This information on property holding is subject to a number of distortions. Including those who joined churches from 1810–1849 has the effect of skewing the results, since church joiners would be expected to be wealthier than the general population, just as a function of age. In addition, church joiners would generally have been in their teens or older, and so the group would not include those younger who were unlikely to own real property. For these reasons, property holding of the head of household is a more reliable yardstick for comparing church-joiners and the general population.

26. There are a number of possible distortions in these property hold-ing statistics which must be considered. One is that of age—since church joiners are older than the general population, they would be more likely to own property. Comparing the property holding of church joiners with those in the general population over the age of 18 helps establish a more appropriate comparison. But even here church members emerged as a rela-tively propertied segment of the population. (Table 3.1.)

Another possible distortion of property holding statistics is that they may inordinately reflect the accumulated wealth of those who joined in the earliest years. But controlling for year of joining still results in the con-clusion that church joiners owned more property than non-joiners. Of the 23 who joined churches from 1846–50, 17 (73.9 percent) held property, with a mean for the 17 of $3,805. Of the 26 who joined from 1851–55, 16 (61.5 percent) held property, with a mean of $1,987. (Table 3.1.)

27. The statisttics are based on 90 church joiners located in the cen-sus. See Appendix and McTighe, "Embattled Establishment," Tables 12 and 13, pp. 136–37. The categories used in this analysis and the occupations which fit within each of them are drawn from the work of the Philadelphia Social History Project (see Appendix). The categories ("professional," "white collar," "blue collar") are ones more fitting for the twentieth century, but they provide a general sense of the occupational distribution. Blumin, *Emer-gence of the Middle Class*, uses categories more applicable to early nine-teenth-century occupational life, such as "manual" and "nonmanual."

28. See previous note, and McTighe, "Embattled Establishment," Tables 14 and 15, pp. 138–40.

29. For a detailed breakdown of participartion in specific organiza-tions see McTighe, "Embattled Establishment," Table 32, pp. 585–90.

30. William H. Pease and Jane H. Pease, *The Web of Progress: Private Values and Public Styles in Boston and Charleston, 1828–1843* (New York: Oxford University Press, 1985), pp. 135, 301–02. See the next chapters for additional discussions of the interconnected leadership elite and its simi-larities to groups in other cities.

31. Although membership does not necessarily imply commitment or indicate degree of commitment, it is a convenient indication of affilia-tion. In the early nineteenth-century context. membership evidences a level of commitment greater than is assumed in the late twentieth century. The evangelical theology to which, to a greater or lesser degree, almost all Protestant churches adhered, stressed the centrality of individual decision and required that new members be examined for their experience and knowledge of doctrine. To be a member was to make an express commit-

ment to having had a regenerative experience. This meant that membership, at least in theory, was more than a token commitment. We may, therefore, discern some of the potential for influence of Cleveland's Protestants by a detailed look at the membership of the churches.

Barbara Welter, "The Feminization of American Religion, 1800–1860," in *Clio's Consciousness Raised*, ed. by Mary Hartman and Lois Banner (New York: Harper and Row, 1973), pp. 137–55. Ann Douglas, *The Feminization of American Culture* (New York: Avon, 1977), presents a related argument. For the predominance of women in churches, and the effect this had on both, see Richard D. Shiels, "The Feminization of American Congregationalism, 1730–1835," *American Quarterly* 33 (Spring, 1981): 46–62; Mary Maples Dunn, "Saints and Sinners: Congregational and Quaker Women in the Early Colonial Period," in *Women in American Religion*, ed. by Janet Wilson James (Philadelphia: University of Pennsylvania Press, 1980), pp. 27–46; Gerald F. Moran, "'Sisters' in Christ: Women and the Church in Seventeenth-Century New England," in James, pp. 47–65; Rosemary Ruether and Eleanor McLaughlin, *Women of Spirit: Female Leadership in the Jewish and Christian Traditions* (New York: Simon and Schuster, 1979); Barbara J. MacHaffie, *Women in Christian Tradition* (Philadelphia: Fortress, 1986); Curtis D. Johnson, *Islands of Holiness: Rural Religion in Upstate New York, 1790–1860* (Ithaca, NY: Cornell University Press, 1989), pp. 53–66; Suzanne Lebsock, *The Free Women of Petersburg: Status and Culture in a Southern Town, 1784–1860* (New York: Norton, 1984), p. 215; Pease and Pease, *Web of Progress*, p 136; Mark A. Noll, *A History of Christianity in the United States and Canada* (Grand Rapids, MI: Eerdmans, 1992), pp. 181–82.

32. Lebsock, *Free Women of Petersburg*, p. 234; Anne M. Boylan, "Timid Girls, Venerable Widows and Dignified Matrons: Life Cycle Patterns Among Organized Women in New York and Boston, 1797–1840," *American Quarterly* 38 (Winter 1986): 791; Linda K. Kerber, "Separate Spheres, Female Worlds, Woman's Place: The Rhetoric of Women's History," *Journal of American History* 75 (June 1988): 18.

33. Douglas, *Feminization of American Culture*; and Lebsock, *Free Women of Petersburg*, pp. 195–236; see esp. p. 198.

34. Trinity Episcopal Church, Vestry Record, Oct. 31, 1959, Trinity Episcopal Church, Cleveland. For further information about the city's Protestant ministers, see McTighe, "Embattled Establishment," pp. 561–69.

35. Arthur C. Ludlow, *The Old Stone Church: The Story of a Hundred Years, 1820–1920* (Cleveland: Premier Press, 1920), pp. 59–60; *L*, May 18, 1857, p. 3 in WPA, *Annals*, 1857, p. 45; *PD*, Mar. 7, 1857, p. 3. Lebsock, *Women of Petersburg*, p. 223, argues that investing in buildings was part of a larger process by which Southern Protestantism made itself respectable.

36. See McTighe, "Embattled Establishment," pp. 62–64.

37. J. Hyatt Smith in "Circular Letter," Cleveland, or Rocky River Baptist Association, *Minutes, 1852–1860* (n. p., 1852–60), 1854, p. 23, italics and capitalization in original. *PD*, May 30, 1857, p. 3.

38. For a fuller discussion of these disputes see McTighe, "Embattled Establishment," pp. 71–86. Amy Bridges, *A City in the Republic: Ante-Bellum New York and the Origins of Machine Politics* (New York: Cambridge University Press, 1984), pp. 85, 87, refers to tensions among Protestants which kept them from becoming a united anti-Catholic front.

39. Typical examples of evangelical theology can be found in Euclid *P*, Records, Feb. 1, 1853, p. 6; First Baptist Church, *A Declaration of the Faith and Practice, Together With the Rules and Regulations of the First Baptist Church in the City of Cleveland, Ohio* (Cleveland: Harris, Fairbanks and Co., 1857), p. 7; First Baptist Church, Articles of Faith, 1833, in Benjamin Rouse, Life, First Congregational Church, Record Book "A," December 1834 to July 1852, Congregational Library, Boston, Dec. 21, 1834.

40. S. B. Canfield, S. C. Aiken, and H. Blodget, *An Exposition of the Peculiarities, Difficulties and Tendencies of Oberlin Perfectionism Prepared by a Committee of the Presbytery of Cleveland* (Cleveland: T. H. Smead, 1841), p. 79.

41. Cornelius E. Dickenson, "History of Congregationalism in Ohio Before 1852," *Ohio Church History Society Papers* (Oberlin, OH: Ohio Church History Society, 1899), vol. 3 (1896): 32 (the *Papers* have been collected in two volumes, published by the Society in 1899. Citations are to the original volumes); William S. Kennedy, *The Plan of Union, or, A History of the Presbyterian and Congregational Churches of the Western Reserve* (Hudson, OH: Pentagon Steam Press, 1856); Delavan L. Leonard, *A Century of Congregationalism in Ohio*, (Oberlin, OH: Ohio Home Missionary Society, 1896); Ludlow, *Old Stone Church*, pp. 97–104; Rev. [Arthur Clyde] Ludlow and Mrs. Arthur Clyde Ludlow, *History of Cleveland Presbyterianism with Directory of All the Churches* (Cleveland: W.M. Bayne, 1896), p. 12. In May 1822 the male members resolved to adopt the Presbyterian mode of church government, "but under existing circumstances it does not think it prudent to act upon that subject." The confusion persisted in a rule adopted in 1832, which after noting that some members preferred the Congregational mode of government and some the Presbyterian, provided that the church officers were to operate as a Standing Committee of Deacons for those desiring a Congregational system, and as Ruling Elders for those preferring Presbyterian government. In 1833 the members chose a Congregational form of government, 20 to 3. First Presbyterian Church, Records, 1820–37, First

Presbyterian Church, Cleveland, May 11, 1822; Sept. 9, 1832; July 9, 1833; Bourne, *Church of the Covenant*, p. 17. Later in the year thirty-five new members swung the sentiment to Presbyterianism. Ludlow, *Old Stone Church*, p. 57. Kennedy is quoted in E. D. Welsh, and others, *Buckeye Presbyterianism* (n.p.: United Presbyterian Synod of Ohio, 1968), p. 99.

42. For the story of the founding of First Presbyterian, Ohio City, and its difficulty resolving Congregationalist-Presbyterian church government disputes see First Congregational Church, Record Book "A," December 1834 to July 1852 [September, 1841], Congregational Library, Boston, Mar. 20, 1839; John G. Fraser, "A Century of Congregationalism in Cleveland," *Ohio Church History Society Papers*, vol. 8 (1897): 14; Henry M. Tenney, "The History of the First Congregational Church of Cleveland," *Ohio Church History Society Papers*, vol. 2 (1892): 40; Rev. A. B. Cristy, *Cleveland Congregationalists, 1895: Historical Sketches of our Twenty-Five Churches and Missions* (Cleveland: Williams Publishing and Electric Co., 1896), p. 41. Aiken had opposed the formation of a Congregational Union in 1836, which put him in opposition to Pres. Mahan and Prof. Cowles of Oberlin. Aiken lost, and a General Association of the Western Reserve (also known as the Western Reserve Congregational Association) was formed. Kennedy, *The Plan of Union*, p. 196.

43. First P., Record, 1820–37, Nov. 30, 1834; Tenney, "History of the First Congregational Church," vol. 2 (1892): 30–31; William Henry Goodrich, "Fiftieth Anniversary of the Stone Church, September 18, 1870," Western Reserve Historical Society, vertical file, n. p.

44. Bourne, *The Church of the Covenant*, p. 20; Charles S. Pomeroy, *An Historical Sketch Reviewing the Origin and Growth of the Second Presbyterian Church* (Cleveland: Leader Book and Job, 1876), pp. 4–5.

45. A more friendly offshoot of First Presbyterian Church, once again taking the name Second Presbyterian Church, was founded in 1844, and survived the antebellum years. First P., Record, 1837–49, Feb. 22, 1841; Cleveland Presbytery, Minutes, 1830–83, Presbytery of the Western Reserve, Cleveland, Apr. 7, 1841; Pomeroy, *Historical Sketch*, p. 5.

46. Plymouth Church, *Manual, 1860* (Cleveland: E. Cowles and Co., 1860), p. 3. The church took the name Plymouth Congregational in 1854 at the suggestion of Henry Ward Beecher. Roy Edwin Bowers, *Ohio Congregational Christian Story* (n.p., Ohio Conference of Congregational Christian Churches, 1952), p. 76.

47. Trinity Cathedral, *Some Sketches and Statements of Cathedral Work and Ideas* (Cleveland: Trinity Cathedral, 1899), p. 16; F. Washington Jarvis,

St. Paul's Cleveland 1846–1968: A History of the Parish in Its Fortieth Year on the Heights (Cleveland: St. Paul's Episcopal Church, 1967), p. 2; A.H. Washburn, "Some Historical Sketches of Grace Church, Cleveland, Ohio, 1876," in "Historical Sketch of the Diocese of Ohio, 1817–1878," ed. G. T. Bedell, in Archives, Episcopal Diocese of Ohio, Trinity Cathedral, Cleveland, vol. 3: 4; Roderic Hall Pierce, *Trinity Cathedral Parish: The First 150 Years* (Cleveland: Vestry of Trinity Cathedral, 1967), p. 9. Cleveland *Whig and Herald*, Oct. 5, 1847, p. 1, letter, in WPA, *Annals*, 1847, p. 45. See also the votes in the Convention of the Protestant Episcopal Diocese of Ohio on a resolution condemning a "Popish" doctrine, tractarianism: No—Rev. Lloyd Windsor of Trinity and Geo. E. Freeman of Grace; Yes—Rev. Dr. Perry, H.L. Noble and Jas. Kellogg of St. Paul's. George Franklin Smythe, *A History of the Diocese of Ohio Until the Year 1918* (Cleveland: Protestant Episcopal Church, Ohio Diocese, 1931), p. 245; Grace Church, *Past and Present*, pp. 17–18.

48. Washburn, "Historical Sketches of Grace Church," note (E) opposite p. 14, and p. 11.

49. John Hall, Ashtabula Letters, Oct. 24, 1846 to Charles P. McIlvaine, Archives, Episcopal Diocese of Ohio, Trinity Cathedral, Cleveland, Hall Papers; Jarvis, *St. Paul's*, pp. 3–4; Washburn, "Historical Sketches of Grace Church," p. 11; *PD*, Dec. 11, 1846, p. 2.

50. Washburn, "Historical Sketches of Grace Church," p. 11; Hall, Ashtabula Letters, Nov. 26, 1846; Dec. 21, 1846.

51. [Harvey Rice], *Review of Bishop McIlvaine's Opinion Relative to the Official Position of the Clergy of Grace Church, Cleveland, Ohio* (Cleveland: E. Cowles and Co., 1856), p. 5; Grace Church, *Past and Present*, p. 22–23; Washburn, "Historical Sketches of Grace Church," pp. 17–18.

52. Charles P. McIlvaine, *Opinion of the Right Rev. Charles P. McIlvaine, D.D., Bishop of the Protestant Episcopal Church in Ohio in Answer to Certain Questions Regarding the Official Position of the Clergy of Grace Church, Cleveland* (Cleveland: Plain Dealer Book and Job Office, 1856); Rice, *Review of Bishop McIlvaine's Opinion*, pp. 9–10; Washburn, "Historical Sketches of Grace Church," pp. 20, 24.

53. Rice, *Review of Bishop McIlvaine's Opinion*, p. 14.

54. *PD*, Nov. 14, 1856, p. 3.

55. *PD*, Nov. 21, 1856, p. 3; Washburn, "Historical Sketches of Grace Church," p. 19; *PD*, Feb. 4, 1857, p. 3.

56. For a listing of Protestant ministers and terms of service see McTighe, "Embattled Establishment," pp. 561–69.

57. Trinity E., Vestry Record, Jan. 17, 1854 [1855], emphasis in original.

58. These figures are based on a systematic compilation of hundreds of entires from the church records avaiable for the years 1836–60. See Appendix, and McTighe, "Embattled Establishment," Tables 6–9, pp. 124–31.

CHAPTER 4. ANOINTING THE COMMERCIAL ECONOMY

1. S. C. Aiken, *Moral View of Rail Roads: A Discourse* (Cleveland: Harris, Fairbanks, and Co., 1851), pp. 8–9.

2. Worries about the corrosive effects of wealth and the spirit of enterprise had something of a pro forma quality consistent with the Protestant tradition of the jeremiad. Protestants, after all, especially those in the Reformed tradition, were expected to feel guilty about wealth. James H. Moorhead, "Social Reform and the Divided Conscience of Antebellum Protestantism," *Church History* 48 (December, 1979): 428; William McLoughlin, "Charles Grandison Finney," in *Ante-Bellum Reform*, edited by David Brion Davis (New York: Harper and Row, 1967), p. 104; Edmund S. Morgan, "The Puritan Ethic and the American Revolution," in *The Reinterpretation of the American Revolution, 1763–1789*, ed. by Jack P. Greene (New York: Harper and Row, 1968); Beecher is quoted by Clifford E. Clark, Jr., *Henry Ward Beecher: Spokesman for a Middle-Class America* (Urbana, IL: University of Illinois Press, 1978), pp. 77–78; Sandra Sizer, "Politics and Apolitical Religion: The Great Urban Revivals of the Late Nineteenth Century," *Church History* 48 (March, 1979): 81–98. See also Donald M. Scott, *From Office to Profession: The New England Ministry, 1750–1850* (Philadelphia: University of Pennsylvania Press, 1978), pp. 39–41; and Charles Grier Sellers, *The Market Revolution: Jacksonian America, 1815–1846* (New York: Oxford University Press, 1991), pp. 28–31, 202–19.
Cleveland Presbytery, Minutes, 1830–1883, 4 Vols., Presbytery of the Western Reserve, Cleveland. Perry was pessimistic, but ended by hoping that maybe the cultivation of thought would prevent the trend of the age from becoming an overwhelming deluge. Gideon B. Perry, *An Address on the True Character of Mental Greatness* (Gambier, OH: Theological Seminary Press, by the Philomathesian Society of Kenyon College, 1852), pp. 6, 26–27. Other responses to these worries about new forms of economic life are described by J. E. Crowley, *This Sheba, Self: The Conceptualization of Economic Life in Eighteenth-Century America* (Baltimore, MD: Johns Hopkins University Press, 1974); Charles L. Sanford, *The Quest for Paradise: Europe and the American Moral Imagination* (Urbana, IL: University of Illinois Press, 1961), pp. 114–34; John H. Kasson, *Civilizing the Machine: Technology and*

Republican Values, 1776–1900 (New York: Penguin, 1977); Paul E. Johnson, *A Shopkeeper's Millennium: Society and Revivals in Rochester, New York, 1815–1837* (New York: Hill and Wang, 1978); and Nancy F. Cott, *The Bonds of Womanhood: "Woman's Sphere" in New England, 1780–1835* (New Haven, CT: Yale University Press, 1978, pb), p. 97.

See also Levi Tucker, *Lectures on the Nature and Dangerous Tendency of Modern Infidelity* (Cleveland: Francis B. Penniman, 1837), p. 48. These religious views were echoed in republican political thought, which feared that wealth would sap the virtue of citizens upon which the republic depended. John Adams feared that the very qualities which made for success, temperance, and industry, prepared the ground for future difficulties. As he wrote to Jefferson in 1819:

> Will you tell me how to prevent riches from becoming the effects of temperance and industry? Will you tell me how to prevent riches from producing luxury? Will you tell me how to prevent luxury from producing effeminacy intoxication extravagance Vice and folly.

From Lester J. Cappon, ed., *The Adams-Jefferson Letters*, 2 Vols. (Chapel Hill, NC: University of North Carolina Press, 1959), 2: 187, quoted by Daniel T. Rodgers, *The Work Ethic in Industrial America, 1850–1920* (Chicago: University of Chicago Press, pb., 1978), p. 103. See also Gordon Wood, *The Creation of the American Republic, 1776–1787* (Chapel Hill, NC: University of North Carolina Press, 1969).

3. Cleveland *Plain Dealer*, Aug. 21, 1854, p. 3. The Cleveland *Leader* expressed a comparable view: "in truth, people place money before God. They work fast, eat fast, and worship fast." Cleveland *Leader*, Mar. 15, 1856, p. 2 in Work Projects Administration, Ohio [Works Progress Administration in Ohio], *Annals of Cleveland* (Cleveland: Works Progress Administration, 1936–38), 1856, p. 28. Money was the strongest and meanest of passions: "on its altar all the finer and all the nobler attributes of humanity are remorselessly sacrificed." *L*, Oct. 18, 1855, p. 2 in WPA, *Annals*, 1855, p. 101.

4. *PD*, Feb. 4, 1860, p. 3; *L*, Mar. 8, 1856, p. 2 in WPA, *Annals*, 1856, p. 472.

5. *L*, June 4, 1860, p. 1 in WPA, *Annals*, 1860, p. 63; First Baptist Society Record, January 5, 1849–April 1, 1859, First Baptist Church, Shaker Heights, Ohio, Nov. 4, 1853.

6. *PD*, Dec. 14, 1850, p. 2; Mason, I. N., ed., *Smead and Cowles' General Directory for the City of Cleveland* (Cleveland: Smead and Cowles, 1850), p. 46; Western Seamen's Friend Society, "Second Annual Report," *Spirit of the Lakes,*

and *Boatman's Magazine*, Nov. 1849, p. 164; *Knight and Parson's Business Directory of the City of Cleveland* (Cleveland: E.G. Knight and Co., and Parsons and Co., 1853), p. 62; Western Seamen's Friend Society, "Third Annual Report," *Spirit of the Lakes, and Boatman's Magazine*, Oct., 1850, p. 178.

7. Sherman Canfield, *An Address on the Power and Progressiveness of Knowledge* (Painesville, OH: Smythe and Hanna, 1843), pp. 3, 26–27; *PD*, Aug. 24, 1858, p. 3; *PD*, Sept. 8, 1849, quoted by Elbert Jay Benton, *Cultural Story of an American City: Cleveland* (Cleveland: Western Reserve Historical Society, 1943), 2: 71.

8. Leo Marx, *The Machine in the Garden: Technology and the Pastoral Ideal in America* (New York: Oxford University Press, 1964), pp. 195, 150–226. See also Hugo A. Meier, "Technology and Democracy, 1800–1860," *Mississippi Valley Historical Review* 43 (March 1957), pp. 619, 631–34; George H. Daniels, *Science in American Society: A Social History* (New York: Knopf, 1971), pp. 126–45; Kasson, *Civilizing the Machine*, pp. 41–48; Sanford, *The Quest for Paradise*; and William Cronon, *Nature's Metropolis: Chicago and the Great West* (New York: W. W. Norton, 1992), pp. 72–74.

9. Aiken, *Moral View of Rail Roads*, pp. 16–17, 18–20, 26. See also Sherman Canfield, *The Indications of a Divine Purpose to Make Our Country a Model Christian Republic* (Syracuse: T. S. Truair, Daily Journal Office, 1855), p. 46, who described the railroad as ribs of iron binding the states together.

Having succumbed to the lure of the railroad, Protestant leaders expressed no concern about one by-product of the new technology, railroad accidents. The *Plain Dealer* referred to some railroad accidents as "massacres" and "murders" and the Common Council (the city's governing body) passed legislation concerning the noise, disruption, and speed of trains in the city, all without noticeable Protestant participation. *PD*, May 9, 1853, p. 3; *PD*, May 10, 1853, p. 2 refers to "railroad murders." Other complaints: Cleveland *Daily True Democrat*, Jan. 31, 1850, p. 2 in WPA, *Annals*, 1850, p. 331; *L*, Nov. 22, 1855, p. 2 in WPA, *Annals*, 1855, p. 481; *L*, Mar. 5, 1856, p. 2 in WPA, *Annals*, 1856, p. 388. Regulation: City of Cleveland, *Charters of the Village of Cleveland, and the City of Cleveland, With Their Several Amendments: To Which Are Added the Laws and Ordinances of the City of Cleveland* (Cleveland: Harris, Fairbanks and Co., 1851), pp. 162–63, Nov. 12, 1851; B. White, ed., *The Acts to Provide for the Organization of Cities and Villages and the Revised Ordinances of the City of Cleveland* (Cleveland: Harris, Fairbanks and Co., 1855), pp. 167–68, Ordinance LXIV, Sept. 27, 1854; pp. 191–92, Ordinance LXXX, n.d.; Ordinance LXXXI, Sept. 27, 1857; Cleveland, Ohio, *The Acts to Provide for the Organization of Cities and Villages and the Revised Ordinances of the City of Cleveland* (Cleveland: Plain Dealer, 1862), pp. 238–39, Jan. 10, 1856. Alliance railroad crash: *L*, Dec. 10, 1856,

p. 2 in WPA, *Annals*, 1856, p. 8. For other questions about loss of life and injury caused by railroads, see: *DTD*, May 11, 1853, p. 2 in WPA, *Annals*, 1853, p. 392; *H*, Jan, 12, 1843, p. 3 in WPA, *Annals*, 1843, p. 1; *DTD*, May 4, 1853, p. 3 in WPA, *Annals*, 1853, pp. 391–92.

10. *PD*, Aug. 21, 1854.

11. James H. Moorhead, "Between Progress and Apocalypse: A Reassessment of Millennialism in American Religious Thought, 1800–1880," *Journal of American History* 71 (December 1984): 525, 533; Nancy A. Hewitt, *Women's Activism and Social change: Rochester, New York, 1822–1872* (Ithaca, NY: Cornell University Press, 1984), pp. 24–32.

12. Cleveland *Herald*, May 9, 1843, p. 3 in WPA, *Annals*, 1843, p. 286.

13. Protestant Episcopal Church, Ohio Diocese, *Journal, 1835–60*, (n.p., n.d.), 1857, McIlvaine Address, pp. 17–18. Cleveland Bible Society, *Annual Report* (Cleveland: Harris, Fairbanks and Co., 1856), pp. 22, 23.

14. First Presbyterian Church, Records, 1820–37, First Presbyterian Church, Cleveland, Jan. 18, 1837.

15. First Presbyterian Church, Church Record, 1837–49, First Presbyterian Church, Cleveland, June 24, 1839, June 27, 1839, July 16, 1839, Aug. 2, 1839. For others see: Henry M. Tenney, "The History of the First Congregational Church of Cleveland," *Ohio Church History Society Papers* (Oberlin, Ohio: Ohio Church History Society, 1892), 2 (1892): 36. The *Papers* have been collected in two volumes, published by the Society in 1899. Citations are to the original volumes. First P., Record, 1837–49, Oct. 31, 1844.

16. First Congregational Church, Record Book "A," December, 1834 to July, 1852 [September, 1841], Congregational Library, Boston, Aug. 11, 1837, Sept. 9, 1839, Oct. 21, 1839; Cleveland Presbytery, Minutes, 1830–83, Dec. 7, 1841.

17. *PD*, Sept. 19, 1860, p. 3.

18. *The Boatman's Magazine* 1 (Oct., 1834): 29–30.

19. Aiken, *Moral View of Rail Roads*, pp. 23, 24; Cleveland Presbytery, Minutes, 1830–83, Apr. 19, 1837.

20. See the appeal from Harmon Kingsbury reported in *H*, May 7, 1842, p. 2 in WPA, *Annals*, 1842, pp. 56–57. For agreements with individual shipping owners, see the Cleveland *Whig*, Apr. 15, 1835, p. 2 in WPA, *Annals*, 1835, p. 10; *H*, Sept. 15, 1842, p. 2 in WPA, *Annals*, 1842, p. 58; *H*, May 21, 1842, p. 3 in WPA, *Annals*, 1842, p. 359. George M. Young's

announcement was in *H*, Sept. 15, 1842, p. 2 in WPA, *Annals*, 1842, p. 58. Stopping railroad traffic was a little more successful. The Western Seamen's Friend Society's newspaper reported in 1849 that 30 railroad companies had discontinued running on the Sabbath. But this was only a modest number of Sabbath observers in light of the hundreds of small railroad companies in the midwest. The other major companies serving Cleveland continued Sunday service. *Spirit of the Lakes, and Boatman's Magazine* 1, (May, 1849): 72; *L*, Nov. 22, 1855, p. 3 in WPA, *Annals*, 1855, pp. 481–482; Cleveland Presbytery, Minutes, 1830–83, April 19, 1837. Challenges to church enforcement of Sabbath observance were part of a general loss of corporate power by the churches under the impact of individualism brought by more Arminian and "democratic" theologies and by the impact of the market: Curtis D. Johnson, *Islands of Holiness: Rural Religion in Upstate New York, 1790–1860* (Ithaca, NY: Cornell University Press, 1989), pp. 9, 56–57, 71–72, 103–12. See also John S. Gilkeson, Jr., *Middle-Class Providence, 1820–1940* (Princeton, NJ: Princeton University Press, 1986), pp. 65–67.

21. See chapter 2 for a discussion of the social characteristics of the city's Protestants. A fuller discussion of the links between Protestants and the business community is in Michael J. McTighe, "Embattled Establishment: Protestants and Power in Cleveland, 1836–60" (Ph.D. Dissertation, University of Chicago, 1983), pp. 390–451, 585. Had more church membership lists been available, the number linked to business activity would have been even higher. James Herbert Stuckey, "The Formation of Leadership Groups in a Frontier Town: Canton, Ohio, 1805–1855" (Ph.D. Dissertation, Case Western Reserve University, 1976), p. 266. Several studies contend that revivals were stronger among entrepreneurs: Johnson, *A Shopkeeper's Millennium*, p. 106; Anthony F. C. Wallace, *Rockdale: The Growth of an American Village in the Early Industrial Revolution* (New York: Alfred A. Knopf, 1978); Michael Allen McManis, "Range Ten, Town Four: A Social History of Hudson, Ohio, 1799–1840" (Ph.D. Dissertation, Case Western Reserve University, 1976), pp. 100, 143–44.

22. The classic formulation of the Protestant Ethic is in Max Weber, *The Protestant Ethic and the Spirit of Capitalism* (New York: Charles Scribner's Sons, pb., 1958). Cleveland Bible Society, *Annual Report*, 1856, p. 25. Mark A. Noll, *A History of Christianity in the United States and Canada* (Grand Rapids, MI: Eerdmans, 1992), pp. 174–75 sums up much of the dominant historical view in writing that Charles Grandison Finney, the nation's leading evangelist, "formalized ties between conservative theology and industrial wealth that still characterize evangelical culture." See also, Sellers, *Market Revolution*, pp. 225–36.

23. Cleveland Bible Society, *Annual Report*, 1856, pp. 20–21, 22, 23 (emphasis in original).

24. Trinity Church Home for the Sick and Friendless, *Twenty-Second Annual Report, 1880* (Cleveland: Short and Forman, 1881), extract from 1857 appeal. See also Anne C. Loveland, *Southern Evangelicals and the Social Order, 1800–1860* (Baton Rouge, LA: Louisiana State University Press, 1980), p. 105; Martin E. Marty, *Righteous Empire: The Protestant Experience in America* (New York: Dial, 1970, pb.), p. 110; and Sellers, *Market Revolution*, p. 212.

25. Aiken, *Moral View of Rail Roads*, p. 17. For similar sentiments, see Sellers, *Market Revolution*, p. 233.

26. Handy and others developed what Charles Sellers, *Market Revolution*, p. 211, has referred to as a vision of a "Christian capitalist republic."

27. First United Methodist Church, *Commemorating 125 Years of Methodism in Downtown Cleveland* (Cleveland: First Methodist Church, 1952), p. 8; Aiken, *Moral View of Rail Roads*.

28. William H. Boyd, *Boyd's Cleveland City Directory: 1857* (New York: William H. Boyd, 1857), p. 296.

29. Second Presbyterian Church, Record, 1844–69, Church of the Covenant, Cleveland, June 14, 1844; Trinity Episcopal Church, Minutes of Vestry, October 9, 1852 to February 20, 1855 [July 27, 1854], Trinity Cathedral, Cleveland (see, for example, Nov. 26, 1852). See also St. Paul's Episcopal Church, [Vestry Minutes], 1846 to October 20, 1862, Records, Volume 1, St. Paul's Episcopal Church, Cleveland Heights, Ohio, Oct. 6, 1849, Aug. 30, 1849, Sept. 8, 1849, Mar. 18, 1850; First Presbyterian Church, Trustee Minutes, 1855–1909, First Presbyterian Church, Cleveland, May 7, 1855, May 26, 1855, April 9, 1856.

30. *L*, Mar. 6, 1860, p. 2 in WPA, *Annals*, 1860, p. 498; *L* , Sept. 22, 1856, p. 1 in WPA, *Annals*, 1856, p. 227.

31. The city's Presbyterian ministers were most often called upon, with the Baptist and Episcopal ministers also popular. *PD* Feb. 22, 1855, p. 3; *PD* Mar. 8, 1855, p. 3; *PD* Oct. 31, 1857, p. 3; *L*, Dec. 4, 1855, p. 3 in WPA, *Annals*, 1855, p. 233; *L*, Mar. 13, 1855, p. 3 in WPA, *Annals*, 1855, p. 226; *L*, Jan. 1, 1855, p. 4, adv., in WPA, *Annals*, 1855, p. 126; *PD*, Dec. 9, 1856, p. 3; *PD*, Dec. 14, 1855, p. 3; *L*, Dec. 2, 1856, p. 1 in WPA, *Annals*, 1856, p. 163.

32. Handy benefitted from his early sponsorship in 1861, when a grateful Rockefeller provided money for Handy to buy stock in Rockefeller's new company, Standard Oil. Grace Goulder, *John D. Rockefeller: The*

Cleveland Years (Cleveland: Western Reserve Historical Society, 1972), pp. 14, 29, 30, 40, 47–48; Euclid Avenue Baptist Church, *Historical Sketches: Seventy-Five Years of the Euclid Avenue Baptist Church, Cleveland, Ohio, 1851–1926* (Cleveland: Euclid Avenue Baptist Church, 1927), pp. 53–56; Robert A. Wheeler, "Water to Steam: Industry in the Western Reserve, 1800–1860," *Western Reserve Magazine*, Sept.–Oct. 1978, pp. 27–34. See also Johnson, *Shopkeeper's Millennium*, pp. 119–28.

33. St. John's Episcopal Church, Vestry Books, 1836–63, Western Reserve Historical Society (typewritten), Mar. 14, 1850; St. James Episcopal Church, Parish File, Archives, Episcopal Diocese of Ohio, Trinity Cathedral, Cleveland, Nov. 18, 1857, letter from L. Case; Trinity E., Vestry Minutes, July 26, 1854; Arthur C. Ludlow, *The Old Stone Church: The Story of a Hundred Years, 1820–1920* (Cleveland: Premier Press, 1920), p. 59; Third Baptist Church, Record Book, 1852–67, 1884, 1885, Western Reserve Historical Society, Jan. 18, 1856; Trinity Episcopal Church, Records of the Proceedings of the Vestry of Trinity Church Cleveland Commencing Easter May 1839 [to 1864], Trinity Cathedral, Cleveland, Dec. 13, 1852, p. 132; Euclid Street Presbyterian Church, Records of the Euclid Street Presbyterian Church and Society, 1853 to 1870, Church of the Covenant, Cleveland, Sept. 26, 1856, p. 16.

34. Trinity E., Vestry Records, July 3, 1854; Euclid Avenue Presbyterian Church, Society and Trustees Record, [1851], 1853–1906, Dec. 3, 1852; First P., Trustee Record, 1855–1909, June 18, 1855; *PD*, Feb. 15, 1856, p. 3.

35. Trinity E., Vestry Record, 1836–64, May 28, 1855, June 1, 1854; Trinity E., Vestry Minutes, 1852–55, July 26, 1854 ($1500 from Commercial Branch Bank); Ludlow, *Old Stone Church*, p. 59 reports a loan in 1832 to First Presbyterian from the Commercial Bank of Lake Erie which was finally paid in 1848 when it amounted to $3,600. Third B., Record, 1852–67, Nov. 16, 1859; Trinity E., Vestry Record, 1836–64, Articles of Association.

36. There were a few exceptions to the tendency to identify with the perspective of the employer and the needs of the commercial economy. Samuel Aiken lent his help in the early stages of the concern about the plight of sewing women, but dropped from the picture as the sewing women established a cooperative store to bypass the city's merchants. For a detailed account see Michael J. McTighe, "'True Philanthropy' and the Limits of the Female Sphere: Poor Relief and Labor Organizations in Early Nineteenth-Century Cleveland," *Labor History*, 27 (Spring 1986): 227–56, and Chapter 5. Richard B. Stott, *Workers in the Metropolis: Class, Ethnicity and Youth in Antebellum New York City* (Ithaca, NY: Cornell University Press,

1990), pp. 68–86, 240–42, notes the failure of traditional Protestant churches to reach workers.

37. J. A. Thome, *Address at the Ninth Annual Meeting of the Oberlin Agricultural Society* (Oberlin, OH: J. M. Fitch, 1847), pp. 19, 20.

38. The interconnections between traditional churchgoers and the business leadership of cities has been described by William H. Pease and Jane H. Pease, *The Web of Progress: Private Values and Public Styles in Boston and Charleston, 1828–1843* (New York: Oxford University Press, 1985), pp. 38–39, 52–53, 236–37; Amy Bridges, *A City in the Republic: Ante-bellum New York and the Origins of Machine Politics* (New York: Cambridge University Press, 1984), p. 89; and Johnson, *Islands of Holiness*, pp. 77, 80, 148–55.

39. Moorhead, "Social Reform and the Divided Conscience of Antebellum Protestantism," p. 417.

CHAPTER 5. BENEVOLENCE AND THE ESTABLISHMENT OF AN ETHOS OF OBLIGATION

1. J. A. Thome, *Address at the Ninth Annual Meeting of the Oberlin Agricultural Society* (Oberlin, OH: J. M. Fitch, 1847), p. 28.

2. Cleveland or Rocky River Baptist Association, *Minutes, 1832–1869*, (n. p., 1852–60), 1856, pp. 20–21; Robert T. Handy, *A History of the Churches of the United States and Canada* (New York: Oxford University Press, pb., 1979), p. 173; Rocky River Baptist Association, *Minutes*, 1854, pp. 21–23. For a quick overview of the ideology of benevolence, see, Lois Banner, "Religious Benevolence as Social Control: A Critique of an Interpretation," in John M. Mulder and John F. Wilson, *Religion in American History: Interpretive Essays* (Englewood Cliffs, NJ: Prentice-Hall), pp. 218–35; David Brion Davis, ed., *Ante-Bellum Reform* (New York: Harper and Row, 1967). For recent studies see Priscilla Ferguson Clement, *Welfare and the Poor in the Nineteenth Century: Philadelphia, 1800–1854* (Rutherford, NJ: Fairleigh Dickinson University Press, 1985); Nancy A. Hewitt, *Women's Activism and Social Change: Rochester, New York, 1822–1872* (Ithaca, NY: Cornell University Press, 1984); Lori D. Ginzberg, *Women and the Work of Benevolence: Morality, Politics, and Class in the Nineteenth-Century United States* (New Haven, Conn.: Yale University Press, 1990).

Several recent studies survey and analyze benevolence in the United States: Peter Dobkin Hall, "The History of Religious Philanthropy in America," in Robert Wuthnow and Virginia A. Hodgkinson eds., *Faith and Philanthropy in America: Exploring the Role of Religion in America's Voluntary Sector* (San Francisco: Jossey-Bass, 1990), pp. 38–62; Robert Wuthnow, "Religion and the Voluntary Spirit in the United States: Mapping the Terrain," in Wuthnow and Hodgkinson, *Faith and Philanthropy*, pp. 3–21; Timothy T. Clydesdale, "Soul Winning and Social Work: Giving and Caring in the Evangelical Tradition," in Wuthnow and Hodgkinson, *Faith and Philanthropy*, pp. 187–210; James R. Wood and James G. Houghland, "The Role of Religion in Philanthropy," in Jon Van Til et al., *Critical Issues in American Philanthropy* (San Francisco: Jossey-Bass Publishers, 1990), pp. 99–132; and Teresa Odendahl, *Charity Begins at Home: Generosity and Self-Interest Among the Philanthropic Elite* (New York: Basic Books, 1990).

3. See Appendix for a discussion of the information which forms the basis of this portrait of the interconnected elite. See Tables 9 and 11 for church-joining by members of particular benevolent societies. For a compilation of the specific churches the benevolent society officers joined see Michael J. McTighe, "Embattled Establishment: Protestants and Power in Cleveland, 1836–1860" (Ph.D. Dissertation, University of Chicago, 1983), Tables 22, 23, pp. 362–66. Other organizational affiliations of benevolent society officers are in Tables 25 and 26, pp. 369–78.

4. Cleveland *Daily True Democrat*, July 6, 1850, p. 2 in U.S., Work Projects Administration, Ohio [Works Progress Administration in Ohio], *Annals of Cleveland* (Cleveland: Works Progress Administration, 1936–38), 1850: 466.

5. Female Baptist Sewing Society, Records, 1834–36, Jan. 2, 16, 30, 1834; Feb. 13, 27, 1834, Western Reserve Historical Society, Hughes Papers; First Baptist Church, *History of the First Baptist Church of Cleveland, Ohio, 1883* (Cleveland: J. B. Savage, 1883), 65. The social functions of participation in voluntary organizations are discussed by Mary P. Ryan, *Womanhood in America from Colonial Times to the Present* (New York: New Viewpoints, 1979), pp. 85–92, 105–7; Barbara J. Berg, *The Remembered Gate: Origins of American Feminism: The Woman and the City, 1800–1860* (New York: Oxford University Press, 1980), pp. 142, 145, 221; Keith Melder, "Ladies Bountiful: Organized Women's Benevolence in Early 19th-Century America," *New York History* 48 (July 1967): 234, 242–43; Marlene Stein Wortman, "Domesticating the Nineteenth-Century American City," in *Prospects: An Annual of American Cultural Studies*, ed. Jack Salzman (New York: Burt Franklin and Co., 1977), 3: 545; Anne M. Boylan, "Timid Girls, Venerable Widows and Dignified Matrons: Life Cycle Patterns Among Organized Women in New York and Boston, 1797–1840," *American Quarterly* 38 (Winter 1986): 779–97; William H. Pease and Jane H. Pease, *The Web of Progress: Private Values and Public Styles in Boston and Charleston, 1828–1843* (New York: Oxford University Press, 1985), p. 142; Suzanne Lebsock, *The Free Women of Petersburg: Status and Culture in a Southern Town, 1784–1860* (New York: W.W. Norton, 1984), p. 198. A similar argument of the importance of voluntary

groups as bridges between public and private is David Blackbourn and Geoff Ely, *The Peculiarities of German History: Bourgeois Society and Politics in Nineteenth-Century Germany* (New York: Oxford University Press, 1984), pp. 195–98, 226.

6. Ginzberg, *Women and the Work of Benevolence*, pp. 34–35. See also pp. 7, 11–12, 16–17, and 32–69. For the ability of voluntary organizations to provide women avenues to influence see, for example, Berg, *The Remembered Gate*; Nancy A. Hewitt, *Women's Activism and Social Change: Rochester, New York, 1822–1872* (Ithaca, NY: Cornell University Press, 1984); and Peggy Pasco, *Relations of Rescue: The Search for Female Moral Authority in the American West, 1874–1939* (New York: Oxford University Press, 1990), pp. xv–xvi. For an interesting contrast with southern women, who Estelle Friedman argues were unable to sustain benevolent networks, see Friedman, *The Enclosed Garden: Women and Community in the Evangelical South, 1830–1900* (Chapel Hill, NC: University of North Carolina Press, 1985), pp. xi, xii, xiv, 6–7, 19–20; and Anne C. Loveland, *Southern Evangelicals and the Social Order, 1800–1860* (Baton Rouge, LA: University of Louisiana Press, 1980); and Pease and Pease, *Web of Progress*.

7. Mrs. W. A. Ingham, *Women of Cleveland and Their Work* (Cleveland: W. A. Ingham, 1893), p. 109; Cleveland *Plain Dealer*, June 19, 1857, p. 3; *Williston and Company's Directory of the City of Cleveland* (Cleveland: J.H. Williston and Co., 1859–60), p. 28.

8. *Knight and Parson's Business Directory of the City of Cleveland* (Cleveland: E.G. Knight and Co., and Parsons and Co.), 1853, p. 17; Cleveland *Whig*, July 21, 1847, p. 1 in *Annals* 1847: 63.

9. *Forest City Democrat*, Jan. 26, 1854, p. 3 in *Annals*, 1854: 46; *PD*, Jan. 24, 1857, p. 2.

10. Raymond A. Mohl, *Poverty in New York, 1783–1825* (New York: New York University Press, 1971), pp. 37–38.

11. For histories of poor relief in other cities see Clement, *Welfare and the Poor*; Robert E. Cray, Jr., *Paupers and Poor Relief in New York City and Its Rural Environs, 1700–1830* (Philadelphia: Temple University Press, 1988); Christine Stansell, *City of Women: Sex and Class in New York, 1789–1860* (New York: Alfred A. Knopf, 1986), pp. 30–37; Pease and Pease, *Web of Progress*, pp. 144–49, 152.

12. Cleveland Centennial Commission, *History of the Charities of Cleveland: 1796–1896* (Cleveland: Cleveland Centennial Commission, 1896), p. 15; *PD*, Nov. 9, 1847, p. 3. The "Martha Washington" of the society's name suggested it would be the counterpart of the Washingtonian

temperance societies then being formed in the East; the "Dorcas" was for the biblical woman who aided the sick and was "full of good works and charity." Dorcas, from the Greek, or Tabitha in the Aramaic, was a disciple at Joppa who was brought back to life by Peter (Acts 9:36–43) and who was known for making coats and garments. Thus female charitable and sewing societies took the name "Dorcas." A similar organization, the Charitable Society, is discussed by Hewitt, *Women's Activism*, pp. 48–58. Lebsock, *Free Women*, finds a Dorcas Society of First Baptist Church, Petersburg, Virginia. Hewitt, pp. 22, 40, 216–258, finds three self-consciously competing women's networks in Rochester—bourgeois women activists, free blacks, and working class women. In Cleveland only the bourgeois women, such as those active in the Martha Washington and Dorcas society coalesced, since Cleveland trailed Rochester in economic and social organization. Anne M. Boylan, "Women's Benevolence," *Journal of American History* 71 (December 1984), 510 finds a greater degree of cross-cultural backgrounds in the benevolent societies she studied. The evidence for the Cleveland groups was too scanty to test that finding. Cleveland's benevolent workers did branch out into other related interests, like orphan asylums, but did not move as much toward the political as she suggests, pp. 503–04.

13. *PD*, Nov. 9, 1847, p. 3.

14. *DTD*, Dec. 4, 1850, p. 2 in *Annals*, 1850: 464–65.

15. Catharine Lyon, quoted by Ingham, *Women of Cleveland*, pp. 105–7, 111; *DTD*, Dec. 4, 1850, p. 2 in *Annals*, 1850: 464–65; *PD*, Nov. 17, 1849, p. 3.

16. The quote of the Episcopal minister is from Thomas Starkey, *A Sermon in Behalf of Trinity Church Home, 1860, also The Annual Report of the Managers* (Cleveland: Nevins, *Plain Dealer*, 1860), p. 17, emphasis in original. See also *PD*, Jan. 20, 1855, p. 2; Dec. 16, 1857, p. 3; and Feb. 18, 1859, p. 3; *DTD*, Dec. 24, 1850, p. 2, and Dec. 20, 1850, p. 2 in *Annals*, 1850: 465–66; Dec. 7, 1854, p. 3 in *Annals*, 1854: 466; Rector [James A. Bolles], Trinity Episcopal Church, *Fourth Annual Report and Pastoral Letter* (Cleveland: Fairbanks, Benedict and Co., 1858), p. 9; Cleveland Orphan Asylum, *Ninth Annual Report of the Board of Managers* (Cleveland: Fairbanks, Benedict and Co., 1861), p. 6.

The 1850s as a turning point both for the situation of the poor and of efforts to address and conceptualize the issue are discussed in Ginzberg, *Women and the Work of Benevolence*, pp. 98, 129, 201–02, 297, 209, 215; Pease and Pease, *Web of Progress*, pp. 90, 107, 146; Stansell, *City of Women*, p. 35; Michael B. Katz, *In the Shadow of the Poorhouse: A History of Social Welfare in America* (New York: Basic Books, 1986), pp. 11, 16–19, 65–66. In many instances, as in Cleveland, men took over benevolent functions for-merly reserved for women: Lebsock, *Free Women*, pp. 198, 225–29, 234; Stansell, *City of Women*, p. 35; Ginzberg, *Women and the Work of Benevo-lence*, pp. 124, 125; Anne M. Boylan, "Timid Girls, Venerable Widows and Dignified Matrons," pp. 506–08; Pease and Pease, *Web of Progress*, pp. 152, 144–45, and 150–51 describe differences between Boston and Charleston.

17. *PD*, June 19, 1857, p. 3. In the winter of 1858–59, the Sons of Malta distributed $2,000 in aid: *PD*, Sept. 22, 1859, p. 3; Feb. 3, 1859, p. 3; and Apr. 11, 1859, p. 3; Centennial Commission, *History of the Charities*, p. 78; *Directory*, 1959–60, p. 28.

18. Euclid Street Presbyterian Church, Records, 1853–70, Church of the Covenant, Cleveland, Jan. 3, 1859; Jan. 14, 1859; Euclid Presbyterian, Missionary Record, 1859, Church of the Covenant, Cleveland.

19. Pease and Pease, *Web of Progress*, pp. 150–52.

20. *DTD*, Dec. 28, 1850, p. 2 in *Annals*, 1850: 466; *PD*, Dec. 20, 1851, p. 2; Dec. 16, 1851, p. 2; and Dec. 31, 1852, p. 3.

21. *PD*, Dec. 31, 1852, p. 3, emphasis in original. Luce, "Report," Euclid Presbyterian, Missionary Record. The City Mission model of system-atic visitation and assessment of need likewise failed as a plan for poor relief because its effort and resources did not match the need for aid.

22. Cleveland, Ohio, Common (City) Council, "Act of Incorpora-tion," Mar. 1836, Sec. 13 in *Charters of the Village of Cleveland, and the City of Cleveland, with Their Several Amendments: To Which Are Added the Laws and Ordinances of the City of Cleveland* (Cleveland: Sanford and Co., 1842), p. 33; Centennial Commission, *History of the Charities*, p. 9; Clara Anne Kaiser, "Organized Social Work in Cleveland, Its History and Setting" (Ph.D. Diss., Ohio State University, 1936), pp. 90, 91, 403; Samuel P. Orth, *A History of Cleveland, Ohio*, vol. 1 (Chicago and Cleveland: S. J. Clarke Pub-lishing Co., 1910), p. 403; Cleveland *Herald and Gazette*, June 4, 1838, p. 2 in *Annals*, 1838: 356; Apr. 27, 1838, p. 2 in *Annals*, 1838: 49; May 9, 1838, p. 2 in *Annals*, 1838: 53; July 26, 1838, p. 2 in *Annals*, 1838: 59; Mar. 31, 1841, p. 3 in *Annals*, 1841: 255. Cleveland, Ohio, City Council, *Charters of the Village of Cleveland, and the City of Cleveland, with Their Several Amend-ments: To Which Are Added the Laws and Ordinances of the City of Cleveland* (Cleveland: Harris, Fairbanks and Co., 1851), 47; *PD*, Mar. 22, 1849, p. 2. The ordinance which set up the City Infirmary repeated the concern of the decade that poor relief be given only to the deserving and established rules "for the purpose of meeting promptly the wants of meritorious cases, and preventing fraudulent exactions." Directors were to inquire personally

about the circumstances of those who applied for aid. Outdoor relief (aid given outside the confines of the building) was a special concern, since it required an unforeseeable outlay of funds, rather than a manageable, firm commitment to the infirmary building and staff. The ordinance set the limit on outdoor relief at five hundred dollars. Cleveland, Ohio, City Council, *The Acts to Provide for the Organization of Cities and Villages, and the Revised Ordinances of the City of Cleveland* (Cleveland: *Plain Dealer*, 1862), Jan. 19, 1856, pp. 159, 160. A committee appointed by the city council in 1855 recommended changes to correct lack of coordination and loose management; *PD*, Mar. 9, 1855, p. 2.

For an excellent history of the poor house see Katz, *In the Shadow of the Poorhouse*. His claim that "public funds have always relieved more people than private ones" is difficult to determine for Cleveland. Public provisions are difficult to measure, given the random allotments and episodic interest in outdoor and institutional relief by the Common Council.

23. June 12, 1856, p. 3 in *Annals*, 1856: 27–28; *DTD*, Jan. 18, 1850, p. 2 in *Annals*, 1850: 29. For other expressions of concern about abandoned and ill-disciplined children see *Annals* listings under "Juvenile Delinquency," including *Annals*, 1855: 24–25; Sept. 29, 1847, p. 1 in *Annals*, 1847: 99; and Jan. 16, 1855, p. 3 in *Annals*, 1855: 24.

24. For the early history of the institutions see Marian J,. Morton, "Homes for Poverty's Children: Cleveland's Orphanages, 1851–1933," *Ohio History* 98 (Winter–Spring 1989), pp. 5–22. James Leiby, *A History of Social Welfare and Social Work in the United States* (New York: Columbia University Press, 1978), uses the phrase "urban Huckleberry Finns." The Ragged School established by the First Methodist Church is not to be confused with the public elementary school often called the "ragged school." For other children's institutions also see Pease and Peas, *Web of Progress*, pp. 147–49; Lebsock, *Free Women*, pp. 201, 212, 217; and Clement, *Welfare and the Poor*, pp. 118–40. The popularity of institutions and asylums is discussed in David J. Rothman, *The Discovery of the Asylum: Social Order and Disorder in the New Republic* (Boston: Little, Brown, 1971), and Ginzberg, *Women and the Work of Benevolence*, pp. 119–124.

25. For the Catholic orphan asylums, see George F. Houck, *A History of Catholicity in Northern Ohio and in the Diocese of Cleveland from 1749 to December 31, 1900* (Cleveland: J. B. Savage, 1903), 1: 60, 82, 740–44; Michael J. Hynes, *History of the Diocese of Cleveland: Origin and Growth (1847–1952)* (Cleveland: Diocese of Cleveland, 1953), pp. 90–92; and John O'Grady, *Catholic Charities in the United States* (1931; rpt. New York: Arno Press, 1971), pp. 86, 388. The founding of the Cleveland Orphan Asylum is described by Ingham, *Women of Cleveland*, p. 106, and Centennial Com-

mission, *History of the Charities*, p. 35. The institution changed its name to the Cleveland Protestant Orphan Asylum in 1875. For the House of Correction, see Cleveland *Leader*, Mar. 1, 1855, p. 3 in *Annals*, 1855: 216, and Robert M. Mennel, "'The Family System of Common Farmers': The Early Years of Ohio's Reform Farm, 1858–1884," *Ohio History* 89 (Summer 1980): 281. The two Catholic orphan asylums were established directly by the diocese and its bishop, Amadeus Rappe, and they resembled mutual aid organizations in caring for only their own. Cleveland Orphan Asylum, *Report of the Board of Managers* (Cleveland: Fairbanks, Benedict and Co., 1950), p. 9; and *Eighth Annual Report of the Board of Managers* (Cleveland: Fairbanks, Benedict and Co., 1860), p. 7; *PD*, Mar. 13, 1855, p. 2; *L*, Nov. 25, 1857, p. 3 in *Annals*, 1857: 388; Cleveland Orphan Asylum, *Ninth Annual Report*, p. 6.

The pattern of public contributions to private, religious societies is also noted by Ginzberg, *Women and the Work of Benevolence*, pp. 73–75, 122–24.

26. Cleveland Industrial School, *Annual Report of the Superintendent, 1858* (Cleveland: Fairbanks, Benedict and Co., 1859), p. 6, gives the account of the Ragged School's children.

27. Centennial Commission, *History of the Charities*, pp. 26–27; *PD*, Dec. 27, 1856, p. 3; *L*, Dec. 17, 1856, p. 3; Dec. 18, 1856, p. 3; Dec. 24, 1856, p. 3; Dec. 25, 1856, p. 1 in *Annals*, 1856: 532–33.

28. First Methodist Church, *First Methodist Episcopal Church of Cleveland, Ohio, 1827–1884* (Cleveland: J. B. Savage, 1884), pp. 26–27; Orth, *History of Cleveland*, p. 403; Centennial Commission, *History of the Charities*, p. 26; *Annals*, 1857: 387–88; Cleveland Industrial School and Children's Aid Society, *Annual Report of the Superintendent, 1859* (Cleveland: Fairbanks, Benedict and Co., 1860), p. 27; *PD*, May 31, 1858, p. 3; *L*, Oct. 31, 1860, p. 1; Apr. 4, 1860, p. 3; Sept. 14, 1860, p. 1; Oct. 12, 1860, p. 1; in *Annals*, 1860: 527–28. Foote's remark is in *L*, Jan. 21, 1858, p. 3 in *Annals*, 1858: 595. Foote was a founder and long-term commissioner of Ohio's Reform Farm. He served in both houses of the state legislature and on Cleveland's city council.

Mimi Abramovitz, *Regulating the Lives of Women: Social Welfare Policy from Colonial Times to the Present* (Boston: South End Press, 1988), pp. 107–79 comments on the effects of the institutions on children and others.

29. The difficulty of establishing the wealth of the city's benevolent community precludes a firm linking of wealth and involvement in benevolent activity. The few benevolent society officers located in the 1850 census had substantially more property than the average Clevelander over the age

of eighteen, but not enough were located to support anything but a suggestion that wealth and benevolence went hand in hand. Of the six benevolent society officers included in the 1850 census sample, four owned real property. The mean property holding of the four was $3,925.00. Of the 707 men over eighteen in the sample, 115 held property, with a mean property holding of $2,724.00. Two women who were benevolent society officers were found in the census. Neither had any real property, but the head of household of one of them had $33,000.00 in real property. Of the 659 women over eighteen in the sample, 4 owned real property, with a mean of $4,250.00. In addition, 321 of the 659 had heads of household with property, and the mean for them was $1,765.20. See McTighe, "Embattled Establishment," pp. 367–78, 578–79.

30. *PD*, Sept. 22, 1852, p. 3. For examples of contributions by businesses: Cleveland Industrial School, *Annual Report, 1858*, pp. 12–13; Cleveland Orphan Asylum, *Ninth Annual Report, 1861*, p. 8; *Fifth Annual Report* (Harris, Fairbanks and Co., 1857), p. 10; Ingham, *Women of Cleveland*, pp. 107, 109–10; and *PD*, Dec. 10, 1858, p. 3.

31. Ingham, *Women of Cleveland*, pp. 16–19; Harriet Taylor Upton, *History of the Western Reserve* (Chicago: Lewis Publishing Co., 1910), 1: 519; Gertrude Van Rensselaer Wickham, *The Pioneer Families of Cleveland, 1796–1840* (Cleveland: Evangelical Publishing House, 1914), 1: 368; James Harrison Kennedy, *A History of the City of Cleveland, Its Settlement, Rise and Progress, 1796–1896* (Cleveland: The Imperial Press, 1896), p. 236. The church and organizational affiliations of Rebecca Rouse and Benjamin Rouse are drawn from the information described in the Appendix. Bertram Wyatt-Brown, *Lewis Tappan and the Evangelical War Against Slavery* (Cleveland: Case Western Reserve University Press, 1969) describes the work of Lewis and Arthur Tappan.

32. This biography is based on the sources cited in the preceding note, on Upton, *History of the Western Reserve*, 1: 117; on the material cited in connection with the Martha Washington and Dorcas Society and the Protestant Orphan Asylum (notes 9–13, 26–27); and on Female Baptist Sewing Society, Records, Jan. 2, 1834.

33. Benjamin Rouse, A Record, Western Reserve Historical Society, Adella Prentiss Hughes Papers; Benjamin Rouse, Manuscript Record of the Life of Benjamin Rouse, 1801–1837, 1839, 1862 and of the First Baptist Church, 1862, WRHS, Hughes Papers, pp. 6, 7, 21; Benjamin Rouse, Account Book of Benjamin Rouse, 1836–1863, WRHS, Hughes Papers; First Baptist, *History, 1883*, pp. 52–55; Arthur C. Ludlow, *The Old Stone Church: The Story of a Hundred Years, 1820–1920* (Cleveland: Pioneer Press, 1920), p. 62.

34. Grace Goulder, *John D. Rockefeller, The Cleveland Years* (Cleveland: Western Reserve Historical Society, 1972), p. 14; O. J. Hodge, *Reminiscences* (Cleveland: Imperial Press, 1902), 1: 120. Based on sources in Appendix and *H*, Oct. 5, 1844, p. 2 in *Annals*, 1844: 619; Hodge, *Reminiscences*, 1: 122.

35. M. J. Heale, "From City Fathers to Social Critics: Humanitarianism and Government in New York, 1790–1860," *Journal of American History* 61 (June 1976), p. 33; Pease and Pease, *Web of Progress*, p. 146.

36. Starkey, *Sermon*, p. 12; Ingham, *Women of Cleveland*, pp. 77–81, 83; Upton, *History of the Western Reserve*, p. 518. For the Western Seamen's Friend Society, see *The Boatmen's Magazine* 1 (Oct. 1834): 7; Centennial Commission, *History of the Charities*, p. 16; "1st Annual Report," in *Spirit of the Lakes, and Boatman's Magazine* 1 (Sept. 27, 1848): 3–10; "Third Annual Report," in *Spirit of the Lakes* 2 (Oct. 14, 1850): 173–81; Euclid Presbyterian, Missionary Record, Nov. 30, 1859; and Luce, "Report," Euclid P., Missionary Record.

37. *PD*, Jan. 20, 1855, p. 2.

38. *PD*, Nov. 25, 1848, p. 3; Jan. 16, 1852, p. 3. See also *PD*, Dec. 20, 1854, p. 3. Catholic opposition to the Ragged School is discussed by Lucius Mellen in Early Settlers' Association of Cuyahoga County, *Annals of the Early Settlers' Association of Cuyahoga County, Ohio* (Cleveland: Mount and Carroll, 1880–1931) 5, no. 4 (1906): 293.

39. *PD*, Feb. 2, 1853, p. 3. See also *L*, Nov. 28, 1857, p. 2 in *Annals*, 1857: 39–40; and Dec. 16, 1857, p. 2 in *Annals*, 1857: 41.

40. William H. Boyd, *Boyd's Cleveland City Directory: 1857* (New York: William H. Boyd, 1857), p. 303; Early Settlers' Association, *Annals*, 5, no. 4 (1906): 293.

41. Ludlow, *The Old Stone Church*, pp. 121–22.

42. *L*, Nov. 11, 1856, p. 3 in *Annals*, 1856, p. 31; *L*, Nov. 8, 1856, p. 3 in *Annals*, 1856: 532; Ludlow, *The Old Stone Church*, pp. 121–22.

43. *PD*, Nov. 17, 1849, p. 3; *PD*, Nov. 17, 1849, p. 3; Nov. 25, 1848, p. 3; Dec. 18, 1852, p. 3. For similar attention to individuals in straitened circumstances aided by the MWDS, see *PD*, Nov. 17, 1849, p. 3; *PD*, Nov. 25, 1848, p. 3.

44. Cleveland Industrial School, *Annual Report of the Superintendent, 1859*, p. 14; *PD*, June 19, 1857, p. 3.

45. Bernard Wishy, *The Child and the Republic: The Dawn of Modern American Child Nurture* (Philadelphia: University of Pennsylvania Press,

1968), p. 32; Cleveland Industrial School, *Report, 1858*, p. 7; Cleveland Industrial School, *Annual Report of the Superintendent, 1859*, pp. 8–10; Early Settlers' Association, *Annals*, 5, no. 3 (1906): 293; Cleveland Centennial Commission, *History of the Charities*, p. 26; First Methodist Church, *Commemorating 125 Years of Methodism in Downtown Cleveland* (Cleveland: First Methodist Church, 1952), p. 7; First Methodist Church, *First Methodist Episcopal Church, 1827–1884*, p. 25; *PD*, June 19, 1857, p. 3; *PD*, Jan, 17, 1859, p. 3; *L*, Jan. 20, 1859, p. 1 in *Annals*, 1859: 491; *L*, Feb. 10, 1857, p. 1 in *Annals*, 1857: 1; *FCD*, Jan. 13, 1854, p. 3 in *Annals*, 1854: 464–65; *PD*, June 19, 1857, p. 3. Ragged and industrial schools were common in antebellum America: Joseph Lee Lukonic, "Evangelicals in the City: Evangelical Protestant Social Concerns in Early Chicago, 1837–1860" (Ph.D. Dissertation, University of Wisconsin, 1979), pp. 179–81; Berg, *The Remembered Gate*, p. 232; Philip M. Hosay, *The Challenge of Urban Poverty: Charity Reformers in New York City, 1835–1890* (New York: Arno Press, 1980), p. 57; Joseph M. Hawes, *Children in Urban Society: Juvenile Delinquency in Nineteenth Century America* (New York: Oxford University Press, 1971), pp. 65–67, 75.

46. James H. Moorhead, "Social Reform and the Divided Conscience of Antebellum Protestantism," *Church History* 48 (December 1979): 780; Paul E. Johnson, *A Shopkeeper's Millennium: Society and Revivals in Rochester, New York, 1815–1837* (New York: Hill and Wang, 1978), pp. 6, 8, 136–41; Anthony F. C. Wallace, *Rockdale: The Growth of an American Village in the Early Industrial Revolution* (New York: Alfred A. Knopf, 1978); Alan Dawley, *Class and Community: The Industrial Revolution in Lynn* (Cambridge, MA: Harvard University Press, 1976), pp. 113–22.

47. For a fuller account of the FPU see Michael J. McTighe, "'True Philanthropy' and the Limits of the Female Sphere: Poor Relief and Labor Organizations in Ante-Bellum Cleveland," *Labor History* 27 (Spring 1986), pp. 227–56; *PD*, Jan. 25, 1851, p. 3; *PD*, Jan. 29, 1851, p. 3; *DTD*, Sept. 4, 1850, p. 2 in *Annals*, 1850: 113. Similar concern or efforts to organize sewing women are described by Berg, *The Remembered Gate*, pp. 167–71; Elizabeth Leitch Bonkowsky, "The Church and the City: The Protestant Concern for Social Problems, 1800–1840" (Ph.D. Dissertation, Boston University, 1973), pp. 169–70; Mary Blewett, *Men, Women, and Work: Class, Gender, and Protest in the New England Shoe Industry, 1700–1910* (Urbana: University of Illinois Press, 1988), pp. 39–43, 79; Ginzberg, *Women and the Work of Benevolence*, pp. 60–61, 214; Stansell, *City of Women*, pp. 133–37, 147; Hewitt, *Women's Activism*, p. 42, and Clement, *Welfare and the Poor*, p. 32.

48. *PD*, Jan. 17, 1851, p. 2; *DTD*, Jan. 17, 1851, p. 2 in *Annals*, 1851: 436.

49. *PD*, Oct. 30, 1851, p. 3; *PD*, Oct. 30, 1851, p. 3. Antebellum America spawned other cooperative stores. The Church of the Messiah in Boston in the mid-1830s set up a project to cut out and prepare garments for poor women to sew: Bonkowsky, "The Church and the City," p. 166. It opened a salesroom, where garments were sold at a small profit. In Rochester, New York, a "Journeymen Tailors' Emporium" was established, but soon collapsed: James Logan McElroy, "Social Reform in the Burned-Over District: Rochester, New York, As a Test Case" (Ph.D. Dissertation, State University of New York at Binghamton, 1974), pp. 31–32. Thomas Dublin, *Women at Work: The Transformation of Work and Community in Lowell, Massachusetts, 1826–60* (New York: Columbia University Press, 1979), pp. 121–22, finds an active cooperative movement in Lowell.

50. *DTD*, Jan. 25, 1851, p. 3 in WPA, *Annals*, 1851: 114.

51. This is based on a comparison of the church joining and organizational affiliations of the officers and members of the Female Protective Union described in McTighe, "'True Philanthropy,'" pp. 231–35.

52. *PD*, Oct. 30, 1851, p. 3. The *Daily True Democrat*, the paper digested in the *Annals* in the early 1850s, covered the Union's activities in its disputes with Morse in 1851 but did not mention it in 1852 and 1853. There are no mentions of the Female Protective Union in the *Annals* for 1854–60, which are digested from the *Leader*. The *Plain Dealer*, another Democratic paper which followed the Union's activities in 1851, did not mention it from 1852–60, a conclusion based on a reading of every issue.

53. Protestant Orphan Asylum, *Report of the Board of Managers, 1857*, p. 6; *PD*, Mar. 14, 1854, p. 3; *PD*, Dec. 10, 1852, p. 2.

54. *PD*, Dec. 10, 1852, p. 2.

55. [Bolles], *Fourth Annual Report*; Episcopal Church Home for Women, *The Church Home, 1856–1956* (Cleveland: Episcopal Church Home for Women, 1956); Cleveland Centennial Commission, *History of the Charities*, p. 50; Trinity Church Home for the Sick and Friendless, *Twenty-Second Annual Report, 1880* (Cleveland: Short and Forman, 1881), p. 29. The contributions of Beecher and Bushnell are described by Clifford E. Clark, Jr., *Henry Ward Beecher: Spokesman for a Middle-Class America* (Urbana: University of Illinois Press, 1978); Wishy, *The Child and the Republic*, pp. 22–23, 43–44; Ann Douglas, *The Feminization of American Culture* (New York: Avon, 1977); Barbara M. Cross, *Horace Bushnell: Minister to a Changing America* (Chicago: University of Chicago Press, 1958); William G. McLoughlin, *The Meaning of Henry Ward Beecher: An Essay on the Shifting Values of Mid-Victorian America, 1840–1870* (New York: Alfred A. Knopf,

1970); and Kathryn Kish Sklar, *Catharine Beecher: A Study in American Domesticity* (New York: W. W. Norton and Co., 1973).

56. Ever since Lois Banner's "Religious Benevolence as Social Control: A Critique of an Interpretation," it has been clear that multi-faceted explanations for benevolence must be developed. Although the term hegemony has sometimes been invoked as a description of the exercise of broad social authority, I find it inappropriate here. As used by Antonio Gramsci in his *Prison Notebooks*, and by historians such as T. J. Jackson Lears, "The Concept of Cultural Hegemony: Problems and Possibilities," *American Historical Review* 90 (June 1985): 567–93, the term hegemony refers to the "spontaneous" consent given by the mass of the population to the direction imposed on social life by a dominant group. By stressing the complex interaction of the intentions of the dominant group and the consent of others, references to hegemony avoid the assumption of the social control metaphor that intentions, actions, and effects can be rigidly linked. Yet the term hegemony, as useful as it may be, must be modified in light of an understanding of the means by which a Protestant elite such as Cleveland's actually exercised its authority. Consent to the direction-setting of the Protestants was by no means spontaneous. As this chapter indicates, Protestants purposefully used their authority to encourage preferred conduct and values and discourage conduct and values inconsistent with a commercial economy. Using the term hegemony almost inevitably moves the discussion in the direction of describing a calculated imposition of a vision by one social group on another. Even if the imposition is described as unconscious or unintended, relying on the term hegemony introduces a degree of rigidity in describing the relation of intentions and consequences that seems excessively reductionist and inflexible. It does not leave enough room for the millennial optimism and confidence of antebellum Protestants for whom interest was not defined solely in terms of economic interest, or for the conflicting tendencies of the Protestant ideology. In order not to weigh this study down with a lengthy theoretical discussion of hegemony, I have chosen to use terms such as influence and authority, and introduce precision by describing the type of influence Protestants achieved and the process by which the influence was established and maintained.

57. Hewitt, *Women's Activism*, p. 231; Lebsock, *Free Women*, p. 197; Ginzberg, *Women and the Work of Benevolence*, pp. 25, 27–35; Boylan, "Timid Girls, Venerable Widows and Dignified Matrons," pp. 778–91.

58. Ginzberg, *Women and the Work of Benevolence*, p. 216; Stansell, *City of Women*, p. 31; Lebsock, *Free Women*, p. 220.

59. The importance of indirect, informal, and "quiet" influence is

suggested by David Blackbourn and Geoff Eley, *The Peculiarities of German History*, pp. 195–98, 224.

CHAPTER 6. TEMPERANCE:
THE COLD WATER ARMY TASTES DEFEAT

1. Nancy Hewitt, *Women's Activism and Social Change: Rochester, New York, 1822–1872* (Ithaca, NY: Cornell University Press, 1984), p. 160 notes that the only social problem which garnered significant attention over a long period of time from all three of the activist groups she studied was intemperance. The divisions between benevolent, perfectionist, and radical women, which Hewitt finds in Rochester (p. 40), do not seem to characterize Cleveland, a newer city with a less diverse and differentiated group of voluntary society activists.

2. Christine Stansell, *City of Women: Sex and Class in New York, 1789–1860* (New York: Alfred A. Knopf, 1986), p. 67. Hewitt, *Women's Activism and Social Change*, pp. 24–37, describes the connections between reform movements and visions of material and moral progress.

3. James Harrison Kennedy, *A History of the City of Cleveland, Its Settlement, Rise and Progress, 1796–1896* (Cleveland: The Imperial Press, 1896), p. 153; Charles Whittlesey, *Early History of Cleveland, Ohio* (Cleveland: Fairbanks, Benedict and Co., 1867), pp. 373–74; Samuel P. Orth, *A History of Cleveland, Ohio* (Chicago and Cleveland: S. J. Clarke Publishing Co., 1910), 1: 99–100.

4. Early Settlers' Association of Cuyahoga County, *Annals* (Cleveland: Mount and Carroll, 1880–1931), 3, no. 1 (1892): 75.

5. Thirty-nine of the 88 male officers of temperance organizations (44.3 percent), and 4 of the 15 female officers were traced to lists of those who joined English-speaking Protestant churches from 1816 to 1860. (Tables 2.3 and 2.5) If membership lists had been available for all churches, it is likely that the percentage traced to Protestant church membership would have been more than 75 percent, particularly since 2/3 of the temperance leaders served as church officers. (See Appendix.) Temperance groups drew a surprisingly high percentage of their officers from a few churches. First Presbyterian, Second Presbyterian, and First Baptist Churches accounted for almost two-thirds of the 39 male temperance officials who joined churches in the years from 1816–1860. First Presbyterian Church alone contributed 21. Michael J. McTighe, "Embattled Establishment: Protestants and Power in Cleveland, 1836–1860" (Ph.D. Dissertation, University of Chicago, 1983), pp. 247–50; James Logan McElroy, "Social Reform in the Burned-Over District: Rochester, New York As a Test

Case" (Ph.D. Dissertation, State University of New York at Binghamton, 1974), p. 187, found that of 83 moral reformers, 54.2 percent joined evangelical churches and 10.9 percent joined non-evangelical churches.

6. This is based on reports of 70 meetings and addresses in U.S., Work Projects Administration, Ohio [Works Progress Administration in Ohio], *Annals of Cleveland* (Cleveland: Works Progress Administration, 1936–1938), and the *Plain Dealer* from 1841 through 1850. First Baptist Church held 13, First Presbyterian Church 12, and First Methodist Church 8. None were held at an Episcopal Church despite the strong endorsement of total abstinence by Bishop Charles McIlvaine. C. P. McIlvaine, *Address to the Young Men of the United States on Temperance* (n.p., n.d.), pp. 7–14. In the 1850s, the churches' role diminished. Temperance meetings were more likely to be held in Public Square, in public halls, or in the halls owned by organizations like the Sons of Temperance, than in the churches. Only five of the 21 temperance meetings of the 1850s were held in the city's Protestant churches.

7. The characterization of Protestant activity as an evangelical united front is from Charles I. Foster, *An Errand of Mercy: The Evangelical United Front, 1790–1837* (Chapel Hill, NC: University of North Carolina Press, 1960). Cleveland *Leader*, Sept. 3, 1858, p. 3 in WPA, *Annals*, 1858, p. 550. Some ministers were especially prominent. In the early years, Samuel Aiken of the First Presbyterian Church took the lead. His church hosted the most meetings. He personally addressed meetings where temperance societies were founded, and he lectured for the Cuyahoga County Temperance Society and the Cleveland City Temperance Society. Aiken also participated in a temperance meeting at First Baptist Church which was part of a simultaneous, worldwide temperance convention. Cleveland *Whig*, Mar. 16, 1836, p. 1 in WPA, *Annals*, 1836, p. 284; Cleveland *Herald*, Feb. 24, 1841, p. 3 in WPA, *Annals*, 1841, p. 285; Cleveland *Daily True Democrat*, May 1, 1850, p. 2 in WPA, *Annals*, 1850, p. 448; *H*, Apr. 7, 1843, p. 3 in WPA, *Annals*, 1843, p. 336; *H*, Apr. 16, 1842, p. 3 in WPA, *Annals*, 1842, p. 181.

Ministers other than Aiken dominated the temperance cause in the 1850s. For example, J. Hyatt Smith of Second Baptist Church specialized in lecturing to the young. *DTD*, Dec. 8, 1852, p. 3 in WPA, *Annals*, 1852, p. 39; *PD*, Dec. 2, 1852, p. 3. For other Smith lectures: *DTD*, Oct. 1, 1853, p. 3 in WPA, *Annals*, 1853, p. 516; *DTD*, Dec. 8, 1852, p. 3 in WPA, *Annals*, 1852, p. 39. A.H. Nevin of Plymouth Congregational Church addressed the Cuyahoga County Total Abstinence Society, the Sons of Temperance, and large county meetings. *DTD*, Jan. 3, 1855, p. 2 in WPA, *Annals*, 1852, p. 465; *DTD*, May 1, 1850, p. 2 in WPA, *Annals*, 1850, p. 448; *DTD*, June 15, 1852, p. 2 in WPA, *Annals*, 1852, p. 460; *DTD*, June 8, 1850, p. 2 in WPA, *Annals*, 1850, p. 449; *DTD*, Feb. 11, 1853, p. 3 in WPA, *Annals*, 1853, p.

507. J. C. White, also of Plymouth Congregational Church, offered a series of lectures on temperance in 1859 at Plymouth Church. *L*, Feb. 26, 1859, p. 3 in WPA, *Annals*, 1859, p. 465. For the Ladies' Temperance Union see Mrs. W. A. Ingham, *Women of Cleveland and Their Work* (Cleveland: W. A. Ingham, 1893), p. 112.

8. John A. Foote, a pillar of the Cuyahoga County and Cleveland City Total Abstinence Societies, acknowledged their work in 1843, and the *Plain Dealer* praised Father Mathew's untheatrical manner and his work when he visited in 1851. Cleveland *Plain Dealer Weekly*, Mar. 15, 1843 p. 3. See also *PD*, Aug. 11, 1851, p. 2.

9. The Washingtonian temperance movement began in 1840 in Baltimore and had a reputation for dealing directly with the intemperate, whom more traditional, clergy-led societies avoided. Ian R. Tyrrell, *Sobering Up: From Temperance to Prohibition in Antebellum America, 1800–1860* (Westport, CT: Greenwood Press, 1979), pp. 159–71, 191–94; Ronald G. Walters, *American Reformers, 1815–1860* (New York: Hill and Wang, 1978), pp. 130–34, 140; Don Harrison Doyle, *The Social Order of a Frontier Community: Jacksonville, Illinois, 1825–1870* (Urbana, IL: University of Illinois Press, 1978), pp. 213–14; Anne C. Loveland, *Southern Evangelicals and the Social Order, 1800–1860* (Baton Rouge, LA: Louisiana State University Press, 1980), p. 149; Jed Dannenbaum, "Drink and Disorder: Temperance Reform in Cincinnati, 1841–1874" (Ph.D. Dissertation, University of California, Davis, 1978), pp. 30–37; McElroy, "Social Reform in the Burned-Over District," pp. 130–33; *H*, Feb. 24, 1843, p. 3 in WPA, *Annals*, 1843, p. 334; Barbara Leslie Epstein, *The Politics of Domesticity: Women, Evangelicalism, and Temperance in Nineteenth-Century America* (Middletown, CT: Wesleyan University Press, 1981), pp. 92–93; Stuart Blumin, *The Emergence of the Middle Class: Social Experience in the American City, 1760–1900* (New York: Cambridge University Press, 1989), pp. 188, 202–04; Ruth M. Alexander,"'We Are Engaged as a Band of Sisters': The Meaning of Domesticity in the Washingtonian Temperance Movement, 1840–1850," *Journal of American History* 75 (December 1988): 764–85; Amy Bridges, *A City in the Republic: Ante-bellum New York and the Origins of Machine Politics* (New York: Cambridge University Press, 1984), p. 88; William H. Pease and Jane H. Pease, *The Web of Progress: Private Values and Public Styles in Boston and Charleston, 1828–1843* (New York: Oxford University Press, 1985), p. 161; Mary H. Blewitt, *Men, Women, and Work: Class, Gender, and Protest in the New England Shoe Industry, 1780–1910* Urbana, IL: University of Illinois Press, 1988), pp. 78–80; John S. Gilkeson, Jr., *Middle-Class Providence, 1820–1940* (Princeton, NJ: Princeton University Press, 1986), pp. 23–35.

10. *PD Weekly*, Mar. 15, 1843, p. 3, John A. Foote letter. Meetings of

Washingtonians in First Presbyterian Church: *H*, Mar. 13, 1843, p. 2 in WPA, *Annals*, 1843, p. 335; *H*, July 6, 1842, p. 3 in WPA, *Annals*, 1842, p. 421; in First Baptist Church: *H*, May 8, 1843, p. 2 in WPA, *Annals*, 1843, p. 337; *H*, Mar. 20, 1844, p. 3 in WPA, *Annals*, 1844, p. 791; *H*, Oct. 23, 1845, p. 2 in WPA, *Annals*, 1845, p. 365; in First Methodist Church: *H*, Feb. 20, 1843, p. 2 in WPA, *Annals*, 1843, p. 334; *H*, Mar. 27, 1843, p. 2 in WPA, *Annals*, 1843, p. 336; in First Presbyterian Church, Ohio City: *H*, Jan. 26, 1842, p. 2 in WPA, *Annals*, 1842, p. 410. For disputes between Washingtonians and temperance regulars in other cities, see Tyrrell, *Sobering Up*, pp. 191–94; *PD Weekly*, Mar. 15, 1843, p. 3.

11. Paul E. Johnson, *A Shopkeeper's Millennium: Society and Revivals in Rochester, New York, 1815–1837* (New York: Hill and Wang, 1978), pp. 79–83; Jed Dannenbaum, "Immigrants and Temperance: Ethnocultural Conflict in Cincinnati, 1845–1960," *Ohio History* 87 (Spring, 1978), p. 20; Walters, *American Reformers*, pp. 140–41. Another Washingtonian officer (1842), Buckley Steadman, had also been a director of the Cleveland City Temperance Society (1836–38, 1847). Steadman was also a director of the Western Seamen's Friend Society (1850, 1853, 1857), a member of the City Council (1850, 1852, 1853) as a Whig, and the Whig candidate for mayor in 1853. Steadman's church involvement kept pace. He was an elder of First Presbyterian Church (1841) and First Presbyterian Church, Ohio City (1834), and a trustee of Plymouth Congregational Church (1853, 1855).

12. These figures come from McTighe, "Embattled Establishment," Tables 19–21, 26, pp. 251–58, 378. The temperance society officers ran most often as Whigs. (Table 20.) Twelve temperance officers (13.6 percent) were nominated by the Whigs for major offices, and seven (8.0 percent) for minor ones. (Table 20.) Temperance officials can also be found in the Republican Party (six, or 6.8 percent nominated for minor positions), and to a lesser extent in the Liberty, Citizens', and Union parties. (Table 20.) Surprisingly, given the opposition of the Democrats to temperance, two temperance officials were nominees of the Democrats. (Table 20.) Tyrrell, *Sobering Up*, p. 109, finds that no Democrats supported the temperance (no-license) position, and that Whigs were split on the licensing questions. Temperance officials not only ran for office, they won. Close to a third (27, or 30.7 percent) served as government officials in the years from 1836 to 1860. (Table 19.) Fifteen of the temperance officials (17.0 percent) held major Cleveland offices, and 9 held minor ones. (Table 20.)

After politics and government, the next most likely spot to find a temperance official was in business (24, or 27.3 percent). (Table 19.) Nineteen (21.6 percent) could be found in lists of bank officers and almost as many, 11 (12.5 percent), were officers of incorporated companies and non-Cleveland railroads. (Table 20.) There was also a great deal of overlap between benevolent society and temperance society officers. Twenty-one (23.9 percent) of the temperance officers were also officers of one or more benevolent groups. (Table 19.) Fifteen (17.0 percent) of the temperance officials were in the Western Seamen's Friend Society, an indication of the temperance orientation of that organization. Smaller numbers were active in the Mona's Relief Society and the Cleveland Orphan Asylum. (Table 20.)

Administrators of public education were also involved in sizeable numbers in temperance activity. Of the 88 male temperance officers, 14 (15.9 percent) were administrators in education. (Table 19.) Cultural groups (13, or 14.8 percent) and fire companies (8, or 9.1 percent) also claimed the attention of significant numbers of male temperance officials. (Table 20.)

The female officers of temperance societies, like the women of benevolent societies (Table 26), were active within a limited sphere. One-fifth (3 of the 15) can be located on lists of benevolent society officers. The Martha Washington and Dorcas Society and the Protestant Orphan Asylum each drew two temperance officers. (Table 21.) For a complete listing of the organizations and organization types temperance society officers joined, see McTighe, "Embattled Establishment," Tables 19–21, pp. 251–58.

13. Foote's name is spelled Foot in many Cleveland records and histories. Early Settlers' Association, *Annals*, 2, no. 12 (1891): 569–70; First Presbyterian Church, *Annals of the First Presbyterian Church, 1820–1895* (Cleveland: Winn and Judson, 1895), p. 208; Robert M. Mennel, "'The Family System of Common Farmers': The Origins of Ohio's Reform Farm, 1840–1858," *Ohio History* 89 (Spring, 1980): 134–35, 149, 154; Samuel P. Orth, *History of Cleveland*, 1910), 1: 109, 239; *L*, Jan. 21, 1858, p. 3 in WPA, *Annals*, 1858, p. 595; *L*, Jan. 19, 1859, p. 2 in WPA, *Annals*, 1859, p. 490; *L*, Jan. 17, 1860, p. 3 in WPA, *Annals*, 1860, p. 527; Henry Howe, *Historical Collections of Ohio* (Columbus, OH: Henry Howe & Son, 1889), 1: 524. For more about the Industrial School, see Chapter 5. The description of Foote's organizational and religious activities is also based on the sources cited in the Appendix. Foote's first wife, Frances A. (Hitchcock) Foote, had essentially the same religious affiliations. His second wife, Mary S. (Cutter) Foote, was a member of First Presbyterian Church in 1860. Neither spouse appeared in the lists of organizational activity.

14. Kennedy, *History of the City of Cleveland*, p. 217; Roderic Hall Pierce, *Trinity Cathedral Parish: The First 150 Years* (Cleveland: Vestry of Trinity Cathedral, 1967), p. 18; Arthur C. Ludlow, *The Old Stone Church: The Story of a Hundred Years, 1820–1920* (Cleveland: Premier Press, 1920), pp. 66–67, mentions Andrews' two pews. Andrews' organizational affiliations are based on the sources described in the Appendix.

15. Foster, *An Errand of Mercy*, and Clifford S. Griffin, *Their Brother's Keepers: Moral Stewardship in the United States, 1800–1850* (New Brunswick, NJ: Rutgers University Press, 1960) stress the declining status of temperance reformers. Michael H. Frisch, *Town Into City: Springfield, Massachusetts and the Meaning of Community* (Cambridge, MA: Harvard University Press, 1972), pp. 36–38; Susan E. Hirsch, *Roots of the American Working Class: The Industrialization of Crafts in Newark, 1800–1860* (Philadelphia: University of Pennsylvania Press, 1978), p. 104; Tyrrell, *Sobering Up*, pp. 7, 273; and James Herbert Stuckey, "The Formation of Leadership Groups in a Frontier Town: Canton, Ohio, 1805–1855" (Ph.D. Dissertation, Case Western Reserve University, 1976), p. 257, describe temperance reformers as a current elite.

16. Donald G. Mathews, *Religion in the Old South* (Chicago: University of Chicago Press, 1977), p. 44.

17. First Congregational Church, Record Book "A," December, 1834 to July, 1852, Congregational Library, Boston, Nov. 13, 1840, p. 89; First Baptist Church, Minutes, March 31, 1837 to Dec. 18, 1848, First Baptist Church, Shaker Heights, Ohio, Jan. 26, 1846; Jan. 29, 1846; Apr. 30, 1846. The member, E. T. Nichols, was investigated because of "the various reports in circulation respecting his want of integrity in his business transactions."

18. Sherman Canfield, *The Temporal Blessings of Christianity* (Cleveland: Smead and Cowles, 1850), p. 7; *H*, Jan. 12, 1832, p. 3, adv., in *Annals*, 1832, p. 43.

19. *L*, Aug. 16, 1859, p. 3 in WPA, *Annals*, 1859, pp. 46, 180–81; *L*, Aug. 11, 1859, p. 2 in WPA, *Annals*, 1859, p. 181; *PD*, Aug. 10, 1859, p. 3.

20. *L*, Aug. 16, 1859, p. 3 in WPA, *Annals*, 1859, p. 46; *L*, Aug. 16, 1859, p. 3 in WPA, *Annals*, 1859, p. 52; *PD*, Aug. 15, 1859, p. 3.

21. *L*, Aug. 16, 1859, p. 3 in WPA, *Annals*, 1859, p. 46. See also *L*, Aug. 12, 1859, p. 3 in WPA, *Annals*, 1859, p. 54.

22. *PD*, Mar. 15, 1843, p. 3; *H*, April 9, 1844, p. 2 in WPA, 1844, p. 792; *H*, May 17, 1843, p. 3 in WPA, *Annals*, 1843, p. 337. See Pease and Pease, *Web of Progress*, p. 158, for similar arguments. Richard B. Stott, *Workers in the Metropolis, Class, Ethnicity and Youth in Antebellum New York City* (Ithaca, NY: Cornell University Press, 1990), pp. 143–44, 217–22, and 239–40, describes the role of saloons and drinking in workers' lives.

23. *PD*, May 8, 1847, p. 3. The Washingtonian Society had presented similar arguments in petitions to the state legislature in 1843: *H*, Nov. 29, 1843, p. 2 in WPA, *Annals*, 1843, p. 341; *PD Weekly*, Dec. 6, 1843, p. 2; Loveland, *Southern Evangelicals and the Social Order*, p. 135; *H*, Apr. 17, 1846, p. 2 in WPA, *Annals*, 1846, p. 333. See also David J. Rothman, *The*

Discovery of the Asylum: Social Order and Disorder in the New Republic (Boston: Little Brown and Co., 1970), pp. 66–67, 163, 177; *H*, Oct. 22, 1845, p. 2 in WPA, *Annals*, 1845, p. 364; Robert S. Pickett, *House of Refuge: Origins of Juvenile Reform in New York State, 1815–1857* (Syracuse, NY: Syracuse University Press, 1969), pp. 103–05; John K. Alexander, *Render Them Submissive: Responses to Poverty in Philadelphia, 1760–1800* (Amherst: University of Massachusetts Press, 1980), pp. 52, 166.

24. See *L*, May 31, 1856, p. 1 in WPA, *Annals*, 1856, p. 31 for an example which identified Catholics with intemperance, murder and illegitimate births. Rappe is quoted by Henry B. Leonard, "Ethnic Conflict and Episcopal Power: The Diocese of Cleveland, 1847–1870," *Catholic Historical Review* 62 (July 1976): 398.

25. John G. Fraser, "A Century of Congregationalism in Cleveland," *Ohio Church History Society Papers* (Oberlin, OH: Ohio Church History Society, 1897), 8: 13. Citations are to the original volumes of the papers. The *Papers* were later collected in two volumes, published by the Society in 1899. See also First Presbyterian Church, Records, 1820–37, First Presbyterian Church, Cleveland, Sept. 29, 1834; June 27, 1835; First Baptist Church, Records, 1833–37, in Benjamin Rouse, Manuscript Record of the Life of Benjamin Rouse, 1801–37, 1839, 1862, and of the First Baptist Church, 1862, Western Reserve Historical Society, Adella Prestiss Hughes Family Papers, Jan. 5, 1835, May 31, 1837; Third Baptist Church, Church Record Book, 1852–67, Western Reserve Historical Society, Cleveland, Feb. 23, 1854; First Methodist Episcopal Church, Official Board 1856–1864, First United Methodist Church, Cleveland, Sept. 16, 1858. For examples of the process, see First Presbyterian Church, Church Record, 1837–1849, First Presbyterian Church, Cleveland, Oct. 6, 1846; and entries for Oct. 26, 1843; Apr. 25, 1844; and Aug. 24, 1843; First B., Minutes, 1837–48, Mar. 4, 1842; Second Presbyterian Church, Record, 1844–69, Church of the Covenant, Cleveland, Dec. 31, 1852. For examples of repeated infractions, see First C., Record Book "A", Apr. 28, 1837; Dec. 8, 1837; June 30, 1838; Oct. 7, 1838; and First B., Minutes, 1837–48, Feb. 28, 1838; Apr. 3, 1838; and First B., Minutes, 1837–48, Oct. 19, 1837; Nov. 23, 1837; Feb, 28, 1838; Dec. 19, 1838; Nov. 3, 1839. Only after repeated infractions were members excommunicated. First Baptist Church suspended a future church officer, Abbee Perlee, for trafficking in liquor in 1837. First B., Records, 1833–1837, May 31, 1837, Apr. 19, 1836 [sic: 1837].

26. *PD*, Sept. 24, 1845, p. 3; *PD*, Sept. 9, 1845, p. 2; *PD*, Sept. 24, 1845, p. 3. For efforts to enforce licensing, see *H*, Apr. 14, 1843, p. 2 in WPA, *Annals*, 1843, p. 336; *H*, Sept. 13, 1845, p. 3 in WPA, *Annals*, 1845, p. 361; *H*, Oct. 18, 1845, p. 3 in WPA, *Annals*, 1845, p. 361.

27. *H*, June 14, 1843, p. 2 in WPA, *Annals*, 1843, p. 388; *PD Weekly*, Apr. 10, 1844, p. 3; Apr. 17, 1844, p. 3; *H*, Mar. 19, 1844, p. 2 in WPA, *Annals*, 1844, p. 792; *H*, Nov. 14, 1844, p. 3 in WPA, *Annals*, 1844, p. 797; *DTD*, Dec. 9, 1848, p. 2 in WPA, *Annals*, 1848, p. 33; *H*, June 25, 1844, p. 3 in WPA, *Annals*, 1844, p. 794; *PD*, Aug. 2, 1845, p. 3; *PD*, Oct. 6, 1845, p. 3; *H*, Oct. 14, 1846, p. 2 in WPA, *Annals*, 1846, p. 336. For a fuller discussion of Protestants reaction to theaters and entertainments, including the criticisms of the theater by Rev. Samuel Aiken of First Presbyterian Church, see McTighe, "Embattled Establishment," pp. 161–74.

28. *PD*, Sept. 17, 1845, p. 2; *H*, Aug. 23, 1845, p. 3 in WPA, *Annals*, 1845, p. 358; *PD*, Sept. 18, 1845, p. 2; Sept. 17, 1845, p. 3; Aug. 25, 1845, p. 2; *H*, Sept. 13, 1845, pp. 2–3 in WPA, *Annals*, 1845, p. 361. For information on street dramas and their functions, see Susan G. Davis, *Parades and Power: Street Theatre in Nineteenth-Century Philadelphia* (Philadelphia: Temple University Press, 1986), pp. 5, 11–12, 103–09, 163.

29. *H*, June 15, 1841, p. 3 in WPA, *Annals*, 1841, pp. 118–19; *H*, July 4, 1843, p. 3 in WPA, *Annals*, 1843, p. 128. Maybe only male members marched: *H*, July 2, 1841, p. 2 in WPA, *Annals*, 1841, p. 289; *H*, July 6, 1841, p. 2 in WPA, *Annals*, 1841, p. 120. Catholics in the early 1840s bonded temperance principles to another holiday, St. Patrick's Day. The members and band of the Father Mathew Temperance Society marched in St. Patrick's Day parades and then held a dinner on temperance principles. The *Herald* approved: "A dinner was served—song, sentiment, and good feeling abounded—with no stimulant save the notable occasion and the glow of feeling which ever bubbles fresh from the Irish man's warm heart." *H*, Mar. 22, 1841, p. 2 in WPA, *Annals*, 1841, p. 286. For the social functions of parades, see Davis, *Parades and Power*.

30. Foster, *An Errand of Mercy*; Griffin, *Their Brother's Keepers*; Joseph R. Gusfield, *Symbolic Crusade: Status Politics and the American Temperance Movement* (Urbana, IL: University of Illinois Press, 1966); McElroy, "Social Reform in the Burned-Over District," pp. 111–33; Dannenbaum, "Immigrants and Temperance," p. 61; and Doyle, *The Social Order of a Frontier Community*, pp. 194–95, 212–23. Walters, *American Reformers*, p. 194, locates the turn to coercive reform in the 1830s.

31. Tyrrell, *Sobering Up*, p. 227; Walters, *American Reformers*, p. 135, contends that political action went against the evangelical belief that goodness could flow only from a converted heart.

32. *H*, Sept. 10, 1844, p. 2 in WPA *Annals*, 1844, p. 796; Cleveland Presbytery, Minutes, 1830–83, Presbytery of the Western Reserve, Cleveland (photocopy), Sept. 3, 1844. For the licensing question in other cities

see Tyrrell, *Sobering Up*, pp. 225–51; Dannenbaum, "Immigrants and Temperance," pp. 82, 85; Loveland, *Southern Evangelicals*, pp. 151–55.

33. Cleveland, Ohio, *Charters of the Village of Cleveland and the City of Cleveland, With Their Several Amendments: To Which Are Added the Laws and Ordinances of the City of Cleveland* (Cleveland: Sanford & Co., 1842), pp. 25–26, Act of Incorporation, March 1836, Section 6; see also *PD*, Sept. 24, 1850, p. 3, letter by S. E. Adams; Cleveland *Herald and Gazette*, July 25, 1837, p. 2 in WPA, *Annals*, 1837, p. 401; Aug. 5, 1837, p. 2 in WPA, *Annals*, 1837, p. 402; July 20, 1837, p. 2 in WPA, *Annals*, 1837, p. 57; July 28, 1837, p. 2 in WPA, *Annals*, 1837, p. 58; Aug. 2, 1837, p. 2 in WPA *Annals*, 1837, pp. 161–62; Aug. 4, 1837, p. 2 in WPA, *Annals*, 1837, p. 59.

34. *H&G*, Apr. 9, 1839, p. 2 in WPA, *Annals*, 1839, p. 103.

35. *PD*, Sept. 24, 1850, p. 3, letter by S. E. Adams; Cleveland, Ohio, *Charters of the Village*, 1842, pp. 25–26, Act of Incorporation, March 1836, Section 6; Cleveland, Ohio, *Charters of the Village*, pp. 44–45, amendment passed by General Assembly, Mar. 18, 1839; Cleveland, Ohio, *Charters of the Village*, pp. 48–49, ordinance passed May 9, 1840; Kennedy, *A History of the City of Cleveland*, pp. 274–75.

36. Julius P. Bolivar MacCabe, *Directory: Cleveland and Ohio City, For the Years 1837–38* (Cleveland: Sanford and Lott, 1837), pp. 105, 106. For a list of the city's temperance organizations, see McTighe, "Embattled Establishment," pp. 571–72.

37. *H*, Nov. 2, 1841, p. 3 in WPA, *Annals*, 1841, p. 296; Oct. 19, 1841, p. 3 in WPA, *Annals*, 1841, p. 295. The Cleveland City Temperance Society reported 1088 members in 1842, including 392 added during the previous year. The Cuyahoga County Temperance Society claimed in 1842 that 2000 of the city's 6000 residents had signed temperance pledges. Washingtonian societies were also flourishing. The Washingtonian Total Abstinence Society led the way with 1388 members. The Young People's Washingtonian Total Abstinence Society, which began in March of 1844 with ten members, had 450 by July. Washingtonians chalked up remarkable successes in 1842. They signed 120 to pledges in eight days in Cleveland, while in Ohio City, at a meeting in First Presbyterian Church at the same time, 47 signed. *H*, Jan. 19, 1842, p. 2 in WPA, *Annals*, 1842, p. 410; Sept. 10, 1842, p. 2 in WPA, *Annals*, 1842, p. 425; July 6, 1844, p. 3 in WPA, *Annals*, 1844, pp. 794–95; July 6, 1844, p. 3 in WPA, *Annals*, 1844, p. 795; *H*, Jan. 26, 1842, p. 2 in WPA, *Annals*, 1842, p. 410. For the Washingtonians in other cities, see Tyrrell, *Sobering Up*, pp. 159–90; Walters, *American Reformers*, pp. 130–31; Dannenbaum, "Immigrants and Temperance," pp. 30–37; McElroy, "Social Reform in the Burned-Over District," pp. 130–33;

and Loveland, *Southern Evangelicals*, p. 149. The Catholic temperance effort kept pace in these years. Father Peter McLaughlin, the priest of the city's lone Catholic church, St. Mary's, promoted temperance in 1841 and 1842. He took pledges from parishioners and, in one case, from a captain and his crew. McLaughlin claimed 415 members for the Father Mathew Temperance Society in 1842. Catholic efforts are described in *H*, June 1, 1841, p. 3 in WPA, *Annals*, 1841, p. 288; Mar. 15, 1841, p. 3 in WPA, *Annals*, 1841, p. 286; Apr. 12, 1842, p. 2 in WPA, *Annals*, 1842, p. 416. Cleveland's Father Mathew Society was one of many formed by Catholics throughout the North. They were named after Father Theobald Mathew, an Irish Capuchin priest active in temperance in Ireland in the 1840s. Walters, *American Reformers*, p. 133; Tyrrell, *Sobering Up*, pp. 299–305; Sister Joan Bland, *Hibernian Crusade: The Story of the Catholic Total Abstinence Union of America* (Washington, DC: Catholic University of America Press, 1951), pp. 21–42.

38. In announcing a meeting to organize the Society in 1841, the *Herald* referred to it as the Cuyahoga County Total Abstinence Society, but it was founded as the Cuyahoga County Temperance Society, *H*, Oct. 19, 1841, p. 3 in WPA, *Annals*, 1841, p. 295. When it went on record as in favor of the prohibition of intoxicating liquor as a beverage in 1843, the *Herald* referred to it as a total abstinence society, *H*, Sept. 13, 1843, p. 2 in WPA, *Annals*, 1843, p. 340. See Tyrrell, *Sobering Up*, pp. 10, 225, and *passim*, for a similar shift nationwide; Loveland, *Southern Evangelicals*, pp. 133–34, dates the shift to the mid-1830s. Tyrrell, *Sobering Up*, pp. 135–45, gives three reasons for the shift: it was an answer to the charge that temperance proscribed the drink of the poor, liquor, but not the drink of the rich, wine; abstinence was more effective in dealing with drunkards than temperance; and abstinence was more effective in bringing new converts.

39. *PD*, Sept. 18, 1845, p. 2; Sept. 17, 1845, p. 3; Aug. 25, 1845, p. 2; *H*, Sept. 13, 1845, pp. 2–3 in WPA, *Annals*, 1845, p. 361. While in Cleveland, Dean and McDowell lent their efforts to more conventional temperance activities, too. They addressed a meeting of the Young Men's Washingtonian Total Abstinence Society at First Methodist Church.

40. *H*, Apr. 30, 1841, p. 3 in WPA, *Annals*, 1841, p. 288; *PD Weekly*, Mar. 15, 1843, p. 3. Getting hotels to accede to temperance principles was an important victory of the early and mid-1840s. Hotel proprietors were a prime target for temperance agitation, and a welcome addition to the ranks. The first temperance hotel, the Eagle Temperance House, had opened about 1830. Conversions of proprietors and their hotels to temperance principles multiplied in the years from 1840 to 1846. By the mid-1840s, temperate Clevelanders and travelers could patronize one of the eleven hotels conducted in accordance with temperance principles. In

1842, after the Phoenix Hotel, the Scots House, the Commercial House and the Mansion House adopted temperance and repudiated the selling of ardent spirits, the *Plain Dealer* reported that only three "rum-selling" establishments remained. U.S., Works Projects Administration, [Works Progress Administration in Ohio], Ohio Historical Records Survey Project, *Historic Sites of Cleveland: Hotels and Taverns* (Columbus: Ohio Historical Records Survey Project, 1942), pp. 156–232; *H*, Dec. 17, 1841, p. 2 in WPA, *Annals*, 1841, p. 298; *H*, July 8, 1841, p. 2 in WPA, *Annals*, 1841, p. 290; *H*, July 14, 1842, p. 4 in WPA, *Annals*, 1842, p. 162; *H*, Sept. 2, 1845, p. 3 in WPA, *Annals*, 1845, p. 137; *H*, Jan. 24, 1846, p. 2 in WPA, *Annals*, 1846, p. 118; *PD*, July 20, 1846, p. 3; *H*, July 21, 1846, p. 3 in WPA, *Annals*, 1846, p. 334; *PD Weekly*, Mar. 26, 1842, p. 2.

41. *H*, July 28, 1841, p. 2 in WPA, *Annals*, 1841, p. 293; *H*, Mar. 19, 1841, p. 2 in WPA, *Annals*, 1841, p. 286; *H*, Oct. 22, 1845, p. 2 in WPA, *Annals*, 1845, p. 364.

42. Cleveland *Whig and Herald*, Apr. 7, 1847, p. 2 in WPA, *Annals*, 1847, p. 255; *PD*, May 8, 1847, p. 3.

43. In the 1847 voting, the second ward and the township, whose votes were reported together, voted against granting licenses by a wide margin (368–171). The first ward voted against licenses by a small margin (338–280), and the third ward voted decisively for licenses (301–195). In the 1849 vote, all three wards voted in favor of granting licenses by decisive margins (first, 215–22; second, 105–20; third, 178–22). *WH*, Apr. 7, 1847, p. 2 in WPA, *Annals*, 1847, p. 255; *DTD*, Feb. 17, 1849, p. 2 in WPA, *Annals*, 1849, p. 353. Two noticeable features of the 1849 vote might help account for the reversal of the previous vote. First, since the rest of the township did not participate, the opponents of licensing lost a stronghold. Second, turnout was significantly lower—562 compared to 1653 in 1847. The 1847 voting was held in April with other elections, while the 1849 voting was held separately, and in February. The increased percentage in the vote in favor of granting licenses might have been the result of liquor interests taking advantage of the February voting date to mobilize their strength. Other explanations for the vote suggest themselves, too: displeasure with the effects of the no-license law, the realization of how difficult it was to enforce the law, or the possible decline of the temperance movement. Whatever the explanation, the renewed granting of liquor licenses was a step backward for the temperance cause.

44. Elijah Peet, *Peet's General Business Directory of the Cities of Cleveland and Ohio for the Years 1845–6* (Cleveland: Sanford and Hayward, 1845), pp. 116–17. See also *DTD*, Dec. 19, 1848, p. 2 in WPA, *Annals*, 1848, p. 263;

PD, Sept. 9, 1845, p. 2; *Directory*, 1845–46, p. 120; Wm. Stephenson, comp., *Smead and Cowles General Business Directory of the City of Cleveland for 1848–49* (Cleveland: Smead and Cowles, 1848), pp. 30–31; *WH*, Dec. 22, 1847, p. 1 in WPA, *Annals*, 1847, p. 256; Western Seamen's Friend Society, "First Annual Report," *Spirit of the Lakes, and Boatman's Magazine*, 1 (Sept., 1848): 26; *WH*, Dec. 29, 1847, p. 2 in WPA, *Annals*, 1847, p. 44; *DTD*, Apr. 8, 1848, p. 2 in WPA, *Annals*, 1848, p. 235. Catholic temperance efforts maintained their momentum in the last half of the 1840s. Just after being appointed Bishop in 1847 Amadeus Rappe reported that he had convinced 500 to enroll in the temperance cause. *PD*, Sept. 9, 1845, p. 2; also *DTD*, Dec. 19, 1848, p. 2 in WPA, *Annals*, 1848, p. 263; *DTD*, Feb. 28, 1850, p. 2 in WPA, *Annals*, 1850, p. 447; *WH*, Oct. 20, 1847, p. 4 in WPA, *Annals*, 1847, p. 99.

45. For the Maine Law and its effects, see Walters, *American Reformers*, pp. 136–39; Tyrrell, *Sobering Up*, pp. 263–65; *DTD*, Jan. 3, 1852, p. 2 in WPA, *Annals*, 1852, p. 465; *DTD*, Aug. 23, 1853, p. 3 in WPA, *Annals*, 1853, p. 514; *PD*, May 3, 1853, p. 3; *DTD*, May 3, 1853, p. 3 in WPA, *Annals*, 1853, p. 509; *DTD*, July 29, 1853, p. 3 in WPA, *Annals*, 1853, p. 511; *DTD*, July 29, 1853, p. 3 in WPA, *Annals*, 1853, p. 512; the Wesleyan Methodist Church's support for the Maine Law is described in *DTD*, July 29, 1853, p. 3 in WPA, *Annals*, 1853, p. 511.

46. The state did pass a bill designed to discourage social drinking associated with taverns. The bill made it unlawful to sell any liquor to be drunk on the premises. Further, no sales were to be made to persons who were intoxicated or in the habit of getting intoxicated. Fines were set at $20–100, and/or 10–50 days in jail. Wine, as long as it was made in Ohio, ale, beer, and cider were allowed. One new feature of the law was that it punished the seller for the sufferings caused by drinkers, a long-time desire of temperance advocates. Anyone injured by someone who was intoxicated, including married women hurt by their husbands, could sue the seller. The Cuyahoga County Temperance Alliance stressed that this fell short of being a Maine Law, but that it "meets our approbation as far as it goes." *PD*, May 1, 1854, p. 2; *PD*, July 1, 1854, p. 3. The third ward of Cleveland was one of only three jurisdictions in Cuyahoga County to vote yes. *PD*, May 3, 1851, p. 2; *PD*, June 18, 1851, p. 2; *PD*, June 21, 1851, p. 2. Anthony Gene Carey, "The Second Party System Collapses: The 1853 Maine Law Campaign in Ohio," *Ohio History* 100 (Summer–Autumn 1991): 129–153, describes the campaign and its broader implications.

47. *DTD*, July 1, 1852, p. 3 in WPA, *Annals*, 1852, p. 467; North Ohio Conference, Methodist Episcopal Church, *Minutes, 1839–1860* (N. p.: North Ohio Annual Conference, Methodist Episcopal Church, 1839–60),

1851, pp. 26–27; 1855, p. 54; *DTD*, Sept. 29, 1853, p. 2 in WPA, *Annals*, 1853, p. 516.

48. *DTD*, June 3, 1853, p. 3 in WPA, *Annals*, 1853, p. 383; *DTD*, June 3, 1853, p. 3 in WPA, *Annals*, 1853, p. 439; *DTD*, Aug. 11, 1853, p. 3 in WPA, *Annals*, 1853, p. 439; *PD*, Aug. 25, 1853, p. 3; B. White, ed., *The Acts to Provide for the Organization of Cities and Villages, and the Revised Ordinances of the City of Cleveland* (Cleveland: Harris, Fairbanks, and Co.), 1855, p. 26, May 3, 1852.

49. Carson Leagues were formed to raise funds and provide informers and evidence in prosecutions under state Maine Laws. The first of the Leagues was founded by Thomas L. Carson of Syracuse, New York. Tyrrell, *Sobering Up*, pp. 293–95, 310; McElroy, "Social Reform in the Burned-Over District," pp. 122–25, and note 26. *L*, July 4, 1854, p. 2 in WPA, *Annals*, 1854, p. 411; *PD*, Dec. 23, 1854, p. 3; *L*, Nov. 7, 1854, p. 2 in WPA, *Annals*, 1854, p. 1; *PD*, July 19, 1855, p. 3; *L*, Aug. 22, 1854, p. 3 in WPA, *Annals*, 1854, p. 349.

50. For the Cleveland Ladies' Temperance Union: *DTD*, July 8, 1850, p. 2 in WPA, *Annals*, 1850, p. 450; *Directory*, 1850, pp. 49–50; Ingham, *Women of Cleveland*, p. 112; *Directory*, 1853, p. 66. The Roman Catholic temperance group, the Father Mathew Society, was even larger than the Cleveland Ladies' Temperance Union. When Father Mathew visited Cleveland in 1851 as part of an American trip sponsored by the American Temperance Union, "upwards of two thousand renounced for life, intoxicating drinks." For Father Mathew Societies in Cleveland and elsewhere, see *PD*, Aug. 4, 1851, p. 2; Michael J. Hynes, *History of the Diocese of Cleveland: Origin and Growth (1847–1952)* (Cleveland: Diocese of Cleveland, 1953), p. 104; George F. Houck, *A History of Catholicity in Northern Ohio and In the Diocese of Cleveland from 1749 to December 31, 1900* (Cleveland: J.B. Savage, 1903), 1: 82; and Bland, *Hibernian Crusade*, pp. 21–42.

51. Dannenbaum, "Immigrants and Temperance," p. 162, remarks that prohibition dominated Ohio life in 1853, yet four years later it was practically forgotten. *PD*, Sept. 19, 1860, p. 3; *L*, Sept. 19, 1860, p. 1 in WPA, *Annals*, 1860, p. 410. Stott, *Workers in the Metropolis*, pp. 239–40, describes the difficulties of enforcing Sunday closing laws.

52. The Sons of Temperance began in New York in 1842; Walters, *American Reformers*, p. 133; Dannenbaum, "Immigrants and Temperance," describes their work in Cincinnati, pp. 37, 41; Tyrrell, *Sobering Up*, pp. 203–06, 211–15; Loveland, *Southern Evangelicals*, pp. 149–51; William H. Boyd, *Boyd's Cleveland City Directory*, (New York: William H. Boyd, 1857), p. 304; [*J. H.*] *Williston and Co.'s Directory of the City of Cleveland* (Cleveland:

J.H. Williston and Co., 1859–60), pp. 26–27; *PD*, July 2, 1857, p. 3; *PD*, July 6, 1857, p. 3; see also *PD*, July 6, 1858, p. 3; *PD*, July 3, 1860, p. 3. Temperance July 4th celebrations were popular in the antebellum years: Tyrrell, *Sobering Up*, p. 178; Judith M. Wellman, "The Burned-Over District Revisited: Benevolent Reform and Abolitionism in Mexico, Paris, and Ithaca, New York, 1825–1842" (Ph.D. Dissertation, University of Virginia, 1874), pp. 264–65; Dannenbaum, "Immigrants and Temperance," p. 130. In 1860 the Father Mathew Temperance Society, with Bishop Rappe as its president, claimed 1115 members. The Father Mathew Society began marching and holding its own July 4th celebrations in the late 1850s.

53. *PD*, July 20, 1857, p. 2; *PD*, July 27, 1857, p. 3.

54. *PD*, Aug. 23, 1845, p. 3; Aug. 25, 1845, p. 2; Sept. 17, 1845, p. 2 and Sept. 18, 1845, p. 2; *H*, Sept. 4, 1845, p. 3 in WPA, *Annals*, 1845, p. 36.

55. *PD*, Feb. 6, 1847, p. 3; *Directory*, 1845–6, p. 111; *DTD*, July 27, 1850, p. 3 in WPA, *Annals*, 1850, p. 53.

56. *PD*, Feb. 17, 1855, p. 3; *PD*, Feb. 16, 1855, p. 3; *PD*, Mar. 24, 1847, p. 3; *DTD*, June 7, 1853, p. 3 in WPA, *Annals*, 1853, p. 439.

57. *L*, Nov. 7, 1854, p. 3 in WPA, *Annals*, 1854, p. 1; WPA, *Annals*, 1856, pp. 411–14; *DTD*, June 11, 1853, p. 3 in WPA, *Annals*, 1853, p. 439; *PD*, June 9, 1854, p. 3. The arrests may have had the desired effect, even without convictions and substantial penalties, since reports in the *Leader* three months later found the public houses and liquor dealers obeying the law. *L*, Jan. 29, 1855, p. 3 in WPA, *Annals*, 1855, p. 11; *L*, Feb. 3, 1855, p. 3 in WPA, *Annals*, 1855, p. 510. The anti-Carson League is described in *PD*, Nov. 7, 1854, p. 3; and Nov. 8, 1854, p. 3.

58. Early Settlers' Association, *Annals* 2, no. 8 (1887): 113.

59. Dannenbaum, "Immigrants and Temperance," pp. 82, 85, describes problems of enforcement in Cincinnati; Hirsch, *Roots of the American Working Class*, p. 104, concludes that many if not most of those in Newark ignored the preachments of the Protestant ministers and their adherents, but lawmakers still responded to their influence.

60. *PD*, Oct. 14, 1853, p. 2; *PD*, Sept. 19, 1860, p. 2.

61. *W&H*, Mar. 31, 1847, p. 3 in WPA, *Annals*, 1847, pp. 8–9; *PD*, Feb. 21, 1857, p. 2.

62. Johnson, *Shopkeeper's Millennium*, finds a similar development. He concludes that the sober and moral part of the community no longer determined what happened in Rochester in the 1830s.

63. Jean E. Friedman, *The Enclosed Garden: Women and Community in the Evangelical South, 1830–1900* (Chapel Hill, NC: University of North Carolina Press, 1985), p. 19 finds that in the South temperance societies were male-only organizations. Sara M. Evans, *Born for Liberty: A History of Women in America* (New York: Free Press, 1989), p. 75; and Keith Melder, *Beginnings of Sisterhood: The American Woman's Rights Movement, 1800–1850* (New York: Schocken Books, 1977), pp. 53, 54 suggest that temperance activity represented an effort to control male behavior. The development of notions of sisterhood and the move to movements for women's rights are described by Melder, pp. 31, 157; Hewitt, *Women's Activism and Social Change*, p. 164; and Evans, *Born For Liberty*, p. 103. There is little evidence of women's rights activity in Cleveland in the years before 1860. Hewitt's characterization of women at the juncture of the public and private spheres is on p. 22.

64. Epstein, *The Politics of Domesticity*, p. 3 argues that the evangelical and temperance movements of these years shaped what might be loosely called the middle class, and established individual morality, self-control, piety, sobriety and domesticity as means of upward mobility.

CHAPTER 7. COWARDLY CASTLES

1. Ethnocultural approaches are used perceptively by Paul Kleppner, *The Cross of Culture: A Social Analysis of Midwestern Politics, 1850–1900* (New York, Free Press, 1970); and Ronald P. Formisano, *The Birth of Mass Political Parties: Michigan, 1827–1861* (Princeton, NJ: Princeton University Press, 1971). Kenneth J. Winkle, *The Politics of Community: Migration and Politics in antebellum Ohio* (New York: Cambridge University Press, 1988), offers another angle of vision by stressing the role of migration as the context for Ohio's political life. As "persisters," Cleveland's Protestants would expect to have their influence magnified, pp. 9–10, 109–10, 121, 131, 147.

2. This characterization is drawn from A. James Reichley, *Religion and Public Life* (Washington, DC: Brookings Institution, 1983), pp. 112–13.

3. Constitution, preamble, Euclid Street Presbyterian Church, Records of the Euclid Street Presbyterian Church and Society, 1853–70, Church of the Covenant, Cleveland, pp. 3–4; Sherman Canfield, *The Temporal Blessings of Christianity* (Cleveland: Smead and Cowles, 1852), p. 32. For other examples: Constitution of the Episcopalian Church, Nov. 16, 1816, Trinity Episcopal Church, Trinity Parish Register, [Records], Vol. 1, January 1, 1854 to December 16, 1876, Trinity Cathedral, Cleveland; Arthur C. Ludlow, *The Old Stone Church: The Story of a Hundred Years, 1820–1920* (Cleveland: Premier Press, 1920), pp. 44–45. See also Anne C.

Loveland, *Southern Evangelicals and the Social Order, 1800–1860* (Baton Rouge, LA: Louisiana State University Press, 1980), p. 109.

4. Sherman Canfield, *The Indications of a Divine Purpose to Make Our Country a Model Christian Republic* (Syracuse, NY: T. S. Truair, Daily Journal Office, 1855), pp. 14, 18–19.

5. J.P. Bishop, *Memoir of Rev. Seymour W. Adams, D.D.* (Cleveland: Fairbanks, Benedict and Co., 1866), pp. 25–26; Cleveland *Plain Dealer*, March 27, 1854, p. 2.

6. Sandra Sizer, *Gospel Hymns and Social Religion: The Rhetoric of Nineteenth-Century Revivalism* (Philadelphia: Temple University Press, 1978), pp. 145–46; Joseph Lee Lukonic, "Evangelicals in the City: Evangelical Protestant Social Concerns in Early Chicago, 1837–1860" (Ph.D. Dissertation, University of Wisconsin, 1979), p. 179.

7. First Baptist Society, Minutes, March 31, 1837 to December 18, 1848, First Baptist Church, Shaker Heights, Aug. 3, 1846.

8. J. Hyatt Smith of Second Baptist Church was elected to Congress from Brooklyn, New York after leaving Cleveland. O. J. Hodge, *Reminiscences* (Cleveland: Imperial Press, 1902), 1: 52–53; Ann Douglas, *The Feminization of American Culture* (New York: Avon, 1979), pp. 35–37, concludes that there was an increasing tendency to substitute political rhetoric for genuine political leadership.

9. See the Appendix for a discussion of the statistics about church joiners, political party candidates and government officeholders, and for comments about why the figures are imprecise. Unfortunately, the numbers of political party candidates linked to church membership is not large enough to justify any firm conclusion about the link between church membership and specific parties, although there is a suggestive concentration of Protestant church members in the anti-Democratic parties (Whig, Free Soil, Liberty, Peoples', and Republican.) (Table 3.3.)

The evidence of antislavery activity is too spotty for the type of detailed survey which marks ethnocultural studies of political realignments. This account of antebellum Cleveland politics offers a snapshot of the tumultuous political maneuvering of the 1850s by Protestants and their critics over the slavery issue. This snapshot describes the cultural milieu in which political party alignments were formed and in which some of the central values of the parties were forged.

10. Eight of the eleven anti-slavery officers held government office, and eight were political party candidates in the years from 1836 to 1860. They also joined reform efforts: five took part in benevolence, and four in

moral reform. Officers of antislavery societies show a special affinity for temperance. Of the eleven officers included in the newspapers and organization lists, five were traced to temperance groups. Three of the eleven were active in banks, three in the Whig Party, and three in cultural organizations. Two held major Cleveland government positions.

11. Samuel P. Orth, *A History of Cleveland, Ohio* (Chicago and Cleveland: S. J. Clarke Publishing Co., 1910), 1: 290; Cleveland *Herald and Gazette*, June 30, 1837, p. 2 adv. in U.S., Works Progress Administration [Works Progress Administration in Ohio], *Annals of Cleveland* (Cleveland: Works Progress Administration, 1936–38), 1837, p. 391; Cleveland *Herald*, Jan. 19, 1841, p. 2 in WPA, *Annals*, 1841, p. 275; Cleveland *Leader*, Jan. 11, 1859, p. 3 in WPA, *Annals*, 1859, p. 396.

12. Rev. A. B. Cristy, *Cleveland Congregationalists, 1895: Historical Sketches of Our Twenty-five Churches and Missions* (Cleveland: Williams Publishing and Electric Co., 1896), p. 73; Canfield, *Indications*, pp. 12, 42; John G. Fraser, "A Century of Congregationalism in Cleveland," *Ohio Church History Society Papers* (Oberlin, OH: Ohio Church History Society, 1899), 8 (1897): 21. For a more complete discussion of antislavery in antebellum Cleveland see Michael J. McTighe, "Embattled Establishment: Protestants and Power in Cleveland, 1836–1860" (Ph.D. Dissertation, University of Chicago, 1983), pp. 481–505. Bertram Wyatt-Brown, "Abolition and Antislavery in Hudson and Cleveland: Contrasts in Reform Styles," in David D. Van Tassel and John J. Grabowski, eds., *Cleveland: A Tradition of Reform* (Kent, OH: Kent State University Press, 1986), pp. 91–112, finds the rest of the Western Reserve more strongly antislavery than Cleveland.

13. Despite the impression left by the refusal to grant sanctuary to the fugitive slave, Aiken can be counted among the antislavery clergy. The hiding-behind-the-pillar incident is described in Roy Edwin Bowers, *Ohio Congregational Christian Story* (n. p., Ohio Conference of Congregational Christian Churches, 1952), p. 75; Plymouth Church, "Plymouth Church of Shaker Heights, 1916–1923," Plymouth Church, Shaker Heights, Ohio (photocopy); Cristy, *Cleveland Congregationalists, 1895*, pp. 71–73. The most visible antislavery minister was James A. Thome, of First Congregational Church, Ohio City. His activity involving the much publicized Oberlin-Wellington Rescue case are described in Nat Brandt, *The Town that Started the Civil War* (Syracuse, NY: Syracuse University Press, 1990), pp. 163–64, 199. The Rescuers were imprisoned in Cleveland.

14. W. H. Brewster, *God's Law Supreme: A Sermon of the Higher Law* (Cleveland: E. Cowles & Co., 1859), pp. 6, 8.

15. The Oberlin-Wellington rescue trial brought national slavery agi-

tation to Cleveland. A fugitive slave hidden in Oberlin had been caught and placed in jail in Wellington. Groups from Oberlin and Wellington then freed the slave from jail. For this act, 37 were indicted and brought to trial in Cleveland in 1859. The first rescuer to be tried was found guilty, sentenced to 60 days in jail and fined $60 plus court costs. The rest were put in jail after refusing to post bail and declining to be released on their own recognizance. Three of the rescuers eventually pled no contest to the charges in return for a sentence of 24 hours in jail, a $25 fine and payment of court costs. The rest were freed after serving their sentences. A full account of the case is provided by Brandt, *The Town that Started the Civil War*. Thome's role is detailed on pp. 163–64 and 199. Supporters held a number of rallies at the jail while the Rescuers were in jail. See also, Bowers, *Ohio Congregational Christian Story*, p. 77; Elroy McKendree Avery, *A History of Cleveland and Its Environs: The Heart of New Connecticut* (Chicago: Lewis, 1918) 1: 237–41; James Harrison Kennedy, *A History of the City of Cleveland, Its Settlement, Rise and Progress, 1796–1896* (Cleveland: The Imperial Press, 1896), pp. 382–83; Fraser, "A Century of Congregationalism," p. 22; and *PD*, Apr. 18, 1859, p. 2. The report of the mass meeting is in the *PD*, May 24, 1859, p. 2. The meeting is mentioned by Elbert Jay Benton, *Cultural Story of an America City: Cleveland* (Cleveland: Western Reserve Historical Society, 1943), 3: 52, who says that the leaders of public opinion remained aloof, although Avery, *History of Cleveland and Its Environs*, 1: 238, mentions speeches by two state leaders, Joshua R. Giddings and Gov. Salmon Chase.

16. *PD*, Nov. 30, 1859, p. 3; *PD*, Dec. 3, 1859, p. 3; Henry M. Tenney, "The History of the First Congregational Church of Cleveland," *Ohio Church History Society Papers* 2 (1892): 40; Fraser, "A Century of Congregationalism," p. 16. Other support for John Brown's raid is described in *PD*, Dec. 2, 1859, p. 3. According to later accounts, Clevelanders did their part in the Underground Railroad. Contemporary references to the work are slight, and later claims by churches perhaps inflated. Still, there is enough evidence to conclude that much of the work of harboring runaways was conducted by churches. See Cleveland *Daily True Democrat*, Feb. 26, 1853, p. 2 in WPA, *Annals*, 1853, pp. 474–75, for a letter to the editor about the help of the pastor of a Methodist Church for a fugitive. Early Settlers' Association of Cuyahoga County, *Annals* (Cleveland: Mount and Carroll, 1880–1931), 5, no. 6 (1907): 590, includes a description by L. F. Mellen of members of Plymouth Church conducting an underground railroad. Histories of St. John's Episcopal Church describe tunnels and cells to hide runaways. A later investigation concluded that there never was a tunnel, although it is possible the belfry was used as a hiding place: Tom McGuire, "Historic St. John's," *Western Reserve Magazine* (November–December

1978), pp. 31–32, 64–65. See also William Dinwoodie, "St. John's Episcopal Mirrors Life and History of City for 125 Years," Cleveland *News*, November 30, 1941, Archives, Episcopal Diocese of Ohio, Trinity Cathedral, Cleveland. Thomas A. Knight, "Re: Underground Railroad—St. John's Church Tunnel, September 1943," Western Reserve Historical Society (typewritten), p. 2 found the claims for a tunnel unsubstantiated. See also Gertrude Van Rensselaer Wickham, *Memorial to the Pioneer Women of the Western Reserve* (Cleveland: Woman's Department, Cleveland Centennial Commission, 1896–1924), 1: 202; and *L*, Nov. 29, 1859, p. 3 in WPA, *Annals*, 1859, p. 49.

17. *PD*, July 23, 1856, p. 2; *PD*, Dec. 13, 1860, p. 3. Other letter-writers complained to the paper about ministerial impertinence and the desecration of the church by politics: *PD*, July 7, 1856, p. 3; *PD*, June 21, 1847, p. 2. See also Bradburn lecture at the Melodeon on "The Functions of the Pulpit," in *L*, Nov. 7, 1857, p. 2 in WPA, *Annals*, 1857, p. 159.

18. *PD*, June 1, 1857, p. 2; *PD*, Mar. 9, 1854, p. 3.

19. *PD*, Mar. 20, 1854, p. 2; *PD*, May 10, 1854, p. 2; *PD*, June 1, 1857, p. 2; *PD*, Feb. 20, 1855, p. 2; *PD*, Mar. 9, 1854, p. 3; *PD*, Aug. 13, 1853, p. 2; Lukonic, "Evangelicals in the City," p. 81, discusses criticisms of clerical involvement.

20. *PD*, Feb. 20, 1855, p. 2.

21. Luke 22: 17; I Timothy 4: 15–26; II Timothy 24–26; *PD*, May 10, 1854, p. 2; *PD*, Mar. 9, 1854, p. 2, emphasis in original.

CHAPTER 8. RITUALS OF COMMUNITY LIFE

1. Susan G. Davis, *Parades and Power: Street Theatre in Nineteenth-Century Philadelphia* (Philadelphia: Temple University Press, 1986), pp. 5, 6. Davis provides especially perceptive descriptions of the uses of ritual and ceremony in the public culture. See esp. pp. 3–5, 14, 22, 48, 164. Davis employs the term public culture much as it is used in this work to describe "a context of contest and confrontation" (p. 6) and "contested terrain, shifting and continually being redefined" (p. 14). She refers to public culture throughout (see, for example, pp. 9–12, 36–38, 67–72).

2. Davis, *Parades and Power*, pp. 22, 14.

3. David Glassberg, "History and the Public Legacies of the Progressive Era," *Journal of American History* 73 (March 1978), 957–80, suggests many of these functions for public ceremonies. See esp. pp. 958–59.

4. *Boatman's Magazine* 1 (Oct. 1834): 33, emphasis in original; Levi

Tucker, *Lectures on the Nature and Dangerous Tendency of Modern Infidelity* (Cleveland: Francis B. Penniman, 1837), p. 147. See also Cleveland *Herald*, May 7, 1842, p. 2 in U.S. Works Progress Administration, Ohio [Works Progress Administration in Ohio], *Annals of Cleveland* (Cleveland: Works Progress Administration, 1936–38), 1842, pp. 56–57; *H*, Feb. 17, 1843, p. 2 in WPA, *Annals*, 1843, p. 285. The Cuyahoga County Sabbath Society resolved that the "Legislator of the universe" had appointed and sanctified the Sabbath. The Society warned that "all secular employments on the Sabbath, excepting works of mercy, by individuals, chartered companies, or governments, call down the wrath of Heaven, impoverish the land, and inflict cruelty and injustice on all the people, but especially on the laboring poor." *H*, Mar. 14, 1844, p. 2 in WPA, *Annals*, 1844, p. 732; Cleveland *Plain Dealer Weekly*, Mar. 13, 1844, p. 3; and *PD Weekly*, Mar. 13, 1844, p. 3; *H*, Mar. 14, 1844, p. 2 in WPA, *Annals*, 1844, p. 732.

5. B. White, ed., *The Acts to Provide for the Organization of Cities and Villages, and the Revised Ordinances of the City of Cleveland* (Cleveland: Harris, Fairbanks and Co., 1855), Ordinance XCVIII, Aug. 21, 1855, pp. 219–20; Cleveland, Ohio, *The Acts to Provide for the Organization of Cities and Villages and the Revised Ordinances of the City of Cleveland* (Cleveland: *Plain Dealer*, 1862), Jan. 10, 1856, Sec. II, p. 116.

6. Cleveland *Leader*, May 14, 1858, p. 1 in WPA, *Annals*, 1858, p. 17.

7. For the 1840s, see *The Boatman's Magazine* 1 (Oct. 1834): 3–5, emphasis in original. Paul S. Boyer, *Urban Masses and Moral Order in America, 1820–1920* (Cambridge, MA.: Harvard University Press, 1978); Harmon Kingsbury, *The Sabbath: A Brief History of Laws, Petitions, Remonstrances and Reports, With Facts and Arguments, Relating to the Christian Sabbath* (New York: Robert Carter, 1840). Protestant Episcopal Church, Ohio Diocese, *Journal, 1835–60* (n. p., n. d.), Address, Charles McIlvaine, 1857, pp. 17–18; *PD*, Aug. 10, 1850, p. 2.

8. Sabbath advocates had more trouble invoking the law than did temperance reformers. Courts were prone to invoke notions of the separation of church and state when dealing with Sabbath questions. In 1846, for example, the Ohio Supreme Court exempted Jews from a Cincinnati prohibition against trade on Sunday. Cincinnati v. Rice, 15 *Ohio Reports*, p. 225; see also Bloom v. Richards, 2 *Ohio State*, pp. 387–91.

9. Glassberg, "History and the Public," describes the ritual functions of celebrations of historical events. Davis, *Parades and Power*, pp. 40–45, 67, 68.

10. This description of July 4th observances is based on the Cleve-

land *Plain Dealer* and WPA, *Annals,* entries on and around July 4th from 1836 to 1860.

11. Davis, *Parades and Power,* pp. 115, 148. She discusses the participation of temperance groups in July 4th and other parades on pp. 43, 54, 115–16, 148–149. Mary P. Ryan, *Women in Public: Between Banners and Ballots, 1825–1880* (Baltimore: Johns Hopkins University Press, 1990), pp. 35–37 notes the role of women.

12. *H,* July 6, 1843, p. 2 in WPA, *Annals,* 1843, pp. 128–29. Anne C. Loveland, *Southern Evangelicals and the Social Order, 1800–1860* (Baton Rouge, LA: Louisiana State University Press, 1980), p. 126, finds calls for the celebration of July 4th as a political Sabbath. For Fourth of July ceremonies, see Cleveland *Herald and Gazette,* July 6, 1838, p. 2 in WPA, *Annals,* 1838, p. 137; *DTD,* June 27, 1848, p. 2 in WPA, *Annals,* 1848, p. 236; Cleveland *Daily True Democrat,* July 3, 1848, p. 2 in WPA, *Annals,* 1848, p. 236; *PD,* July 5, 1848, p. 2. For temperance participation see Chapter 5. Catholic or non-religious activities are not mentioned in the city's newspapers, including the *Plain Dealer,* which was responsive to Democratic and Catholic concerns and might be expected to report on non-Protestant observances.

13. Cleveland *Plain Dealer,* July 5, 1850, p. 2. The shift may have begun in the 1840s. The *Plain Dealer* description of the 1843 celebration suggested that there may have been parts of the celebration which native Protestants did not take part in, *PD Weekly,* July 5, 1843, p. 2. Descriptions of the July 4th celebration of 1858 are especially complete: WPA, *Annals,* 1858, pp. 214–16; *PD,* June 28, 1858, p. 3; *PD,* July 3, 1858, p. 3; *L,* July 7, 1858, p. 3 in WPA, *Annals,* 1858, p. 60. The *Leader* complained that the religious character of the holiday had been lost sight of: Dec. 20, 1858, p. 1 in WPA, *Annals,* 1858, p. 216. The Bethel Church's excursions are reported in *PD,* June 29, 1853, p. 3; *PD,* June 28, 1858, p. 3; *PD,* July 5, 1854, p. 3. Mary Ryan, *Women in Public,* finds a general native born Protestant retreat from public ceremonies in the 1850s.

14. Thanksgiving also became associated with dispensing aid to the poor. *PD,* Nov. 24, 1852, p. 2; *H,* Nov. 19, 1845, p. 3 in WPA, *Annals,* 1845, p. 128; *H,* Dec. 20, 1842, p. 2 in WPA, *Annals,* 1842, p. 445; *H,* Dec. 2, 1842, p. 2 in WPA, *Annals,* 1842, p. 158; *H,* Nov. 19, 1845, p. 3 in WPA, *Annals,* 1845, p. 128. Joseph Lee Lukonic, "Evangelicals in the City: Evangelical Protestant Social Concerns in Early Chicago, 1837–1860" (Ph.D. Dissertation, University of Wisconsin, 1979), p. 72, discusses the attempt to transform Thanksgiving into a civil-religious festival.

The celebration of another explicitly religious holiday, Christmas, received little attention from newspapers or churches, perhaps because its religious import was clear. A notice in the *Daily True Democrat* in 1850, stating that no paper would be issued because "today is Christmas day and *that* all of us claim as our own" suggests the pervasiveness of a generalized Christianity. *DTD*, Dec. 25, 1850, p. 2 in WPA, *Annals*, 1850, p. 120, emphasis in original.

Washington's birthday and New Year's Day celebrations were not major civic occasions. St. Mary's Catholic Church offered a discourse on "Religious Toleration" and the Father Mathew Temperance Society marched on Washington's birthday in 1843, but usually the holiday was observed with military ceremonies. *H*, Feb. 21, 1843, p. 125 in WPA, *Annals*, 1843, p. 125; Cleveland *Whig & Herald*, Feb. 17, 1847, p. 2 in WPA, *Annals*, 1847, p. 87; *L*, Feb. 24, 1860, p. 3 in WPA, *Annals*, 1860, p. 141.

15. The Cleveland Presbytery called for a day of fasting and prayer in 1835 for the conversion of the world and one in 1838 in view of the low state of religion in the churches. The Erie Methodist Conference voted in 1837 to have a day of fasting and prayer every year. First Baptist Church observed a day of fasting and prayer in 1843 for an outpouring of the "Spirit of Grace" "that the Kingdoms of this World may becom[e] the Kingdoms of our Lord Christ." Cleveland Presbytery, Minutes, 1830–83, Apr. 22, 1835; Apr. 18, 1838; Erie Conference, *Minutes, 1836–55*, 1837, p. 21; First Baptist Church, Minutes, 1837–48, First Baptist Church, Shaker Heights, Ohio, Jan. 2, 1843; First Presbyterian Church, Records, 1820–37, First Presbyterian Church, Cleveland, Feb. 22, 1837; *H*, Apr. 17, 1841, p. 3 in WPA, *Annals*, 1841, p. 91; *H*, May 6, 1841, p. 3 in WPA, *Annals*, 1841, p. 40; WPA, *H*, May 15, 1841, p. 3 in WPA, *Annals*, 1841, pp. 192–93.

16. Rouse, Diary and Letter Book of Benjamin Rouse, Agent for American Sunday School Union, 1830–1860, Western Reserve Historical Society, Adella Prentiss Hughes Family Papers, Aug. 2, 1849; *DTD*, July 10, 1849, p. 2 in WPA, *Annals*, 1849, p. 23. See also *PD*, Aug. 2, 1849, p. 2. The quote is from Rouse, Diary, Aug. 2, 1849, First Baptist Records, emphasis in original.

17. The only fast mentioned in the church records after 1846 is in Euclid Street Presbyterian Church, Records of the Euclid Street Presbyterian Church and Society, 1853–70, Church of the Covenant, Cleveland, Dec. 30, 1860, when the church voted to observe the fast proclaimed by the President for Friday, Jan. 4, 1861. The phrases used to evaluate the hold of the rituals (intellectually convincing, emotionally compelling) are taken from Glassberg, "History and the Legacies of the Progressive Era," p. 977.

18. Davis, *Parades and Power*, pp. 126–29, 130, 157, discusses civic celebrations in Philadelphia.

19. *DTD*, Feb. 3, 1852, p. 2 in WPA, *Annals*, 1852, p. 355; *DTD*, Feb. 4,

228 A Measure of Success

1852, p. 3 in WPA, *Annals*, 1852, p. 41; WPA, *Annals*, 1852, pp. 358–59; *DTD*, Feb. 4, 1852, p. 2 in WPA, *Annals*, 1852, p. 357; *DTD*, Feb. 11, 1852, p. 1 in WPA, *Annals*, 1852, p. 362, says $20 was presented. It is not clear whether Kossuth actually met with the black citizens: *DTD*, Feb. 9, 1852, p. 2 in WPA, *Annals*, 1852, p. 202; *PD*, Nov. 22, 1851, p. 2.

20. *DTD*, Jan. 8, 1852, p. 2 in WPA, *Annals*, 1852, p. 343.

21. *L*, July 4, 1860, p. 1 in WPA, *Annals*, 1860, p. 416; *DTD*, July 13, 1853, p. 3 in WPA, *Annals*, 1853, p. 445; *PD*, Aug. 22, 1860, p. 3; *Herald and Gazette*, Aug. 2, 1839, p. 3 in WPA, *Annals*, 1839, p. 230; *L*, Oct. 24, 1855, p. 3 in WPA, *Annals*, 1855, p. 516; *L*, Apr. 1, 1856, p. 1 in WPA, *Annals*, 1856, p. 415; *PD*, July 10, 1857, p. 3; *DTD*, Mar. 13, 1850, p. 2 in WPA, *Annals*, 1850, p. 350; *L*, July 4, 1860, p. 1 in WPA, *Annals*, 1860, p. 416. Clergy and church supervision of school dedications, commencements, and end-of-year examinations were the visible tip of an iceberg of Protestant involvement in public and private education at all levels, from primary school through college. Cleveland's Protestant ministers, churches, and church members were intimately involved in other aspects of public education, often in conjunction with local authorities. The first school started in the basement of Bethel Church, and schools often used church rooms for classes. Rev. James A. Thome, of First Presbyterian Church, Ohio City, served as president of the Board of Education, and one-third of the "visitors" chosen by the Board to evaluate the schools were ministers. For a more detailed discussion of the involvement of Protestants in public schools, and the similar role they played in private schools, see Michael J. McTighe, "Embattled Establishment: Protestants and Power in Cleveland, 1836–1869," (Ph.D. Dissertation, University of Chicago, 1983), pp. 379–89.

22. Herbert Hovenkamp, *Science and Religion in America, 1800–1860* (Philadelphia: University of Pennsylvania Press, 1978); Theodore Dwight Bozeman, "Inductive and Deductive Politics: Science and Society in Antebellum Presbyterian Thought," *Journal of American History* 64 (December 1977): 704–22; and Bozeman, *Protestants in an Age of Science: The Baconian Ideal in Antebellum Religious Thought* (Chapel Hill, NC: University of North Carolina Press, 1977); Mary Farrell Bednarowski, *American Religion: A Cultural History* (Englewood Cliffs, NJ: Prentice-Hall, 1984), p. 41; George H. Daniels, *American Science in the Age of Jackson* (New York: Columbia University Press, 1968), pp. 52–56, 85, 133, 144, 169–70, 178–83, 199–200; Daniels, *Science in American Society: A Social History* (New York: Alfred A. Knopf, 1971), pp. 77–92; John C. Burnham, *How Superstition Won and Science Lost: Popularizing Science and Health in the United States* (New Brunswick, NJ: Rutgers University Press, 1987), pp. 144–51. The late eigh-

teenth- and early nineteenth-century natural theology built on a long Christian tradition of finding meaning in the created order and in God's activity in the world. This tradition is described in Lynn White, Jr., *Machina ex Deo: Essays in the Dynamism of Western Culture* (Cambridge, MA: Massachusetts Institute of Technology Press, 1971), pp. 88–90, 100–02. For a case study of the role of natural scientists in the U.S. with comparisons to Europe, see Chandos Michael Brown, "A Natural History of the Gloucester Sea Serpent: Knowledge, Power, and the Culture of Science in Antebellum America," *American Quarterly* 42 (September 1990): 402–36.

A typical resolution of religion and natural history can be found in Sherman Canfield, *An Address on the Power and Progressiveness of Knowledge* (Painesville, OH: Smythe and Hanna, 1843), pp. 31, 32; and *The Temporal Blessings of Christianity* (Cleveland: Smead and Cowles, 1852), p. 28. The one exception to the genial accommodation between religion and science was offered by the only representative of Old School Presbyterianism in Cleveland, Westminster Presbyterian Church's minister, Frederick T. Brown. Brown offered a version of the "two revelations" theory which described science and religion as complementary ways of knowing, each with its own sphere. Brown's attempt to discriminate between the grounds of religious knowledge as opposed to those of scientific knowledge marked him as a member of the intellectual vanguard. Cleveland Bible Society, *Annual Report* (Cleveland: Harris, Fairbanks, and Co., 1859), p. 19. Bednarowski, *American Religion*, p. 41; Frederick T. Brown, *The Physician Should Be a Christian* (Cleveland: E. Cowles and Co., 1857), p. 15; Hovenkamp, *Science and Religion in America*, pp. 61–69, tells of others, such as Moses Stuart of Andover, Andrews Norton of Harvard, and the Presbyterian Lewis Taylor, who pushed beyond the usual identification of nature with revelation. See also Daniels, *American Science in the Age of Jackson*, pp. 52–53; and Daniels, *Science in American Society*, pp. 206–22.

23. Cleveland *Herald*, Feb. 22, 1845, p. 3 in WPA, *Annals*, 1845, p. 149; Cleveland *Plain Dealer Weekly*, Feb. 26, 1845, p. 2; *H*, Feb. 25, 1845, p. 3 in WPA, *Annals*, 1845, p. 149; Cleveland *Plain Dealer*, Feb. 18, 1853, p. 3; *H*, Feb. 22, 1845, p. 34 in WPA, *Annals*, 1845, p. 149; *H*, Feb. 25, 1845, p. 3 in WPA, *Annals*, 1845, p. 149. St. John's reconciliation of geology and religion was unremarkable, a distillation of the natural theology arguments of Benjamin Silliman and others who argued for the compatibility of geology and revelation. In lectures from 1845 through the 1850s, St. John pressed his argument that God was the explanation for the successive and higher developments of life, *PD*, Feb. 18, 1853, p. 3. Other lectures by St. John are mentioned in the *Daily True Democrat*, Dec. 23, 1848, p. 2 advertisement in WPA, *Annals*, 1848, p. 50; *DTD*, Jan. 1, 1849, p. 2 in WPA, 1849, p. 137. *PD*, Feb. 18, 1853. Other lectures by St. John are mentioned in an advertise-

ment in the *Daily True Democrat*, Dec. 23, 1848, p. 2 in WPA, *Annals*, 1848, p. 50; and *DTD*, Jan. 1, 1849, p. 1 in WPA, *Annals*, p. 137.

24. *PD*, Nov. 6, 1845, p. 2; *PD*, Nov. 7, 1845, p. 2; *PD*, Nov. 28, 1851, p. 2; *PD*, Jan. 12, 1855, p. 3; *PD*, July 29, 1853, p. 2. Other lectures on science and religion included one at the Young Men's Institute, *H*, Nov. 19, 1842, p. 3 in WPA, *Annals*, 1842, p. 182; and Prof. John Smith on "The Connection Between Science and Morals" at the Cleveland Lyceum, *H*, Mar. 21, 1842, p. 2, advertisement in WPA, 1842, p. 181.

25. *DTD*, Dec. 4, 1849, p. 2 in WPA, *Annals*, 1849, p. 150; *PD*, Dec. 11, 1849, p. 2; *DTD*, Dec. 27, 1849, p. 2 in WPA, *Annals*, 1849, p. 150; *DTD*, Aug. 10, 1850, p. 2 in WPA, 1850, p. 161; *PD*, Dec. 1, 1849, p. 2. For other accounts of mesmerism as a cure for illness, see Robert C. Fuller, *Mesmerism and the American Cure of Souls*, (Philadelphia: University of Pennsylvania Press, 1982), pp. 43, 49. Cleveland was one of the stops on the nationwide tours of spiritualists and mesmerists such as Andrew Jackson Davis, the Fox sisters, and the Burr brothers: *PD*, Aug. 14, 1850, p. 2; *PD*, June 20, 1851, p. 2; *PD*, Nov. 8, 1852, p. 3; *PD*, Nov. 9. 1852, p. 3; *DTD*, Nov. 11, 1852, p. 2, advertisement in WPA, *Annals*, 1852, p. 457; *DTD*, Dec. 11, 1852, p. 2 in WPA, 1852, p. 547; *DTD*, Aug. 5, 1853, p. 3 in WPA, 1853, p.496; *PD*, Feb. 2, 1855, p. 3. An overview of antebellum spiritualism and mesmerism is provided by Robert S. Ellwood, Jr., *Alternative Altars: Unconventional and Spiritual Religion in America* (Chicago: University of Chicago Press, 1979), pp. 95–103; R. Laurence Moore, *In Search of White Crows: Spiritualism, Parapsychology, and American Culture* (New York: Oxford University Press, 1977); Whitney R. Cross, *The Burned-Over District: The Social and Intellectual History of Enthusiastic Religion in Western New York, 1800–1850* (New York: Harper and Row, Torchbook, 1965), pp. 341–52; Ernest Isaacs, "The Fox Sisters and American Spiritualism," in Howard Kerr and Charles L. Crow, *The Occult in America: New Historical Perspectives* (Urbana, IL: University of Illinois Press, 1983), pp. 79–110; and Fuller, *Mesmerism and the American Cure of Souls*; Burnham, *How Superstition Won and Science Lost*, pp. 86–87, 150. Ann Braude, *Radical Spirits: Spiritualism and Women's Rights in Nineteenth-Century America* (Boston: Beacon Press, 1989) offers a full account of spiritualism and stresses its challenge to traditional roles of women. Mesmerism and spiritualism are treated here as one phenomenon. Many demonstrations incorporated both mesmerism and spiritualism and it is difficult to isolate the appeal of each. For mesmerists who believed in a new means of communicating through magnetic fluid or animal magnetism, contacting spirits seemed unscientific. The Burrs, for example, were critics of the Foxes and their rappings. They charged that the Foxes were a fraud and a delusion, and claimed to be able to produce rappings 17 differ-

ent ways: Isaacs, "The Fox Sisters and American Spiritualism," in Kerr and Crow, *The Occult in America*, pp. 93, 95.

26. For the appeal of mesmerism and spiritualism see Fuller, *Mesmerism and the American Cure of Souls*, pp. 21, 73–79, 81, 99–100; Mary Farrell Bednarowski, "Women in Occult America," in Kerr and Crow, *The Occult in America*; Kerr and Crow, "Introduction," p. 4; Catherine L. Albanese, *America: Religions and Religion* (Belmont, CA: Wadsworth, 1981), p. 175; and Bednarowski, *American Religion*, pp. 40, 42–43.

27. *PD*, Apr. 9, 1857, p. 2; *PD*, May 8, 1858, p. 3; *L*, Mar. 23, 1857, p. 3 in WPA, *Annals*, 1857, p. 332. For cynical responses to the Davenport Boys, see *L*, Mar. 23, 1857, p. 3 in WPA, *Annals*, 1857, pp. 332–33; WPA 1856, pp. 463–65. The doubts about a medium who produced rappings are described in *PD*, Dec. 1, 1853, p. 3; *PD*, Dec. 3, 1853, p. 3; *L*, Mar. 20, 1854, p. 3 in WPA, *Annals*, 1854, p. 401; *PD*, Mar. 20, 1854, p. 3.

28. *H*, Sept. 2, 1846, p. 3 in WPA, *Annals*, 1846, p. 148.

29. *PD*, Feb. 28, 1855, p. 2; *PD*, Mar. 2, 1855, p. 2; *PD*, Feb. 23, 1855, p. 2.

30. *PD*, Feb. 28, 1855, p. 2.

31. *PD*, Feb. 21, 1855, p. 2; *PD*, Feb. 22, 1855, p. 2; *PD*, Feb. 21, 1855, p. 2; *PD*, Feb. 22, 1855, p. 2. Mahan was later a publicist for the holiness movement in England. Moore, *In Search of White Crows*, pp. 30–33, discusses Mahan and the notion of the odic force.

32. *PD*, June 17, 1857, p. 3; *L*, Jan. 15, 1859, p. 1 in WPA, *Annals*, 1859, p. 449. Sherman Canfield, minister of Second Presbyterian Church, also lectured against spiritualism, *PD*, Feb. 8, 1851, p. 2. For Thome's lecture and the letter critical of spiritualism, see *PD*, June 17, 1857, p. 3; *L*, Feb. 24, 1859, p. 3 in WPA, *Annals*, 1859, p. 449; *L*, Feb. 26, 1859, p. 3 in WPA, *Annals*, 1859, p. 450. For criticisms of White, see *PD*, Jan. 31, 1859, p. 1; and *PD*, Feb. 3, 1859, quoted by John J. Pullen, "Artemus Ward and the Moral Majority," Cleveland *Plain Dealer Magazine*, Feb. 21, 1982, p. 26. The *Western Pilot*, the newspaper of the Western Seamen's Friend Society, wrote against spiritualism, Apr. 1853, pp. 97–101 and May, 1853, pp. 132–34. Moore, *In Search of White Crows*, pp. 40–69, lists the complaints Christian orthodoxy lodged against spiritualism: there was no guidance from Scripture or church, it mocked forms of worship and miracles, the divinity of Christ was not stressed, there was little belief in a personal God, it was empiricist and rationalist, and there was no notion of sin.

33. Kerr and Crow, "Introduction," in Kerr and Crow, *The Occult in America*, pp. 4–5; Ellwood, *Alternative Altars*, pp. 1–41; Albanese, *America:*

Religions and Religion, p. 169. This pattern of reconciliation is typical of Protestant responses to science. Bednarowski, *American Religion*, pp. 39, 46, notes that "the dialogue between science and religion in America, sometimes bitter but often fruitful, appears to be a continuing feature of the culture." While there has been a pattern of opposition and suspicion between science and religion, she concludes that, more often, a "creative dialogue" has characterized the relationship between the two. The "warfare" image was popularized by Andrew Dickson White, *A History of the Warfare of Science With Theology in Christendom* (New York: D. Appleton and Company, 1919).

34. Davis, *Parades and Power*, p. 48.

CHAPTER 9. A SUBSTANTIAL BUT ERODING PRESENCE

1. George M. Thomas, *Revivalism and Cultural Change: Christianity, Nation-Building, and the Market in the Nineteenth-Century United States* (Chicago: University of Chicago Press, 1989), p. 9, argues that "the market, the primary carrier of sociocultural change, was the plausibility structure of revivalism.

2. For an extensive analysis of the development and effects of pluralism, see David Gerber, *The Making of an American Pluralism: Buffalo, New York, 1825–60* (Urbana, IL: University of Illinois Press, 1989).

APPENDIX

1. For a more detailed discussion, see Michael J. McTighe, "Embattled Establishment: Protestants and Power in Cleveland, 1836–1860 (Ph.D. Dissertation, University of Chicago, 1983), pp. 575–82, 618–23.

2. Theodore Hershberg and Robert Dockhorn, "Occupational Classification," *Historical Methods Newsletter* 9 (March–June 1976): 59–98.

3. Getchen Condran and Jeff Seaman, "Linkage of the 1880–81 Philadelphia Death Register to the 1880 Manuscript Census: A Comparison of Hand- and Machine-Record Linkage Techniques," *Historical Methods*, 14, no. 2 (Spring 1981): 73–84; Theodore Hershberg, Alan Burstein and Robert Dockhorn, "Record Linkage," *Historical Methods Newsletter* 9 (March–June 1976): 137–63; Theodore Hershberg and Robert Dockhorn, "Occupational Classification," *Historical Methods Newsletter* 9 (March–June 1976): 59–98; Michael B. Katz and John Tiller, "Record Linkage for Everyman: A Semi-Automated Process," *Historical Methods Newsletter* 5 (September 1972): 144–50.

BIBLIOGRAPHY

The Bibliography is divided into five sections: "English-Speaking Protestant Churches, Major Denominations," "Other English-Speaking Protestant Churches," "Other Religious Bodies," "Ministers' Sermons and Speeches," and "Secondary and Other Sources." The church sections are arranged by denomination and church.

English-Speaking Protestant Churches, Major Denominations

BAPTIST

General

Cleveland, or Rocky River Baptist Association. *Minutes, 1852–1860.* N.p., 1852–60.

Female Baptist Sewing Society. Records, 1835–36. Western Reserve Historical Society, Adella Prentiss Hughes Family Papers.

Malvin, John. *North Into Freedom: The Autobiography of John Malvin, Free Negro,1795–1880.* Edited by Allan Peskin. Cleveland: The Press of Western Reserve University, 1966.

McTighe, Michael J., "Baptists." In *Encyclopedia of Cleveland History*, David D. Van Tassel, ed., John J. Grabowski, managing ed. Bloomington, IN: Indiana University Press, 1987, pp. 75–76.

Rocky River Baptist Association. *Minutes, 1832–1851.* N.p., 1832–51.

Rouse, Benjamin. Account Book of Benjamin Rouse, 1836–1863. Western Reserve Historical Society, Adella Prentiss Hughes Family Papers.

Rouse, Benjamin. Diary and Letter Book of Benjamin Rouse, Agent for American Sunday School Union, 1830–1860. Western Reserve Historical Society, Adella Prentiss Hughes Family Papers.

Rouse, Benjamin. Journal [1832]. Western Reserve Historical Society, Adella Prentiss Hughes Family Papers.

Rouse, Benjamin. Manuscript Recort of the Life of Benjamin Rouse, 1801, 1837, 1839, 1862, and of the First Baptist Church, 1862. Western Reserve Historical Society, Adella Prentiss Hughes Family Papers.

Rouse, Benjamin. A Record. Western Reserve Historical Society, Adella Prentiss Hughes Family Papers.

First Baptist Church

Adams, Mary E. *First Baptist Church of Cleveland, Ohio, Historical Sketch.* Cleveland: First Baptist Church, 1903.

Bishop, J. P. *Memoir of Rev. Seymour W. Adams, D.D.* Cleveland: Fairbanks, Benedict and Co., 1866.

First Baptist Church. *A Declaration of the Faith and Practice, Together With the Rules and Regulations of the First Baptist Church in the City of Cleveland, Ohio.* Cleveland: Harris, Fairbanks and Co., 1857.

First Baptist Church. *History of the First Baptist Church of Cleveland, OH: And an Account of the Celebration of its Semi-Centennial, February 16th–20th, 1883.* Cleveland: J. B. Savage, 1883.

First Baptist Church. *History of the First Baptist Church, Cleveland, Ohio, 1833–1922.* Cleveland: E. S. Schulte, 1922.

First Baptist Church. *History of the First Baptist Church of Greater Cleveland,1833–1933.* N.p., n.d.

First Baptist Church. *History of the First Baptist Church of Greater Cleveland, 1833–1968.* Cleveland: First Baptist Church, 1968.

First Baptist Church. *In Memoriam: Deacon Moses White.* N.p., n.d.

First Baptist Church. Membership Lists, 1852–56. First Baptist Church, Shaker Heights, Ohio.

First Baptist Church. Membership Record, 1846–64. First Baptist Church, Shaker Heights, Ohio.

First Baptist Church. Minutes, December 21, 1854–March 19, 1883. First Baptist Church, Shaker Heights, Ohio.

First Baptist Church. Minutes, March 31, 1837 to December 18, 1848. First Baptist Church, Shaker Heights, Ohio.

First Baptist Church. Records, 1833–1837, in Benjamin Rouse, Manuscript Record of the Life of Benjamin Rouse, 1801–37, 1839, 1862, and of the First Baptist Church, 1862. Western Reserve Historical Society, Adella Prentiss Hughes Family Papers.

First Baptist Church. Record, January 5, 1849–April 1, 1859. First Baptist Church, Shaker Heights, Ohio.

First Baptist Church. Treasurer's Accounts, 1833–1837. First Baptist Church, Shaker Heights, Ohio.

First Baptist Church. Trustee Minutes, 1855–1883. First Baptist Church, Shaker Heights, Ohio.

Second Baptist Church

Euclid Avenue Baptist Church. *Historical Sketches: Seventy-Five Years of the Euclid Avenue Baptist Church, Cleveland, Ohio, 1851–1926.* Cleveland: Euclid Avenue Baptist Church, 1927.

Schaller, Lyle E. "Euclid Avenue: Limiting the Church." *The City Church*, May–June, 1962, 3–5, 7.

Third Baptist Church

Third Baptist Church. Church Record Book, 1852–67, 1884, 1885. Western Reserve Historical Society.

CONGREGATIONAL

General

Brand, James. "History of the Congregational Association of Ohio." In *Ohio Church History Society Papers*, 3: 56–75. Oberlin, OH: Ohio Church History Society, 1896.

Bowers, Roy Edwin. *Ohio Congregational Christian Story*. N.p.: Ohio Conference of Congregational Christian Churches, 1952.

Cleveland Congregational Conference. *Minutes Book, 1853–60*. N.p., 1853–60.

Congregational Conference of Ohio. *Minutes, 1852–67*. N.p., 1852–67.

Cleveland Congregational Conference. *Minutes, 1860–1873*. N.p.,1860–73.

Dickinson, Cornelius E. "History of Congregationalism in Ohio Before 1852." In *Ohio Church History Society Papers*, 3: 31–55. Oberlin, OH: Ohio Church History Society, 1896. The *Papers* have been collected in two volumes, published by the Society in 1899. Citations are to the original volumes.

Cristy, Rev. A. B. *Cleveland Congregationalists, 1895: Historical Sketches of Our Twenty-Five churches and Missions*. Cleveland: Williams Publishing and Electric Co., 1896.

Fraser, John G. "A Century of Congregationalism in Cleveland." In *Ohio Church History Society Papers*, 8: 1–44. Oberlin, OH: Ohio Church History Society, 1897.

Leonard, Delavan L. *A Century of Congregationalism in Ohio*. Oberlin: Ohio Home Missionary Society, 1896.

McTighe, Michael J., "Congregationalists." In *Encyclopedia of Cleveland History*, David D. Van Tassel, ed. Bloomington, IN: Indiana University Press, 1987, pp. 293–94.

Tenney, Henry M. "The History of the First Congregational Church of Cleveland." In *Ohio Church History Society Papers*, 2: 40. Oberlin, OH: Ohio Church History Society, 1892.

Western Reserve Agency of the American Home Missionary Society. *Ninth Annual Statement of the Western Reserve Agency of the American Home Missionary Society*. Hudson, OH: D. Marshall and Co., 1854.

Western Reserve Agency of the American Home Missionary Society. *Third Annual Statement of the Western Reserve Agency of the American Home Missionary Society.* Hudson, OH: Ohio Observer, 1848.

Whitlock, Frank M. "The Bible Christian Church and Its Relations to Congregationalism, Particularly in Ohio." *Ohio Church History Society Papers*, 1: 61–77. Oberlin, OH: Ohio Church History Society, 1890.

First Congregational Church (Avery)

First Congregational Church. *Manual.* Cleveland: Smead and Cowles, 1852.

Pilgrim Congregational Church

Hart, Jeanette. "A History of Pilgrim Church." Pilgrim Congregational Church. *Jubilee Year Book, 1859–1909.* Cleveland: Pilgrim Congregational Church 1909.

Jennings Avenue Congregational Society. Records of the Congregational Society, University Heights. Pilgrim Congregational Church, Cleveland.

Pilgrim Congregational Church. *History and Directory, 1859–1929.* Cleveland, OH: Pilgrim Congregational Church, 1929.

Pilgrim Congregational Church. *Jubilee Year Book, 1859–1909.* Cleveland, OH: Pilgrim Congregational Church, 1909.

Pilgrim Congregational Church. *Our First One Hundred Years, 1859–1959.* Cleveland: Pilgrim Congregational Church, 1959.

University Heights Union Sabbath School. [Records]. Pilgrim Congregational Church, Cleveland.

Plymouth Congregational Church

Plymouth Church. *Annual Report of the Plymouth Church, Cleveland, January,1865.* Cleveland: Plymouth Church, 1865.

Plymouth Church. *Manual, 1860.* Cleveland: E. Cowles and Co., 1860.

Plymouth Church. *Manual of the Plymouth Church, Cleveland, Ohio.* Cleveland: Smead and Cowles, 1852.

Plymouth Church. "Plymouth Church of Shaker Heights, 1916–1923" (Photocopy).

EPISCOPAL

General

Episcopal Church Home for Women. *The Church Home, 1856–1956.* Cleveland: Episcopal Church Home for Women, 1956.

Hall, John. Ashtabula Letters. Archives, Episcopal Diocese of Ohio, Trinity Cathedral, Cleveland, Hall papers.

Hall, John. Letters to and from John Hall, 1846–49, 1846–53, 1850–65. Archives, Episcopal Diocese of Ohio, Trinity Cathedral, Cleveland, Hall papers.

Hall, John. Letter to G. T. Bedell, 1868. "Historical Notes, Diocese of Ohio, 1816–1863." Archives, Episcopal Diocese of Ohio, Trinity Cathedral, Cleveland, Hall papers.

Memorial of the Rev. Gideon Babcock Perry at Hopkinsville, K. N.p., 1879.

Protestant Episcopal Church, Ohio Diocese. *Journal, 1835–60.* 4 Vols. N.p., 1835–60.

Smythe, George Franklin. *A History of the Diocese of Ohio Until the Year 1918.* Cleveland: Protestant Episcopal Church, Ohio Diocese, 1931.

Wells, Michael V., "Episcopalians," in *Encyclopedia of Cleveland History,* David D. Van Tassel, ed., John J. Grabowski, managing editor. Bloomington, IN: Indiana University Press, 1987, pp. 375–77.

Grace Episcopal Church

Grace [Episcopal] Church. *Past and Present of Grace Church.* Cleveland: Grace Episcopal Church, 1898.

McIlvaine, Charles P. *Opinion of the Right Rev. Charles P. McIlvaine, D.D., Bishop of the Protestant Episcopal Church in Ohio in Answer to Certain Questions Regarding the Official Position of the Clergy of Grace Church, Cleveland.* Cleveland: Plain Dealer Book and Job Office, 1856.

[Rice, Harvey]. *Review of Bishop McIlvaine's Opinion Relative to the Official Position of the Clergy of Grace Church, Cleveland, Ohio.* Cleveland: E. Cowles and Co., 1856.

Varian, Alexander. *Pastoral Letter to the Parishioners of Grace Church.* Cleveland: Smead and Cowles, 1847.

Washburn, A. H. "Some Historical Sketches of Grace Church, Cleveland, Ohio, 1876." Historical Sketch of the Diocese of Ohio, 1817–1878. Edited by G. T. Bedell. Vol. 3. Archives, Episcopal Diocese of Ohio, Trinity Cathedral, Cleveland.

St. James Episcopal

St. James Episcopal Church. Parish File. Archives, Episcopal Diocese of Ohio, Trinity Cathedral, Cleveland.

St. John's Episcopal

Church, Ransom M. "Notes on the History of St. John's Church Cleveland." Compiled by Alfred Mewitt, 1930. Cleveland Public Library (Typewritten).

Daughters of the American Revolution. "Index: St. John's Episcopal Church Records, 1835–71." Western Reserve Historical Society (Typewritten).

Dinwoodie, William. "St. John's Episcopal Mirrors Life and History of City for 125 Years." Cleveland *News.* November 20, 1941. Archives, Episcopal Diocese of Ohio, Trinity Cathedral, Cleveland.

Knight, Thomas A. "Re: Underground Railroad—St. John's Church Tunnel, September 1943." Western Reserve Historical Society (Typewritten).

McGuire, Tom. "Historic St. John's." *Western Reserve Magazine* (November–December, 1978): 31–32, 64–65.

Rusk, Sarah E. "Ezekiah Eldredge, Architect-Builder of St. John's Church, Cleveland, Ohio." *Journal of the Society of Architectural Historians,* 25 (March 1966): 50–58.

St. John's Episcopal Church. Records, 1835–1871. Western Reserve Historical Society (Photocopy).

St. John's Episcopal Church. Parish File. Archives, Episcopal Diocese of Ohio, Trinity Cathedral, Cleveland.

St. John's Episcopal Church. "History." Parish File. Archives, Episcopal Diocese of Ohio, Trinity Cathedral, Cleveland.

St. John's Episcopal Church. Vestry Books, 1836–63. Western Reserve Historical Society (Typewritten).

St. Paul's Episcopal Church

Jarvis, F. Washington. *St. Paul's, Cleveland, 1846–1968: A History of the Parish in Its Fortieth Year on the Heights.* Cleveland: St. Paul's Episcopal Church, 1967.

Perkins, Litta F. "History of St. Paul's Church, 1846–1918." Archives, Episcopal Diocese of Ohio, Trinity Cathedral, Cleveland (Typewritten).

St. Paul's Episcopal Church. Parish Files. Archives, Episcopal Diocese of Ohio, Trinity Cathedral, Cleveland.

St. Paul's Episcopal Church. Parish Register, 1846–52. St. Paul's Episcopal Church, Cleveland Heights, Ohio.

St. Paul's Episcopal Church. Parish Register, 1853–75. St. Paul's Episcopal Church, Cleveland Heights, Ohio.

St. Paul's Episcopal Church. Records, 1848–62. St. Paul's Episcopal Church, Cleveland Heights, Ohio.

St. Paul's Episcopal Church. [Trustees Minutes], 1852–1865. Records. Vol. 2. St. Paul's Episcopal Church, Cleveland Heights, Ohio.

St. Paul's Episcopal Church. [Vestry Minutes], 1846 to October 20, 1862. Records. Vol. 1. St. Paul's Episcopal Church, Cleveland Heights, Ohio.

Trinity Episcopal Church

Pierce, Roderic Hall. *Trinity Cathedral Parish, The First 150 Years*. Cleveland: Vestry of Trinity Cathedral, 1967.

Trinity Cathedral. *Some Sketches and Statements of Cathedral Work and Ideas*. Cleveland: Trinity Cathedral, 1899.

Trinity Cathedral. Parish Files. Archives, Episcopal Diocese of Ohio, Trinity Cathedral, Cleveland.

Trinity Church Home for the Sick and Friendless. *Twenty-Second Annual Report, 1880*. Cleveland: Short and Forman, 1881.

Trinity Episcopal Church. Minutes of Vestry, October 9, 1852 to February 20, 1855 [July 27, 1854]. Trinity Cathedral, Cleveland.

Trinity Episcopal Church. Records of the Proceedings of the Vestry of Trinity Church Cleveland Commencing Easter May 1839 [to 1864]. Trinity Cathedral, Cleveland.

Trinity Episcopal Church. [Records], November 16, 1816 to February 12, 1837, And Minutes of Vestry [1816–1839]. Trinity Parish Register. Vol. 1. Trinity Cathedral, Cleveland.

Trinity Cathedral. [Records], September 22, 1833 to December 27, 1853. Trinity Parish Register. Vol. 2. Trinity Cathedral, Cleveland.

Trinity Episcopal Church. [Records], January 1, 1854 to December 16, 1876. Trinity Parish Register. Vol. 3. Trinity Cathedral, Cleveland.

METHODIST

General

Barker, John Marshall. *History of Ohio Methodism: A Study in Social Science*. Cincinnati: Curts and Jennings, 1898.

Church of the Cross. *Dedicatory Services, 1926*. Cleveland: Church of the Cross, 1926.

Erie Conference, Methodist Episcopal Church. *Minutes, 1856–1866*. N.p.: Erie Conference, Methodist Episcopal Church, 1856–66.

Erie Conference, Methodist Episcopal Church. *Minutes of the First Twenty Sessions of the Erie Annual Conference of the Methodist Episcopal Church, 1836–55*. Meadville, PA: Erie Conference, 1907.

Fradenburgh, Rev. J.N. *History of the Erie Conference*. 2 Vols. Oil City, PA: Derrick Publishing Co., 1907.

Gregg, Samuel. *The History of Methodism Within the Bounds of the Erie Annual Conference of the Methodist Episcopal Church*. 2 Vols. New York: Nelson and Phillips, 1873.

Ingham, Mary Bigelow. "Methodism in Cleveland." In *History of Ohio Methodism*, pp. 346–55. Edited by John Marshall Barker. Cincinnati: Curts and Jennings, 1898.

King, I. F. "Introduction of Methodism in Ohio," In *Ohio Archeological and Historical Publications* 10: 165–219. Columbus: Ohio Archeological and Historical Society, 1902.

McTighe, Michael J., "Methodists." In *Encyclopedia of Cleveland History*, David D. Van Tassel, ed. Bloomington, IN: Indiana University Press, 1987, pp. 678–79.

North Ohio Conference, Methodist Episcopal Church. *Minutes, 1839–1860* N.p.: North Ohio Annual Conference, Methodist Episcopal Church, 1839–60.

Scoville Avenue Methodist Church. "Historical Record of the Scoville Avenue M.E. Church, 1882." Membership Record Book, 1882–1892. First United Methodist Church, Cleveland.

Stevenson, R. T. *One Hundred Years of Methodism in Ohio.* Cincinnati: Curts and Jennings, 1898.

Versteg, John M., ed. *Methodism: Ohio Area (1812–1962).* N.p.: Ohio Area Sesquicentennial Committee, Methodist Church, 1962.

"Willson Methodist Church." Baldwin-Wallace College, Berea, Ohio Methodist Archives, Local Church History Collection.

Bridge Street Methodist Church

Bridge Street Methodist Episcopal Church. Records 1860–1876. People's Methodist Church, Cleveland.

Elgin, W. T. "Short History of the People's Methodist Episcopal Church." People's Methodist Episcopal Church. *Official Directory*. Cleveland: People's Methodist Church, 1923.

People's Methodist Episcopal Church. *Official Directory*. Cleveland: People's Methodist Church, 1932.

Yates, Rev. Clarence M. "Brief History of People's Methodist Church." Baldwin-Wallace College, Berea, Ohio. Methodist Archives, Local Church History Collection.

Church Street Methodist Church

Benton, Horace. "Franklin Avenue M.E. Church, 1870–1895." Western Reserve Historical Society, Hope-Wesley United Methodist Church Papers, 1895.

Benton, Horace. "Hanover Street M.E. Church, 1833–1869." 1895. Western Reserve Historical Society, Hope-Wesley United Methodist Church Papers.

"The Ohio City Methodists." Western Reserve Historical Society, Hope-Wesley United Methodist Church Papers (Typewritten).

Erie Street Methodist Church

Erie Street Methodist Episcopal Church. Records. [1853–1868]. Epworth-Euclid Methodist Church, Cleveland.

Erie Street Methodist Episcopal Church. Minutes, 1850–1868. Epworth-Euclid Methodist Church, Cleveland.

Erie Street Methodist Episcopal Church. Record of the Proceedings of the Trustees, 1844–1884. Epworth-Euclid Methodist Church, Cleveland.

McMillan, Janice. Historical Record of the Erie Street Methodist Episcopal Church. Epworth-Euclid Methodist Church, Cleveland (Typewritten).

Truesdell, A. I. "Historical Record." Central Methodist Episcopal Church. Records, 1883–91. Epworth-Euclid Methodist Church, Cleveland.

First Methodist Church

Burwell, George P. Pastoral History, 1871. First Methodist Church, Records 1900–1942. Western Reserve Historical Society, Talmage Papers.

First Methodist Episcopal Church. Incorporation, 1839: The Book of Records for the First Methodist Episcopal Church of Cleveland, 1839–1845. First United Methodist Church, Cleveland.

First Methodist Episcopal Church. Membership, 1843–1854: Register for M.E. Church of Cleveland Station. First United Methodist Church, Cleveland.

First Methodist Episcopal Church. Membership Record Book, 1858–1867. First United Methodist Church, Cleveland.

First Methodist Episcopal Church. Official Board 1856–1864. First United Methodist Church, Cleveland.

First Methodist Episcopal Church. Steward's Recording Book, Cleveland Station, August 15th 1840 to 1855. First United Methodist Church, Cleveland.

First Methodist Episcopal Church. Trustees, 1839–1886: Record of the Proceedings of the Trustees of the First Methodist Episcopal Church of Cleveland. First United Methodist Church, Cleveland.

First Methodist Episcopal Church of Cleveland, Ohio, 1827–1884. Cleveland: J.B. Savage, 1884.

First United Methodist Church. *Commemorating 125 Years of Methodism in Downtown Cleveland.* Cleveland: First Methodist Church, 1952.

First United Methodist Church. *Commemorating 150 Years of Methodism in Downtown Cleveland, June 1977.* Cleveland: First United Methodist Church, 1977.

Talmage, W. C., comp. [Documents, Histories and Articles, January 24,

1918.] First Methodist Episcopal Church Records, 1900–1942. Western Reserve Historical Society, Talmage Papers.

Wesleyan Methodist Church

Kelly, S. J. "The Oldest Church on Euclid." Western Reserve Historical Society, Vertical File, Wesleyan Methodist Church.

Kelly, S. J. "Preachers of an Early Day." Western Reserve Historical Society, Vertical File, Wesleyan Methodist Church.

Skiles, Charles N. ["History of Wesley Methodist Church, Cleveland."] Baldwin-Wallace College, Berea, Ohio. Methodist Archives, Local Church History Collection.

Wesleyan Methodist Church. *Constitution, Articles and Covenant of the Wesleyan Methodist Church.* Cleveland: Francis B. Penniman, 1840.

PRESBYTERIAN

General

Baird, Samuel J. *A Collection of the Acts, Deliverances, and Testimonies of the Supreme Judicatory of the Presbyterian Church.* Philadelphia: Presbyterian Board of Publication, 1858.

Barnum, George D., "Presbyterians." In *Encyclopedia of Cleveland History,* David D. Van Tassel, ed. Bloomington, IN: Indiana University Press, 1987, pp. 789–90.

Brown, James Haldane. "Presbyterian Social Influences in Early Ohio." *Journal of the Presbyterian Historical Society* 30 (December 1952): 209–35.

Brown, James Haldane. "United Church Work in Ohio." *Journal of the Presbyterian Historical Society* 30 (June 1952): 73–94.

Cleveland Presbytery. Minutes, 1830–1883. 4 Vols. Presbytery of the Western Reserve, Cleveland (Photocopy).

Fairchild, Rev. James H. "The Story of Congregationalism in the Western Reserve." *Ohio Church History Society Papers,* 1: 1–27. Oberlin, OH: Ohio Church History Society, 1890.

Griffin, Joseph W. *History of Cleveland Presbytery of the United Presbyterian Church.* Cleveland: Cleveland Presbytery, 1933.

Griffin, Joseph W., and MacDonald, James A. "History of Cleveland Presbytery of the United Presbyterian Church." Western Reserve Historical Society, 1956.

Hall, John G. "Brief Historical Sketch of the Cleveland Presbytery, Ohio." Presbyterian Historical Society, Philadelphia.

Haydn, Hiram C. "The History of Presbyterianism in Cleveland." First

Presbyterian Church. *Annals of the First Presbyterian Church, 1820–1895*. Cleveland: Winn and Judson, 1895.

Kennedy, William S. *The Plan of Union, or, A History of the Presbyterian and Congregational Churches of the Western Reserve*. Hudson, OH: Pentagon Steam Press, 1856.

Ludlow, A. C. "Scrapbook of Clippings on Presbyterian Churches of Cleveland, 1901–1910." Western Reserve Historical Society.

Ludlow, Rev. [Arthur Clyde], and Ludlow, Mrs. Arthur Clyde. *History of Cleveland Presbyterianism with Directory of All the Churches*. Cleveland: W. M. Bayne, 1896.

Presbytery of the Western Reserve [Old School]. Records, 1858–70. Western Reserve Historical Society.

Synod of Ohio [New School]. *Historical Sketch of the Synod of Ohio, (N.S.) From 1838 to 1868*. Cincinnati: Elm St. Printing Co., 1870.

Thompson, K. O. *The Congregational Churches of Greater Cleveland*. Western Reserve Historical Society, 1951 (Typewritten).

Welsh, E. B., and others. *Buckeye Presbyterianism*. N.p.: United Presbyterian Synod of Ohio, 1968.

Wood, James. *Facts and Observations Concerning the Organization and State of the Churches in the Three Synods of Western New-York, and the Synod of the Western Reserve*. Saratoga Springs, NY: G.M. Davison, 1837.

Euclid Street Presbyterian Church

Euclid Street Presbyterian Church. *Manual*. Cleveland: Fairbanks, Benedict and Co.,1859.

Euclid Street Presbyterian Church. *Manual*. Cleveland: Leader Steam Printing House, 1870.

Euclid Street Presbyterian Church. Missionary Record. Church of the Covenant, Cleveland.

Euclid Street Presbyterian Church. Records of the Euclid Street Presbyterian Church and Society, 1853 to 1870. Church of the Covenant, Cleveland.

Euclid Avenue Presbyterian Church. Society and Trustees Record, [1851] 1853-1906. Church of the Covenant, Cleveland.

First Presbyterian Church

"An Act to Incorporate the First Presbyterian Society in the village of Cleveland, in the County of Cuyahoga, January 5, 1827." Western Reserve Historical Society.

First Presbyterian Church. *Annals of the First Presbyterian Church, 1820-1895*. Cleveland: Winn and Judson, 1895.

First Presbyterian Church. *Anniversary Celebration of the Woman's Missionary Society, Old Stone Church.* Cleveland: First Presbyterian Church, 1931.

First Presbyterian Church. Church Record, 1837–1849. First Presbyterian Church, Cleveland.

First Presbyterian Church. Church Record, 1849–1878. First Presbyterian Church, Cleveland.

First Presbyterian Church. *Church Manual.* Cleveland: Smead, 1842.

First Presbyterian Church. *The History of The Ladies' Society of the First Presbyterian Church.* Cleveland: Fairbanks and Co., 1881.

First Presbyterian Church. *In Memoriam: Rev. Wm. A. Goodrich.* Cleveland: Fairbanks, Benedict and Co., 1874.

First Presbyterian Church. *Manual.* Cleveland: Fairbanks, Benedict and Co., 1868.

First Presbyterian Church. Membership Records, 1820–1855 [1820–60]. First Presbyterian Church, Cleveland.

First Presbyterian Church. Records, 1820–1837. First Presbyterian Church, Cleveland.

First Presbyterian Church. "Souvenir of the First Presbyterian Church, March 15, 1886." Western Reserve Historical Society, Vertical File, First Presbyterian Church.

First Presbyterian Church. Trustees Minutes, 1855–1909. First Presbyterian Church, Cleveland.

Goodrich, William Henry. "Fiftieth Anniversary of the Stone Church, September 18, 1870." Western Reserve Historical Society, Vertical File.

Ludlow, Arthur C. *The Old Stone Church: The Story of a Hundred Years, 1820–1920.* Cleveland: Premier Press, 1920.

First Presbyterian Church, Ohio City

First Congregational Church. *Eightieth Anniversary of the First Congregational Church.* Cleveland: First Congregational Church, 1914.

First Congregational Church. Minutes of Church Society, January 6, 1857 to June 1, 1885. Congregational Library, Boston.

First Congregational Church. Record Book "A," December, 1834 to July, 1852 [September, 1841]. Congregational Library, Boston.

First Congregational Church. Register, 1883–92. Congregational Library, Boston.

First Presbyterian Church, Ohio City. *The History, Confession and Covenant of the First Presbyterian Church of Ohio City: With the Names of Its Members.* Ohio City: Timothy H. Smead, 1837.

Tenney, Henry M. "The History of the First Congregational Church of Cleveland." *Ohio Church History Society Papers*, 2: 26–44. Oberlin, OH: Ohio Church History Society, 1892.

Second Presbyterian Church

Bourne, Henry E. *The Church of the Covenant: The First Hundred Years.* Cleveland: Church of the Covenant, 1945.

Dockstader, C. J. *Historical Sketch of the Second Presbyterian Sunday School.* Cleveland: Leader Printing, 1883.

"The Early History of the Second Presbyterian Church of Cleveland, Ohio." Western Reserve Historical Society, Vertical File, Second Presbyterian Church.

In Memoriam: James Eells. Cleveland: W. W. Williams, 1886.

Pomeroy, C. S. "A Church History: The Growth of Second Presbyterian Church." Cleveland *Leader*, July 11, 1876, 7–8.

Pomeroy, Charles S. *An Historical Sketch Reviewing the Origin and Growth of the Second Presbyterian Church.* Cleveland: Leader Book and Job, 1876.

Second Presbyterian Church. Annual Statistics of the Second Presbyterian Church et al. at Cleveland, Ohio Since Its Organization June 12, 1844 to October 6, 1920. Church of the Covenant, Cleveland.

Second Presbyterian Church. Index, 1844–1920. Church of the Covenant, Cleveland.

Second Presbyterian Church. *Manual and Catalogue of the Second Presbyterian Church in Cleveland, Ohio from June 1844 to April 1864.* Cleveland: E. Cowles and Co., 1864. Compiled in Second Presbyterian Church, Reports and Statistics, 1844–1889. Bound collection.

Second Presbyterian Church. *Manual.* Cleveland: Harris and Fairbanks, 1854.

Second Presbyterian Church. "Manual for the communicants of the Second Presbyterian Church in Cleveland, January 1854." Cleveland: Harris and Fairbanks, 1854. Compiled in Second Presbyterian Church, Reports and Statistics, 1844–1889. Bound collection.

Second Presbyterian Church. Record, 1844–69. Church of the Covenant, Cleveland.

Second Presbyterian Church. *The Semi-Centennial Celebration.* Cleveland: Second Presbyterian Church, 1894.

Westminster Presbyterian

Handyside, James. "Westminster Presbyterian Church." January, 1916. Western Reserve Historical Society, Vertical File, Westminster Presbyterian Church.

Westminster Presbyterian Church. Session and Congregational Meeting Minutes, 1853–1880. Presbyterian Historical Society, Philadelphia.

Other English-Speaking Protestant Churches

BETHEL CHURCH

Floating Bethel City Mission. *Forty-third Thanksgiving and Christmas Appeal of the Floating Bethel and City Mission* Cleveland: Floating Bethel City Mission, [1911].

Floating Bethel and City Mission. *Chaplain J. D. Jones' 25th Annual Report and Review*. Cleveland: S. Barker and Son, 1893.

FRANKLIN CIRCLE DISCIPLES OF CHRIST CHURCH

"A Decade of Work." Cleveland *Plain Dealer*, April 9, 1894.

Flick, Marjorie R. *100th Anniversary, 1842–1942, Franklin Circle Church of Christ*. Cleveland: Franklin Circle Church of Christ, 1942.

Franklin Circle Church of Christ. *Diamond Jubilee, 1842–1917*. Cleveland: Franklin Circle Church of Christ, 1917.

Hayden, A. S. *Early History of the Disciples in the Western Reserve*. Cincinnati: Chase & Hall, 1875.

McTighe, Michael J., "Disciples of Christ." In *Encyclopedia of Cleveland History*, David D. Van Tassel, ed. Bloomington, IN: University of Indiana Press, 1987, pp. 345–46.

Peskin, Allan, *Garfield: A Biography*. Kent, OH: Kent State University Press, 1978.

Shaw, Henry K. *Buckeye Disciples: A History of the Disciples of Christ in Ohio*. St. Louis: Christian Board of Publication, Ohio Christian Missionary Society, 1952.

Wilcox, Alanson. *A History of the Disciples of Christ in Ohio*. Cincinnati: The Standard Publishing Co., 1918.

ST. JOHN AFRICAN METHODIST EPISCOPAL CHURCH

African Methodist Episcopal Church, Annual Conference. *Proceedings, 1847–1860*. N.p., n.d.

Hicks, Josephus Franklin. *St. John African Methodist Episcopal: Yesterday and Today, 1830–1955*. Cleveland: St. John A.M.E. Church, 1955.

UNITARIAN AND UNIVERSALIST

Robinson, Elmo Arnold. *The Universalist Church in Ohio*. N.p.: Ohio Universalist Convention, 1923.

Unitarian Church. *History of the Unitarian Church in Cleveland*. Cleveland: Unitarian Church, 1930.

Universalist Companion and Almanac. 1841–52.
Universalist Register and Almanac. 1837–40.
Western Reserve Association of Universalists. Minutes, 1832–1852. Andover Library, Harvard Divinity School, Cambridge, Massachusetts.

Other Religious Bodies

CATHOLIC

Bland, Joan. *Hibernian Crusade: The Story of the Catholic Total Abstinence Union of America.* Washington, DC: Catholic University Press, 1951.
Houck, George F. *A History of Catholicity in Northern Ohio and In the Diocese of Cleveland From 1749 to December 31, 1900.* Vol. 1. Cleveland: J. B. Savage, 1903.
Hynes, Michael J. *History of the Diocese of Cleveland: Origin and Growth (1847–1952).* Cleveland: Diocese of Cleveland, 1953.
Leonard, Henry B. "Ethnic Conflict and Episcopal Power: The Diocese of Cleveland, 1847–1870." *Catholic Historical Review*, 62 (July 1976): 388–407.
Leonard, Henry B. "Roman Catholics." In *Encyclopedia of Cleveland History*, David D. Van Tassel, ed. Bloomington, IN: Indiana University, 1987, pp. 162–64.
O'Grady, John. *Catholic Charities in the United States.* New York: Arno Press, 1971, orig. ed. 1931.

JEWISH

Cline, Scott. "Jews & Judaism." In *Encyclopedia of Cleveland History*, David D. Van Tassel, ed. Bloomington, IN: Indiana University Press, 1987, pp. 572–75.
Euclid Avenue Temple. *Congregation Anshe Chesed: Centennial Program.* Cleveland: Euclid Avenue Temple, 1946.
Gartner, Lloyd P. *History of the Jews of Cleveland.* Cleveland: Western Reserve Historical Society and Jewish Theological Seminary of America, 1978.
Peskin, Allan. *This Tempting Freedom: The Early Years of Cleveland Judaism and Anshe Chesed Congregation.* Cleveland: [Fairmount Temple], 1973.
Tifereth Israel Congregation. *The Temple: Fiftieth Anniversary Services.* Cleveland: Tifereth Israel Congregation, 1900.
Vincent, Sidney Z.; and Rubenstein, Judah. *Merging Traditions: Jewish Life in Cleveland.* Cleveland: The Western Reserve Historical Society and the Jewish Community Federation of Cleveland, 1978.

GERMAN LUTHERAN

Mechling, George Washington. *History of the Evangelical Lutheran District, Synod of Ohio, Covering 53 Years, 1857–1910.* Dayton, OH: Evangelical Lutheran District Synod of Ohio, 1911.

Ministers' Sermons and Speeches

Adams, Rev. S. W. *Address Before the Society of Religious Inquiry of Granville College, July 7th 1850.* Cleveland: Smead and Cowles, 1850.

Adams, S. W. *The Crowned Year: A Discourse Delivered on the Day of Annual Thanksgiving, November 25th, 1858.* Cleveland: Fairbanks, Benedict and Co., 1859.

Aiken, S. C. *Moral View of Rail Roads: A Discourse.* Cleveland: Harris, Fairbanks and Co., 1851

[Aiken] Aikin, Samuel C. *Theatrical Exhibitions: A Sermon.* Cleveland: Francis B. Penniman, 1836.

Bittenger, J. B. [Nebraska:] *A Plea for Humanity: A Sermon.* Cleveland: Medill, Cowles and Co., 1854.

Bittenger, J. B. *The True Mission of the Physician: An Address Delivered at the Commencement of the Western Reserve Medical College.* Cleveland: Cowles, Pinkerton & Co., 1856.

[Bolles, James A.] Rector, Trinity Episcopal Church. *Fourth Annual Report and Pastoral Letter.* Cleveland: Fairbanks, Benedict and Co., 1858.

[Bolles, James A.] Rector, Trinity Episcopal Church. *The Daily Worship of God in His Temple: A Sermon.* Cleveland: Cleveland Herald Printing, 1857.

Bolles, James A. *Free Churches: A Valedictory Sermon Preached in Trinity Church, Cleveland, Ohio, July 3, 1859.* Boston: Henry W. Dutton & Son, 1859. Compiled in James A. Bolles, *Sermons.* 2 Vols. N.p., n.d.

Bolles, James A. *A Free Memorial Church Salutory Address.* N.p., n.d. Compiled in James A. Bolles, *Sermons.* 2 Vol. N.p., n.d.

Bolles, James A. *Trinity Church Home for the Sick and Friendless, Twenty-Ninth Annual Report: Sermon, 1885.* Cleveland: William A. Williams, 1886. Compiled in James A. Bolles, *Sermons.* 2 Vols. N.p., n.d.

Bolles, James A, and McIlvaine, C. P. *Correspondence Between the Right Rev. C. P. McIlvaine and the Rev. James A. Bolles.* Cleveland: Harris, Fairbanks, 1857.

Brewster, W. H. *God's Law Supreme: A Sermon of the Higher Law.* Cleveland: E. Cowles and Co., 1859.

Brown, Frederick T. *Blessings of the Fig-Tree and Vine: A Thanksgiving Sermon.* Madison, WI: Courier, 1852.

Brown, Frederick T. *The Physician Should Be a Christian*. Cleveland: E. Cowles and Co., 1857.

Brown, Frederick T. *The Importance of Christian Missions*. Columbus: Statesman Steam Press, 1856.

Brown, Frederick T. *A Sermon, on the Doctrinal Differences in the "Old" and "New" School Parties in the Presbyterian Church*. Cleveland: Harris and Fairbanks, 1853.

Canfield, S. B.; Aiken, S. C.; and Blodget, H. *An Exposition of the Peculiarities, Difficulties and Tendencies of Oberlin Perfectionism Prepared By a Committee of the Presbytery of Cleveland*. Cleveland: T. H. Smead, 1841.

Canfield, Sherman. *An Address on the Power and Progressiveness of Knowledge*. Painesville, OH: Smythe and Hanna, 1843.

Canfield, Sherman. *The Indications of a Divine Purpose to Make Our Country a Model Christian Republic*. Syracuse: T. S. Truair, Daily Journal Office, 1855.

Canfield, Sherman B. *The Temporal Blessings of Christianity*. Cleveland: Smead and Cowles, 1852.

McIlvaine, C. P. *Address to the Young Men of the United States on Temperance*. N.p., n.d.

McIlvaine, C. P. *Bishop McIlvaine on the Revival of Religion*. Philadelphia: Episcopal Book Depository, 1858.

Perry, Gideon B. *An Address on the True Character of Mental Greatness*. Gambier, Ohio Theological Seminary Press, by the Philomathesian Society of Kenyon College, 1852.

Starkey, Thomas. *A Sermon in Behalf of Trinity Church Home, 1860, also The Annual Report of the Manager*. Cleveland: Nevins, Plain Dealer, 1860.

Strong, A. H. *Blessed Are the Dead Which Die in the Lord: A Sermon Preached in the First Baptist Church, Cleveland, July 7th, 1871 at the Funeral of Deacon Benjamin Rouse*. Cleveland: Fairbanks, Benedict and Co., 1872.

Thome, J. A. *Address at the Ninth Annual Meeting of the Oberlin Agricultural Society*. Oberlin, OH: J. M. Fitch, 1847.

Thome, J. A. *The Christian Teacher: On the Death of Miss Laura W. Ayer*. Cleveland: Fairbanks, Benedict and Co., 1861.

Thome, James A. *Debate at the Lane Seminary, Cincinnati: Speech of James A. Thome, May 6, 1834*. Boston: Garrison and Knapp, 1834.

Tucker, Levi. *Lectures on the Nature and Dangerous Tendency of Modern Infidelity*. Cleveland: Francis B. Penniman, 1837.

Secondary and Other Sources

Abramovitz, Mimi. *Regulating the Lives of Women: Social Welfare Policy From Colonial Times to the Present*. Boston: South End Press, 1988.

Abzug, Robert H. *Passionate Liberator: Theodore Dwight Weld and the Dilemma of Reform.* New York: Oxford University Press, 1980 (paper).

Ahlstrom, Sydney E. *A Religious History of the American People.* New Haven, CT: Yale University Press, 1972.

Albanese, Catherine L. *America: Religions and Religion.* Belmont, CA: Wadsworth, 1981.

Alburn, Wilfred Henry and Alburn, Miriam Russell. *This Cleveland of Ours.* Vol. 1. Chicago: S. J. Clarke, 1933.

Alexander, John K. *Render Them Submissive: Responses to Poverty in Philadelphia, 1760–1800.* Amherst: University of Massachusetts Press, 1980.

Alexander, Ruth M. "We Are Engaged as a Band of Sisters: Class and Domesticity in the Washingtonian Temperance Movement, 1840–1850." *Journal of American History* 75 (December 1988): 763–85.

American Seamen's Friend Society. *Thirty-Ninth Annual Report of the American Seamen's Friend Society, Including the Thirty-Ninth Annual Report of the Boston Seamen's Friend Society, the Thirty-First Annual Report of the American Bethel Society, and the Nineteenth Annual Report of the Western Seamen's Friend Society.* New York: Hallet and Breen, 1867.

Andrew, John A., III. *Rebuilding the Christian Commonwealth: New England Congregationalists and Foreign Missions, 1800–1830.* Lexington, KY: The University Press of Kentucky, 1976.

Andrews, John. Scattered Papers, 1833–1852. Ohio Historical Society.

Andrews, John B. and W. D. P. Bliss. *History of Women in Trade Unions.* New York: Arno Press, 1974; orig. ed. 1911.

Andrews, Sherlock James. Letter to Benjamin Silliman, April 20, 1844. Ohio Historical Society.

Ashworth, John. "The Relationship Between Capitalism and Humanitarianism." *American Historical Review* 92 (October 1987): 813–28.

Avery, Elroy McKendree. *A History of Cleveland and Its Environs: The Heart of New Connecticut.* Vol. 1. Chicago: Lewis, 1918.

Baghdadi, Mania Kleinburd. "Protestants, Poverty and Urban Growth: A Study of the Organization of Charity in Boston and New York, 1820–1865." Ph.D. Dissertation, Brown University, 1975.

Baker, Paula. "The Domestication of Politics: Women and American Political Society, 1780–1920." *American Historical Review* 89 (June 1984): 620–47.

Banner, Lois. "Religious Benevolence as Social Control: A Critique of an Interpretation." *Religion in American History: Interpretive Essays.* Edited by John M. Mulder and John F. Wilson. Englewood Cliffs, NJ: Prentice-Hall, 1978 (paper).

Baron, Ava, and Klepp, Susan E. "'If I Didn't Have My Sewing Machine . . . ': Women and Sewing Machine Technology." In Joan M. Jensen and Sue Davidson, eds., *A Needle, A Bobbin, A Strike: Woman Needleworkers in America* (Philadelphia: Temple University Press, 1984), pp. 20–59.

Barton, W. E. "Early Ecclesiastical History of the Western Reserve." In *Ohio Church History Society Papers* 1: 67–98.

Baum, Dale. "Know-Nothingism and the Republican Majority in Massachusetts: The Political Realignment of the 1850's." *Journal of American History* 64 (March 1978): 959–86.

Beeman, Richard R. "The New Social History and the Search for 'Community' in Colonial America." *American Quarterly* 29 (Fall 1977): 422–43.

Bell, Marion L. *Crusade in the City: Revivalism in Nineteenth-Century Philadelphia.* Lewisburg, PA: Bucknell University Press, 1977.

Bellah, Robert N., and Hammond, Phillip E. *Varieties of Civil Religion.* San Francisco: Harper and Row, 1980.

Bender, Thomas. "Making History Whole Again." *New York Times Book Review*, October 6, 1985, pp. 1, 42–43.

Bender, Thomas. *New York Intellect: A History of Intellectual Life in New York City, from 1750 to the Beginnings of Our Own Time.* Baltimore, MD: Johns Hopkins University Press, 1987.

Bender, Thomas. *Toward an Urban Vision: Ideas and Institutions in Nineteenth-Century America.* Lexington, KY: University Press of Kentucky, 1975.

Bender, Thomas. "Wholes and Parts: Continuing the Conversation." *Journal of American History* 74 (June 1987): 123–30.

Bender, Thomas. "Wholes and Parts: The Need for Synthesis in American History." *Journal of American History* 73 (June 1986): 120–36.

Benton, Elbert Jay. *Cultural Story of an American City: Cleveland.* 3 Vols. Cleveland: Western Reserve Historical Society, 1943.

Berg, Barbara J. *The Remembered Gate: Origins of American Feminism: The Woman and the City, 1800–1860.* New York: Oxford University Press, 1980 (paper).

Bilhartz, Terry D. *Urban Religion and the Second Great Awakening: Church and Society in Early National Baltimore.* Rutherford, NJ: Fairleigh Dickinson University Press, 1986.

Blackbourn, David, and Eley, Geoff. *The Peculiarities of German History: Bourgeois Society and Politics in Nineteenth-Century Germany.* New York: Oxford University Press, 1964.

Bledstein, Burton J. "Humanistic Pieties, Historical Counterpieties." *Reviews in American History* 15 (September 1987): 412–20.

Blewett, Mary. *Men, Women, and Work: Class, Gender, and Protest in the New*

England Shoe Industry, 1780–1910. Urbana: University of Illinois Press, 1988.

Blewett, Mary H. "Work, Gender, and the Artisan Tradition in New England Shoemaking, 1780–1860." *Journal of Social History* 14 (Winter 1983): 221–48.

Blumin, Stuart. "The Historical Study of Vertical Mobility." *Historical Methods Newsletter* 1 (September 1968): 1–13.

Blumin, Stuart M. *The Emergence of the Middle Class: Social Experience in the American City, 1760–1900.* New York: Cambridge University Press, 1989.

Blumin, Stuart M. "The Hypothesis of Middle-Class Formation in Nineteenth-Century America: A Critique and Some Proposals." *American Historical Review* 90 (April 1985): 299–338.

Blumin, Stuart M. *The Urban Threshold: Growth and Change in a Nineteenth-Century American Community.* Chicago: University of Chicago Press, 1976.

Boase, Paul H. "Moral Policemen on the Ohio Frontier." *Ohio Historical Quarterly* 68 (January 1959): 38–53.

The Boatman's Magazine 1 (October 1834).

Bodo, John R. *The Protestant Clergy and Public Issues, 1812–1848.* Princeton, NJ: Princeton University Press, 1954.

Bond, Beverley Waugh, Jr. *The Foundations of Ohio.* Vol. 1 of *The History of the State of Ohio.* Edited by Carl Wittke. 6 Vols. Columbus: Ohio State Archeological and Historical Society, 1941–44.

Bonkowsky, Elizabeth Leitch. "The Church and the City: The Protestant Concern for Social Problems, 1800–1840." Ph.D. Dissertation, Boston University, 1973.

Bouchard, Gerard, and Pouyez, Christian. "Name Variations and Computerized Record Linkage." *Historical Methods* 13 (Spring 1980): 119–25.

Boyd, William H., *Boyd's Cleveland City Directory: 1857.* New York: William H. Boyd, 1857.

Boyer, Paul S. *Urban Masses and Moral Order in America, 1820–1920.* Cambridge, MA: Harvard University Press, 1978.

Boylan, Anne M. "Sunday Schools and Changing Evangelical Views of Children in the 1820's." *Church History* 48 (September 1979): 320–33.

Boylan, Anne M. "Timid Girls, Venerable Widows and Dignified Matrons: Life Cycle Patterns Among Organized Women in New York and Boston, 1797–1840." *American Quarterly* 38 (Winter 1986): 779–97.

Boylan, Anne M. "Women in Groups: An Analysis of Women's Benevolent

Organizations in New York and Boston, 1797–1840." *Journal of American History* 71 (December 1984): 497–523.

Bozeman, Theodore Dwight. "Inductive and Deductive Politics: Science and Society in Antebellum Presbyterian Thought." *Journal of American History* 64 (December 1977): 704–22.

Brandt, Nat. *The Town That Started the Civil War.* Syracuse, NY: Syracuse University Press, 1990.

Braude, Ann. *Radical Spirits: Spiritualism and Women's Rights in Nineteenth-Century America.* Boston: Beacon Press, 1989.

Bremner, Robert H. *From the Depths: The Discovery of Poverty in the United States.* New York: New York University Press, 1956.

Bremner, Robert H. *The Public Good: Philanthropy and Welfare in the Civil War Era.* New York: Alfred A. Knopf, 1980.

Bridges, Amy. *A City in the Republic: Ante-bellum New York and the Origins of Machine Politics.* New York: Cambridge University Press, 1984.

Browne, Gary Lawson. *Baltimore in the Nation, 1789–1861.* Chapel Hill, NC: University of North Carolina Press, 1980.

Brown, Chandos Michael. "A Natural History of the Gloucester Sea Serpent: Knowledge, Power, and the Culture of Science in Antebellum America." *American Quarterly* 42 (September 1990): 402–36.

Brown, Richard D. *Modernization: The Transformation of American Life, 1600–1865.* New York: Hill and Wang, 1976 (paper).

Brunkow, Robert deV. "Officeholding in Providence, Rhode Island, 1646 to 1686: A Quantitative Analysis." *William and Mary Quarterly* 37 (April 1980): 242–60.

Burnham, John C. *How Superstition Won and Science Lost: Popularizing Science and Health in the United States.* New Brunswick, NJ: Rutgers University Press, 1987.

Butler, Jon. *Awash in a Sea of Faith: Christianizing the American People.* Cambridge, MA: Harvard University Press, 1990.

Callahan, Nelson J. and Hickey, William F. *Irish Americans and Their Communities of Cleveland.* Cleveland: Ohio State University Press, 1978.

Campen, Richard. "The Story of Ohio City." Western Reserve Historical Society, 1968 (Typewritten).

Cardinal, Eric. "New England and the Western Reserve in the Nineteenth Century: Some Suggestions." *Western Reserve Studies: A Journal of Regional History and Culture* 1 (1986): 13–19.

Cardinal, Eric J. "The Ohio Democracy and the Crisis of Disunion, 1860–1861." *Ohio History* 86 (Winter 1977): 19–40.

Carey, Anthony Gene. "The Second Party System Collapses: The 1853 Maine Law Campaign in Ohio." *Ohio History* 100 (Summer–Autumn 1991): 129–53.

Chapman, Edmund H. *Cleveland: Village to Metropolis. A Case Study of Problems of Urban Development in Nineteenth-Century America*. Cleveland: The Western Reserve Historical Society and the Press of Western Reserve University, 1964.

Chipman, Samuel. *The Temperance Lectures: Being Facts Gathered from a Personal Examination of All the Jails and Poorhouses of the State of New York and of Numbers in Maine, Pennsylvania, Delaware, Ohio, Indiana, &c.* Albany, NY: N.p., 1842.

Clark, Clifford E., Jr. *Henry Ward Beecher: Spokesman for a Middle-Class America*. Urbana, IL: University of Illinois Press, 1978.

Clebsch, William A. *From Sacred to Profane America: The Role of Religion in American History*. New York: Harper and Row, 1968.

Clement, Priscilla Ferguson. "The Response to Need, Welfare and Poverty in Philadelphia, 1800 to 1850." Ph.D. Dissertation, University of Pennsylvania, 1977.

Clement, Priscilla Ferguson. *Welfare and the Poor in the Nineteenth-Century City: Philadelphia, 1800–1854*. Rutherford, NJ: Fairleigh Dickinson University Press, 1985.

Cleveland, Ohio. *Charters of the Village of Cleveland, and the City of Cleveland, With Their Several Amendments: To Which Are Added the Laws and Ordinances of the City of Cleveland*. Cleveland: Sanford and Co., 1842.

Cleveland, Ohio. *Charters of the Village of Cleveland, and the City of Cleveland, With Their Several Amendments: To Which Are Added the Laws and Ordinances of the City of Cleveland*. Cleveland: Harris, Fairbanks and Co., 1851.

Cleveland, Ohio. *The Acts to Provide for the Organization of Cities and Villages: and the Revised Ordinances of the City of Cleveland*. Cleveland: *Plain Dealer*, 1862.

Cleveland, Past and Present: Its Representative Men. Cleveland: Maurice Joblin, 1869.

Cleveland Bible Society. *Annual Report*. Cleveland: Harris Fairbanks and Co., 1855.

Cleveland Bible Society. *Annual Report*. Cleveland: Harris Fairbanks and Co., 1856.

Cleveland Bible Society. *Annual Report*. Cleveland: Fairbanks, Benedict and Co., 1860.

Cleveland Centennial Commission. *History of the Charities of Cleveland, 1796–1896*. Cleveland: Cleveland Centennial Commission, 1896.

Cleveland Industrial School. *Annual Report of the Superintendent, 1858*. Cleveland: Fairbanks, Benedict and Co., 1859.

Cleveland Industrial School and Children's Aid Society. *Annual Report of the Superintendent, 1859*. Cleveland: Fairbanks, Benedict and Co., 1860.

Cleveland Orphan Asylum. *Eighth Annual Report of the Board of Managers.* Cleveland: Fairbanks, Benedict and Co., 1860.

Cleveland Orphan Asylum. *Fifth Annual Report.* Cleveland: Harris, Fairbanks and Co., 1857.

Cleveland Orphan Asylum. *Ninth Annual Report of the Board of Managers.* Cleveland: Fairbanks, Benedict and Co., 1861.

Cleveland Orphan Asylum. *Report of the Board of Managers.* Cleveland: Fairbanks, Benedict and Co., 1859.

Clinton, Catherine. *The Other Civil War: American Women in the Nineteenth Century.* New York: Hill and Wang, 1984 (paper).

Clinton, Catherine. *The Plantation Mistress: Woman's World in the Old South.* New York: Pantheon Books, 1982.

Clydesdale, Tiimothy T. "Soul Winning and Social Work: Giving and Caring in the Evangelical Tradition." In Robert Wuthrow, Virginia A. Hodgkinson, and Associates, *Faith and Philanthropy in America: Exploring the Role of Religion in America's Voluntary Sector.* San Francisco: Jossey-Bass Publishers, 1990, pp. 187–210.

Coates, William R. *A History of Cuyahoga County and the City of Cleveland: Historical and Biographical.* Vol. 1. Chicago: American Historical Society, 1924.

Cole, Charles C. *The Social Ideas of the Northern Evangelists, 1826–1860.* New York: Columbia University Press, 1954.

Collins, B. W. "Economic Issues in Ohio's Politics During the Recession of 1857–8." *Ohio History* 89 (Winter 1980): 47–64.

Conant, William C. *Narratives of Remarkable Conversions and Revival Incidents: Including. . . . An Account of the Rise and Progress of the Great Awakening of 1857–8 with an Introduction by Henry Ward Beecher.* New York: Derby and Jackson, 1858.

Condran, Gretchen, and Seaman, Jeff. "Linkage of the 1800–81 Philadelphia Death Register to the 1880 Manuscript Census: A Comparison of Hand- and Machine-Record Linkage Techniques." *Historical Methods* 14 (Spring 1981): 73–84.

Condran, Gretchen A., and Seaman, Jeff. "Linkage of the 1880–81 Philadelphia Death Register to the 1880 Manuscript Census: Procedures and Preliminary Results." Paper presented at the annual meeting of the Population Association of America, April 26–28, 1979. Available from Philadelphia Social History Project.

Conzen, Kathleen Neils. *Immigrant Milwaukee, 1836–1860: Accommodation and Community in a Frontier City.* Cambridge, MA: Harvard University Press, 1976.

Cook, Edward M., Jr. *The Fathers of the Towns: Leadership and Community Structure in Eighteenth-Century New England.* Baltimore: The Johns Hopkins University Press, 1976 (paper).

Corrigan, John. *The Hidden Balance; Religion and the Social Theories of Charles Chauncey and Jonathan Mayhew.* New York: Cambridge University Press, 1987.

Cott, Nancy F. *The Bonds of Womanhood: "Woman's Sphere" in New England, 1780–1835.* New Haven: Yale University Press, 1978 (paper).

Cray, Robert E., Jr. *Paupers and Poor Relief in New York City and Its Rural Environs, 1700–1830.* Philadelphia: Temple University Press, 1988.

Cronon, William. *Nature's Metropolis: Chicago and the Great West.* New York: W. W. Norton, 1992.

Cross, Barbara M. *Horace Bushnell: Minister to a Changing America.* Chicago: University of Chicago Press, 1958.

Cross, Whitney. *The Burned-Over District: The Social and Intellectual History of Enthusiastic Religion in Western New York, 1800–1850.* New York: Harper and Row, 1950 (paper).

Daniels, Bruce C. *The Connecticut Town: Growth and Development, 1635–1790.* Middletown, CT: Wesleyan University Press, 1979.

Daniels, George H. *American Science in the Age of Jackson.* New York: Columbia University Press, 1968.

Dannenbaum, Jed. "Drink and Disorder: Temperance Reform in Cincinnati, 1841–1874." Ph.D. Dissertation, University of California, Davis, 1978.

Dannenbaum, Jed. "Immigrants and Temperance: Ethnocultural Conflict in Cincinnati, 1845–1860." *Ohio History* 87 (Spring 1978): 125–39.

Davis, David Brion, ed. *Ante-Bellum Reform.* New York: Harper and Row, 1967 (paper).

Davis, David Brion. "Reflections on Abolitionism and Ideological Hegemony." *American Historical Review* 92 (October 1987): 797–812.

Davis, Russell H. *Black Americans in Cleveland From George Peake to Carl B. Stokes, 1796–1969.* Washington, DC: The Associated Publishers, 1972.

Davis, Susan G. *Parades and Power: Street Theatre in Nineteenth-Century Philadelphia.* Philadelphia: Temple University Press, 1986.

Dawley, Alan. *Class and Community: The Industrial Revolution in Lynn.* Cambridge, MA: Harvard University Press, 1976 (paper).

Dawson, Cole Patrick. "Yankees in the Queen City: The Social and Intellectual Contributions of New Englanders in Cincinnati, 1820–1850." Ph.D. Dissertation, Miami University, 1977.

Degler, Carl N. *At Odds: Women and the Family from the Revolution to the Present.* New York: Oxford University Press, 1981 (paper).

Demming, David W. "A Social and Demographic Study of Cuyahoga County Blacks, 1820–1860." M.A. thesis, Kent State University, 1976.

Dodd, Jill Siegel. "The Working Classes and the Temperance Movement in Antebellum Boston." *Labor History* 19 (Fall 1978): 510–31.

Doherty, Robert W. "Sociology, Religion, and Historians." *Historical Methods Newsletter* 6 (September 1973): 161–69.

Dolan, Jay P. *The Immigrant Church: New York's Irish and German Catholics, 1815–1865*. Baltimore: Johns Hopkins University Press, 1975 (paper).

Douglas, Ann. *The Feminization of American Culture*. New York: Avon, 1977 (paper).

Doyle, Don Harrison. *The Social Order of a Frontier Community: Jacksonville, Illinois, 1825–1870*. Urbana, IL: University of Illinois Press, 1978.

Dublin, Thomas. *Women at Work: The Transformation of Work and Community in Lowell, Massachusetts, 1826–60*. New York: Columbia University Press, 1979 (paper).

Dunn, Mary Maples. "Saints and Sinners: Congregational and Quaker Women in the Early Colonial Period." *Women in American Religion*. Edited by Janet Wilson James. Philadelphia: University of Pennsylvania Press, 1980 (paper).

Dunstan, J. Leslie. *A Light to the City: 150 Years of the City Missionary Society of Boston, 1816–1966*. Boston: Beacon Press, 1966.

Dykstra, Robert. *The Cattle Towns: A Social History of the Kansas Cattle Trading Centers, 1867 to 1885*. New York: Atheneum, 1972.

Early Settlers' Association of Cuyahoga County. *Annals*. 11 Vols. Cleveland: Mount and Carroll, 1880–1931.

Ebner, Michael H. "Urban History: Retrospect and Prospect." *Journal of American History* 68 (June 1981): 69–84.

Elliott, Emery. "The Dove and Serpent: The Clergy in the American Revolution." *American Quarterly* 31 (Summer 1979): 187–203.

Ellwood, Robert S., Jr. *Alternative Altars: Unconventional and Eastern Spirituality in America*. Chicago: University of Chicago Press, Phoenix, 1979.

Epstein, Barbara Leslie. *The Politics of Domesticity: Women, Evangelism, and Temperance in Nineteenth-Century America*. Middletown, CT: Wesleyan University Press, 1981.

Evans, Sara M. *Born for Liberty: A History of Women in America*. New York: Free Press, Macmillan, 1989.

Faler, Paul. "Cultural Aspects of the Industrial Revolution: Lynn, Massachusetts, Shoemakers and Industrial Morality, 1826–1860." *American Workingclass Culture*. Edited by Milton Cantor. Westport, CT: Greenwood Press, 1979.

Farnam, Anne. "A Society of Societies: Associations and Voluntarism in Early Nineteenth-Century Salem." *Essex Institute Historical Collections* 113 (July 1977): 181–90.

Flack, Irwin F. "Who Governed Cincinnati? A Comparative Analysis of Government and Social Structure in a Nineteenth-Century River City: 1819–1860." Ph.D. Dissertation, University of Pittsburgh, 1978.

Formisano, Ronald P. *The Birth of Mass Political Parties: Michigan, 1827–1861.* Princeton: Princeton University Press, 1971.

Foster, Charles I. *An Errand of Mercy: The Evangelical United Front, 1790–1837.* Chapel Hill: University of North Carolina Press, 1960.

Fox-Genovese, Elizabeth. *Within the Plantation Household: Black and White Women of the Old South.* Chapel Hill: University of North Carolina Press, 1988.

Fox, Stephen C. "The Bank War, the Idea of 'Party,' and the Division of the Electorate in Jacksonian Ohio." *Ohio History* 88 (Summer 1979): 253–76.

Fox, Stephen C. "Politicians, Issues, and Voter Preference in Jacksonian Ohio A Critique of an Interpretation." *Ohio History* 86 (Summer 1977): 155–70.

Friedman, Jean E. *The Enclosed Garden: Women and Community in the Evangelical South, 1830–1900.* Chapel Hill: University of North Carolina Press, 1985.

Frisch, Michael H. *Town Into City: Springfield, Massachusetts and the Meaning of Community.* Cambridge, MA: Harvard University Press, 1972.

Fuller, Robert G. *Mesmerism and the American Cure of Souls.* Philadelphia: University of Pennsylvania Press, 1982.

Gardner, Deborah S. "'A Paradise of Fashion': A. T. Stewart's Department Store, 1862–1875." In Joan M. Jensen and Sue Davidson, eds., *A Needle, A Bobbin, A Strike: Women Needleworkers in America.* Philadelphia: Temple University Press, 1984.

Gaustad, Edwin S. *The Rise of Adventism: Religion and Society in Mid-Nineteenth-Century America.* New York: Harper and Row, 1974.

Gaylin, Willard; Glasser, Ira; Marcus, Steven; and Rothman, David. *Doing Good: The Limits of Benevolence.* New York: Pantheon Books, 1976.

Geffen, Elizabeth M. "Philadelphia Protestantism Reacts to Social Reform Movements Before the Civil War." *Pennsylvania History* 30 (April 1963): 192–211.

Gerber, David. *The Making of an American Pluralism, Buffalo, New York, 1825–60.* Urbana: University of Illinois Press, 1989.

Gilkeson, John S., Jr. *Middle-Class Providence, 1820–1940.* Princeton: Princeton University Press, 1986.

Ginzberg, Lori D. "'Moral Suasion is Moral Balderdash': Women, Politics, and Social Activism in the 1850's." *Journal of American History* 73 (December 1986): 601–22.

Ginzberg, Lori D. *Women and the Work of Benevolence: Morality, Politics, and*

Class in the Nineteenth-Century United States. New Haven, CT: Yale University Press, 1990.

Glasco, Laurence A. "Computerizing the Manuscript Census." *Historical Methods Newsletter* 3 (December 1969): 1–4.

Glasco, Laurence A. "Computerizing the Manuscript Census: Part II." *Historical Methods Newsletter* 3 (March 1970): 20–21.

Glassberg, David. "History and the Public: Legacies of the Progressive Era." *Journal of American History* 73 (March 1987): 957–80.

Glazer, Walter S. "Participation and Power: Voluntary Associations and the Functional Organization of Cincinnati in 1840." *Historical Methods Newsletter* 5 (September 1972): 151–68.

Goldfield, David R. *Urban Growth in the Age of Sectionalism: Virginia, 1847–1860*. Baton Rouge, LA: Louisiana State University Press, 1977.

Goodman, Paul. "A Guide to American Church Membership Data Before the Civil War." *Historical Methods Newsletter* 10 (Spring 1977): 85–89.

Gorrell, Donald K. "Presbyterians in the Ohio Temperance Movement of the 1850's." *Ohio Archeological and Historical Quarterly* 60 (July 1951): 292–96.

Goulder, Grace. *John D. Rockefeller: The Cleveland Years*. Cleveland: Western Reserve Historical Society, 1972.

Griffin, Clifford S. *Their Brothers' Keepers: Moral Stewardship in the United States, 1800–1850*. New Brunswick, NJ: Rutgers University Press, 1960.

Griffen, Clyde and Griffen, Sally. *Natives and Newcomers: The Ordering of Opportunity in Mid-Nineteenth-Century Poughkeepsie*. Cambridge, MA: Harvard University Press, 1978.

Griswold, S. O. "The Corporate Birth and Growth of the City of Cleveland." Tract no. 62. Cleveland: Western Reserve and Northern Ohio Historical Society, 1884.

Gusfield, Joseph R. *Symbolic Crusade: Status Politics and the American Temperance Movement*. Urbana, IL: University of Illinois Press, 1966.

Guth, Gloria. "Surname Spellings and Computerized Record Linkage." *Historical Methods Newsletter* 10 (December 1976): 10–19.

Gutman, Herbert G. "Work, Culture, and Society in Industrializing America, 1815–1919." *Work, Culture, and Society in Industrializing America*. New York: Random House, 1977 (paper).

Hall, Peter Dobkin. "The History of Religous Philanthropy in America." In Robert Wuthnow, Virginia A. Hodgkinson, and Associates, *Faith and Philanthropy in America: Exploring the Role of Religion in America's Voluntary Sector*. San Francisco: Jossey-Bass Publishers, 1990, pp. 38–62.

Hammack, David C. "Problems in the Historical Study of Power in the Cities and Towns of the United States, 1800–1960." *American Historical Review* 83 (April 1978): 323–49.

Handler, Joel F. "Assault on the Ablebodied." *Reviews in American History* 15 (September 1987): 394–401.

Handy, Robert T. *A Christian America: Protestant Hopes and Historical Realities.* New York: Oxford University Press, 1971.

Handy, Robert T. *A History of the Churches of the United States and Canada.* New York: Oxford University Press, 1979 (paper).

Handy, Robert T. "The City and the Church: Historical Interlockings." *Will the Church Lose the City?* Edited by Kendig Brubaker Cully and F. Nile Harper. New York: World Publishing, 1969.

Harris, Carl V. "The Underdeveloped Historical Dimension of the Study of Community Power Structure." *Historical Methods Newsletter* 9 (September 1976): 195–200.

Harris, Marc L. "The Process of Voluntary Association: Organizing the Ravenna Temperance Society, 1830." *Ohio History* 94 (Summer–Autumn 1985): 158–70.

Haskell, Thomas L. "Capitalism and the Origins of the Humanitarian Sensibility, Part 1." *American Historical Review* 90 (April 1985): 339–61.

Haskell, Thomas L. "Capitalism and the Origins of the Humanitarian Sensibility, Part 2." *American Historical Review* 90 (June 1985): 547–66.

Haskell, Thomas L. "Convention and Hegemonic Interest in the Debate over Antislavery: A Reply to Davis and Ashworth." *American Historical Review* 92 (October 1987): 829–78.

Hatch, Nathan O. *The Democratization of American Christianity.* New Haven, CT: Yale University Press, 1989.

Hatcher, Harlan. *A Century of Iron and Men.* Indianapolis: Bobbs-Merrill, 1950.

Hatcher, Harlan. *The Western Reserve: The Story of New Connecticut in Ohio.* Cleveland: World Publishing Co., 1966.

Hawes, Joseph M. *Children in Urban Society: Juvenile Delinquency in Nineteenth-Century America.* New York: Oxford University Press, 1971.

Heale, M. J. "From City Fathers to Social Critics: Humanitarianism and Government in New York, 1790–1860." *Journal of American History* 61 (June 1976): 21–41.

Henry, Alice. *The Trade Union Woman.* New York: Burt Franklin, 1973.

Hershberg, Theodore; Burstein, Alan; and Dockhorn, Robert. "Record Linkage." *Historical Methods Newsletter* 9 (March–June 1976): 137–63.

Hershberg, Theodore; Dockhorn, Robert, "Occupational Classification." *Historical Methods Newsletter* 9 (March–June 1976): 59–98.

Hershberg, Theodore, et al., "Occupation and Ethnicity in Five Nineteenth-Century Cities: A Collaborative Inquiry." *Historical Methods Newsletter* 7 (June 1974): 174–216.

Hewitt, Nancy A. *Women's Activism and Social Change: Rochester, New York, 1822–1872*. Ithaca, NY: Cornell University Press, 1984.

Heyrman, Christine Leigh, "The Fashion Among Morally Superior People: Charity and Social Change in Provincial New England, 1700–1740." *American Quarterly* 34 (Summer 1982): 107–24.

Higham, John. "Hanging Together: Divergent Unities in American History." *Journal of American History* 61 (June 1974): 5–28.

Hills, Mrs. Nathan Cushman. *Memories*. Cleveland: Imperial Press, 1899.

Hirsch, Susan E. *Roots of the American Working Class*. Philadelphia: University of Pennsylvania Press, 1978.

Hodge, O. J. *Reminiscences*. 2 Vols. Cleveland: Imperial Press, 1902.

Holt, Edgar Allan. *Party Politics in Ohio*. Columbus: F. J. Heer, 1931.

Hood, Fred J. *Reformed America: The Middle and Southern States, 1783–1837*. University, AL: University of Alabama Press, 1980.

Horowitz, Helen Lefkowitz. *Culture and the City: Cultural Philanthropy in Chicago from the 1880's to 1917*. Lexington: University Press of Kentucky, 1976.

Hosay, Philip M. *The Challenge of Urban Poverty: Charity Reformers in New York City, 1835–1890*. New York: Arno Press, 1980.

Hovenkamp, Herbert. *Science and Religion in America, 1800–1860*. Philadelphia: University of Pennsylvania Press, 1978.

Howe, Henry. *Historical Collections of Ohio*. 2 Vols. Columbus, OH: Henry Howe and Son, 1889, 1891.

Ingham, John H. "Rags to Riches Revisited: The Effect of City Size and Related Factors on the Recruitment of Business Leaders." *Journal of American History* 63 (December 1976): 615–37.

Ingham, Mrs. W. A. *Women of Cleveland and Their Work*. Cleveland: W. A. Ingham, 1893.

Jaker, Frederic Cople. *The Urban Establishment: Upper Strata in Boston, New York, Charleston, Chicago, and Los Angles*. Urbana, IL: University of Illinois Press, 1982.

James, Janet Wilson. "Women in American Religious History: An Overview." *Women in American Religion*. Edited by Janet Wilson James. Philadelphia: University of Pennsylvania Press, 1980 (paper).

Jensen, Joan M. and Davidson, Sue, eds. *A Needle, A Bobbin, A Strike: Women Needleworkers in America*. Philadelphia: Temple University Press, 1984.

Jensen, Richard. "New Presses for Old Grapes: I: Multiple Classification Analysis." *Historical Methods* 11 (Fall 1978): 174–76.

Johnson, Crisfield. *History of Cuyahoga County, Ohio*. Cleveland: D. W. Ensign and Co., 1879.

Johnson, Curtis D. *Islands of Holiness: Rural Religion in Upstate New York, 1790–1860.* Ithaca, NY: Cornell University Press, 1989.

Johnson, Paul E. *A Shopkeeper's Millenium: Society and Revivals in Rochester, New York, 1815–1837.* New York: Hill and Wang, 1978 (paper).

Johnson, R. Christian. "A Procedure for Sampling the Manuscript Census Schedules." *Journal of Interdisciplinary History* 8 (Winter 1978): 515–30.

Johnson, R. Christian. "The 1900 Census Sampling Project: Methods and Procedures for Sampling and Data Entry." *Historical Methods* 11 (Fall 1978): 147–51.

Kaiser, Clara Anne. "Organized Social Work in Cleveland, Its History and Setting." Ph.D. Dissertation, Ohio State University, 1936.

Kasson, John F. *Civilizing the Machine: Technology and Republican Values in America, 1776–1900.* New York: Penguin, 1977 (paper).

Katz, Michael B. "Occupational Classification in History." *Journal of Interdisciplinary History* 3 (Summer 1972): 63–88.

Katz, Michael B. and Tiller, John. "Record Linkage for Everyman: A Semi-Automated Process." *Historical Methods Newsletter* 5 (September 1972): 144–50.

Katz, Michael B. *The People of Hamilton, Canada West: Family and Clan in a Mid-Nineteenth-Century City.* Cambridge, MA: Harvard University Press, 1975.

Katz, Michael B. "Social Class in North American Urban History." *Journal of Interdisciplinary History* 11 (Spring 1981): 579–605.

Katz, Michael B. *In the Shadow of the Poorhouse: A History of Social Welfare in America.* New York: Basic Books, 1986.

Kelly, Dennis. "Linking Nineteenth-Century Manuscript Records: A Computer Strategy." *Historical Methods Newsletter* 7 (March 1974): 72–82.

Kennedy, James Harrison. *A History of The City of Cleveland, Its Settlement, Rise and Progress, 1796–1896.* Cleveland: The Imperial Press, 1896.

Kerber, Linda K. "Separate Spheres, Female Worlds, Woman's Place: The Rhetoric of Women's History." *Journal of American History* 75 (June 1988): 9–39.

Kerr, Howard, and Crow, Charles L. *The Occult in America: New Historical Perspectives.* Urbana, IL: University of Illinois Press, 1983.

Kett, Joseph. "Growing Up in Rural New England, 1800–1840." *Anonymous Americans: Explorations in Nineteenth-Century Social History.* Edited by Tamara K. Hareven. Englewood Cliffs, NJ: Prentice-Hall, 1971.

Kingsbury, Harmon. *The Sabbath: A Brief History of Laws, Petitions, Remonstrances and Reports, With Facts and Arguments, Relating to the Christian Sabbath.* New York: Robert Carter, 1840.

Klassen, William. "The City from a Biblical Standpoint." *Will the Church Lose the City?* Edited by Kendig Brubaker Cully and F. Nile Harper. New York: World Publishing, 1969.

Kleppner, Paul. *The Cross of Culture: A Social Analysis of Midwestern Politics, 1850–1900.* New York: The Free Press, 1970.

Kloppenberg, James T., "The Virtues of Liberalism: Christianity, Republicanism, and Ethics in Early American Political Discourse." *Journal of American History* 74 (June 1987): 9–33.

Knight and Parson's Business Directory of the City of Cleveland. Cleveland: E. G. Knight and Co., and Parsons and Co., 1853.

Knights, Peter K. "Accuracy of Age Reporting in the Manuscript Federal Censuses of 1850 and 1860." *Historical Methods Newsletter* 4 (June 1971): 79–83.

Knights, Peter K. "City Directories as Aids to Ante-Bellum Urban Studies." *Historical Methods Newsletter* 2 (September 1969): 1–10.

Knights, Peter K. "A Method for Estimating Census Under-Enumeration." *Historical Methods Newsletter* 3 (December 1969): 5–7.

Kohl, Lawrence Frederick. "Republicanism Meets the Market Revolution." *Reviews in American History,* 19 (June 1991): 188–93.

Kosher, John Leo. "Cleveland Has Rich Industrial Past." *Cleveland Plain Dealer,* April 17, 1978, p. C–9.

Kranzberg, Melvin. "Prerequisites for Industrialization." In Melvin Kranzberg and Carroll W. Pursell, Jr., *Technology in Western Civilization: The Emergence of Modern Industrial Society, Earliest Times to 1900.* Vol. 1. New York: Oxford University Press, 1967, pp. 217–30.

Kremm, Thomas. "Cleveland and the First Lincoln Election: The Ethnic Response to Nativism." *Journal of Interdisciplinary History* 8 (Summer 1977): 69–86.

Kremm, Thomas W. "Measuring Religious Preferences in Nineteenth-Century Urban Areas." *Historical Methods Newsletter* 9 (September 1975): 137–41.

Kulik, Gary B. "Patterns of Resistance to Industrial Capitalism: Pawtucket Village and the Strike of 1824." *American Workingclass Culture: Explorations in American Labor and Social History.* Edited by Milton Cantor. Westport, CT: Greenwood Press, 1979.

Kusmer, Kenneth L. *A Ghetto Takes Shape: Black Cleveland, 1870–1930.* Urbana, IL: University of Illinois Press, 1976.

Kutolowski, Kathleen Smith. "Antimasonry Reexamined: Social Bases of the Grass-Roots Party." *Journal of American History* 71 (September 1984): 269–93.

Kutolowski, Kathleen Smith. "Identifying the Religious Affiliations of

Nineteenth-Century Local Elites." *Historical Methods Newsletter* 9 (December 1975): 1–13.

Lasser, Carol. "The Domestic Balance of Power: Relations Between Mistress and Maid in Nineteenth-Century New England." *Labor History* 28 (Winter 1987): 5–22.

Laurie, Bruce. "Nothing on Compulsion: Life Styles of Philadelphia Artisans, 1820–1850." *American Workingclass Culture: Explorations in American Labor and Social History.* Edited by Milton Cantor. Westport, CT: Greenwood Press, 1979.

Lears, T. J. Jackson. "The Concept of Cultural Hegemony: Problems and Possibilities." *American Historical Review* 90 (June 1985): 567–93.

Lebsock, Suzanne. *The Free Women of Petersburg: Status and Culture in a Southern Town, 1784–1860.* New York: W. W. Norton, 1984.

Lee, Robert, ed. *Cities and Churches: Readings on the Urban Church.* Philadelphia: Westminster Press, 1962.

Leiby, James. *A History of Social Welfare and Social Work in the United States.* New York: Columbia University Press, 1978.

Leonard, Henry B. "Nineteenth-Century Cleveland: From New England Village to Polyglot Metropolis." *Western Reserve Studies: A Journal of Regional History and Culture* 3 (1988): 1–11.

Lerner, Gerda. "The Lady and the Mill Girl: Changes in the Status of Women in the Age of Jackson." *Our American Sisters: Women in American Life and Thought.* 2nd ed. Edited by Jean E. Friedman and William G. Slade. Boston: Allyn and Bacon, 1976 (paper).

Levine, Susan. "Labor's True Woman: Domesticity and Equal Rights in the Knights of Labor." *Journal of American History* 70 (September 1983): 323–39.

Lindberg, David C. and Numbers, Ronald L. *God and Nature: Historical Essays on the Encounter Between Christianity and Science.* Berkeley: University of California Press, 1986.

Lindenmeyr, Adele. "Why Did They Give? Social Influences on the Motives of Russian Philanthropists." Paper delivered at AAASS National Convention, New Orleans, November 22, 1986.

Lottich, Kenneth V. *New England Transplanted: A Study of the Development of Education and Other Cultural Agencies in the Connecticut Western Reserve in the National and Philosophical Setting.* Dallas, TX: Royal Publishing Co., 1964.

Loveland, Anne C. *Southern Evangelicals and the Social Order, 1800–1860.* Baton Rouge, LA: Louisiana State University Press, 1980.

Lowrey, Robert. Letter to Wm. Lowrey, Aug. 9, 1836. Archives, Ohio Historical Society.

Lukonic, Joseph Lee. "Evangelicals in the City: Evangelical Protestant

Social Concerns in Early Chicago, 1837–1860." Ph.D. Dissertation, University of Wisconsin, 1979.

MacCabe, Julius P. Bolivar. *Directory: Cleveland and Ohio City, For the Years 1837–38*. Cleveland: Sanford and Lott, 1837.

McCarthy, Kathleen D. "Consensus Revisited." *Reviews in American History* 9 (September 1981): 377–81.

McKelvey, Blake. *Rochester, The Water-Power City, 1812–1854*. Cambridge, MA: Harvard University Press, 1945.

McKelvey, Blake. *Rochester, The Flower City, 1855–1890*. Cambridge, MA: Harvard University Press,1949.

McElroy, James Logan. "Social Reform in the Burned-Over District: Rochester, New York, As a Test Case." Ph.D. Dissertation, State University of New York at Binghamton, 1974.

McLoughlin, William G. *The Meaning of Henry Ward Beecher: An Essay on the Shifting Values of Mid-Victorian America, 1840–1870*. New York: Alfred A. Knopf, 1970.

McLoughlin, William G. *Modern Revivalism*. New York: Ronald Press, 1959.

McLoughlin, William G. *Revivals, Awakenings and Reform: An Essay on Religion and Social Change in America, 1607–1977*. Chicago: University of Chicago Press, 1978.

McManis, Michael Allen. "Range Ten, Town Four: A Social History of Hudson, Ohio, 1799–1840." Ph.D. Dissertation, Case Western Reserve University, 1976.

McTighe, Michael J. "Babel and Babylon on the Cuyahoga: Religious Diversity in Cleveland, 1865–1929." In *The Birth of Modern Cleveland, 1865–1929*, ed. Thomas F. Campbell and Edward M. Miggins. Cleveland: Western Reserve Historical Society, 1988, pp. 231–69.

McTighe, Michael J. "Embattled Establishment: Protestants and Power in Cleveland, 1836–1860." Ph.D. Dissertation, University of Chicago, 1983.

McTighe, Michael J. "Leading Men, True Women, Protestant Churches and the Shape of Ante-bellum Benevolence." In *Cleveland: A Tradition of Reform*, ed. David D. Van Tassel and John Grabowski. Kent, OH: Kent State University Press, 1986, pp. 12–28.

McTighe, Michael J. "The Protestant Benevolent Community and the Limits of the Female Sphere: Poor Relief and Labor Organizations in Early Nineteenth-Century Cleveland." *Labor History* 27 (Spring 1986): 227–56.

McTighe, Michael J. "Religion." In *Encyclopedia of Cleveland History*, David D. Van Tassel, ed. Bloomington, IN: Indiana University Press, 1987, pp. 825–29.

Marty, Martin E. *A Nation of Behavers*. Chicago: University of Chicago Press, 1976 (paper).

Marty, Martin E. *Righteous Empire: The Protestant Experience in America*. New York: Dial, 1970 (paper).

Marx, Leo. *The Machine in the Garden: Technology and the Pastoral Ideal in America*. 1976 ed. New York: Oxford University Press, 1964 (paper).

Mason, I. N., ed. *Smead and Cowles' General Business Directory For the City of Cleveland*. Cleveland: Smead and Cowles, 1850.

Mathews, Donald G. *Religion in the Old South*. Chicago: University of Chicago Press, 1977.

Mathews, Donald G. "The Second Great Awakening as an Organizing Process, 1780–1830." *American Quarterly* 21 (Spring 1969): 23–43.

Mathews, Fred. "Hobbesian Populism: Interpretive Paradigms and Moral Vision in American Historiography." *Journal of American History* 72 (June 1985): 92–115.

Mead, Sidney E. *The Lively Experiment: The Shaping of Christianity in America*. New York: Harper and Row, 1963.

Mead, Sidney E. *The Nation With the Soul of a Church*. New York: Harper and Row, 1975.

Mead, Sidney E. *The Old Religion in the Brave New World: Reflections of the Relation Between Christendom and the Republic*. Berkeley, CA: University of California Press, 1977.

Melder, Keith. *Beginnings of Sisterhood: The American Woman's Rights Movement, 1800–1850*. New York: Schocken, 1977.

Melder, Keith. "Ladies Bountiful: Organized Women's Benevolence in Early 19th-Century America." *New York History* 48 (July 1967): 231–54.

Mennel, Robert M. "'The Family System of Common Farmers': The Early Years of Ohio's Reform Farm 1858–1884." *Ohio History* 89 (Summer 1980): 279–322.

Mennel, Robert M. "'The Family System of Common Farmers': The Origins of Ohio's Reform Farm, 1840–1858." *Ohio History* 89 (Spring 1980): 126–56.

Mennel, Robert M. *Thorns and Thistles: Juvenile Delinquents in the Unites States, 1825–1940*. Hanover, NH: University Press of New England, 1973.

Miller, Carol Poh and Robert Wheeler. *Cleveland: A Concise History, 1796–1990*. Bloomington, IN: Indiana University Press, 1990.

Miller, Kenneth D. and Miller, Ethel Prince. *The People Are the City: 150 Years of Religious Concern in New York City*. New York: The Macmillan Company, 1962.

Mohl, Raymond A. *Poverty in New York, 1783–1825*. New York: Oxford University Press, 1971.

Mona's Relief Society. *100th Anniversary of the Mona's Relief Society*. Cleveland: Mona's Relief Society, 1951.

Mona's Relief Society. *The Mona's Relief Society, 75th Anniversary, 1851–1926*. Cleveland: Mona's Relief Society, 1926.

Montgomery, David. "The Working Classes of the Pre-Industrial American City, 1780–1830." *Labor History* 9 (Winter 1968): 3–22.

Moore, James R. "Geologists and Interpreters of Genesis in the Nineteenth Century." In David C. Lindberg and Ronald L. Numbers, *God and Nature: Historical Essays on the Encounter Between Christinity and Science*. Berkeley: University of California Press, 1986, pp. 322–50.

Moore, Paul. *The Church Reclaims the City*. New York: Seabury Press, 1964.

Moore, R. Laurence. *In Search of White Crows: Spiritualism, Parapsychology, and American Culture*. New York: Oxford University Press, 1977.

Moorhead, James H. "Between Progress and Apocalypse: A Reassessment of Millennialism in American Religious Thought, 1800–1880." *Journal of American History* 71 (December 1984): 524–42.

Moorhead, James H. "Social Reform and the Divided Conscience of Antebellum Protestantism." *Church History* 48 (December 1979): 416–30.

Moran, Gerald F. "'Sisters' in Christ: Women and the Church in Seventeenth-Century New England." *Women in American Religion*. Edited by Janet Wilson James. Philadelphia: University of Pennsylvania Press, 1980 (paper).

Morgan, Edmund S. "The Puritan Ethic and the American Revolution." *The Reinterpretation of the American Revolution, 1763–1789*. Edited by Jack P. Greene. New York: Harper and Row, 1968 (paper).

Morton, Marian J. "Homes for Poverty's Children: Cleveland's Orphanages, 1851–1933." *Ohio History* 98 (Winter–Spring 1989): 5–22.

Noll, Mark A. *A History of Christianity in the United States and Canada*. Grand Rapids, MI: Eerdmans, 1992.

Norton, Mary Beth. "The Evolution of White Women's Experience in Early America." *American Historical Review* 89 (June 1984): 593–619.

Norton, Wesley. *Religious Newspapers in the Old Northwest to 1861: A History, Bibliography and Record of Opinion*. Athens, OH: Ohio University Press, 1977.

Odendahl, Teresa. *Charity Begins at Home: Generosity and Self-Interest Among the Philanthropic Elite*. New York: Basic Books, 1990.

"Organization of Churches." Connecticut Land Company. Records. Western Reserve Historical Society.

Ornstein, Michael D., and Darroch, A. Gordon. "Error in Historical Data

Files: A Research Note on the Automatic Detection of Error and on the Nature and Sources of Errors in Coding." *Historical Methods* 12 (Fall 1979): 157–67.

Ornstein, Michael D., and Darroch, A. Gordon. "National Mobility Studies in Past Time: A Sampling Strategy." *Historical Methods* 11 (Fall 1978): 152–61.

Orth, Samuel P. *A History of Cleveland, Ohio.* Vol. 1. Chicago and Cleveland: S. J. Clarke Publishing Co., 1910.

Padernacht, Robert Z. "The Contributions of the New York Association for Improving the Condition of the Poor to Child Welfare, 1843–1939." Ph.D. Dissertation, St. John's University, 1976.

Painter, Nell Irvin; Fox, Richard Wightman; Rosenzweig, Roy; and Bender, Thomas. "A Round Table: Synthesis in American History." *Journal of American History* 74 (June 1987): 107–130.

Pasco, Peggy. *Relations of Rescue: The Search for Female Moral Authority in the American West, 1874–1939.* New York: Oxford University Press, 1990.

Pease, William H. and Pease, Jane H. *The Web of Progress: Private Values and Public Styles in Boston and Charleston, 1828–1843.* New York: Oxford University Press, 1985.

Peet, Elijah. *Peet's General Business Directory of the Cities of Cleveland and Ohio, for the Years 1845–6.* Cleveland: Sanford and Hayward, 1845.

Peet, Elijah. *Peet's General Business Directory of the City of Cleveland for the Years 1846–7.* Cleveland: Smead and Cowles, 1846.

Perlmann, Joel. "Using Census Districts in Analysis, Record Linkage, and Sampling." *Journal of Interdisciplinary History* 10 (Autumn 1979): 279–89.

Pessen, Edward. "The Occupations of the Ante-Bellum Rich: A Misleading Clue to the Sources and Extent of Their Wealth." *Historical Methods Newsletter* 5 (March 1972): 49–52.

Philie, William L. *Change and Tradition: New Haven, Connecticut, 1780–1830.* New York: Garland, 1989.

Phillips, John A. "Achieving a Critical Mass While Avoiding An Explosion: Letter Cluster Sampling and Nominal Record Linkage." *Journal of Interdisciplinary History* 9 (Winter 1979): 493–508.

Pickett, Robert S. *House of Refuge: Origins of Juvenile Reform in New York State, 1815–1857.* Syracuse, NY: Syracuse University Press, 1969.

Piven, Frances Fox and Cloward, Richard A. *Regulating the Poor: The Functions of Public Welfare.* New York: Random House, Vintage, 1971.

Plain Dealer, 1844–60.

Plain Dealer Weekly, 1842–43.

Post, Charles Asa. *Doan's Corners and the City Four Miles West.* Cleveland: The Caxton Company, 1930.

Pred, Allan R. *The Spatial Dynamics of Urban Industrial Growth, 1800–1914.* Cambridge, Mass.: M.I.T. Press, 1966.

R. G. Dun and Co. Collection, Baker Library, Harvard University Graduate School of Business Administration, Ohio, Vols. A, 39, 40, 41.

Ratcliffe, Donald J. "Politics in Jacksonian Ohio: Reflections on the Ethnocultural Interpretation." *Ohio History* 88 (Winter 1979): 5–36.

Rice, Harvey. *Pioneers of the Western Reserve.* Boston: Lee and Shepard, 1883.

Robison, W. Scott, ed. *History of the City of Cleveland, Its Settlement, Rise and Progress.* Cleveland: Robison and Crockett and The Sunday World, 1887.

Rodgers, Daniel T. *The Work Ethic in Industrial America, 1850–1920.* Chicago: University of Chicago Press, 1978 (paper).

Rorabaugh, W. J. *The Alcoholic Republic.* New York: Oxford University Press, 1979.

Rose, William Ganson. *Cleveland: The Making of a City.* Cleveland: World Publishing Co., 1950.

Rosenberg, Carroll Smith. "Beauty, the Beast and the Militant Woman: A Case Study in Sex Roles and Social Stress in Jacksonian America." *American Quarterly* 23 (October 1971): 562–84.

Rosenberg, Carroll Smith. "The Female World of Love and Ritual: Relations Between Women in Nineteenth-Century America." *Signs* 1 (Autumn 1975): 1–29.

Rosenberg, Carroll Smith. *Religion and the Rise of the City: The New York City Mission Movement, 1812–1870.* Ithaca, NY: Cornell University Press, 1971.

Rothman, David J. *The Discovery of the Asylum: Social Order and Disorder in the New Republic.* Boston: Little Brown and Co., 1971 (paper).

Rowe, David L. "A New Perspective on the Burned-Over District: The Millerites in Upstate New York." *Church History* 47 (December 1978): 408–20.

Ryan, Mary P. "A Women's Awakening: Evangelical Religion and the Families of Utica, New York, 1800–1840." *Women in American Religion.* Edited by Janet Wilson James. Philadelphia: University of Pennsylvania Press, 1980 (paper).

Ryan, Mary P. *Cradle of the Middle Class: The Family in Oneida County, New York, 1790–1865.* New York: Cambridge University Press, 1981.

Ryan, Mary P. *Womanhood in America: From Colonial Times to the Present.* 2nd ed. New York: New Viewpoints, 1979.

Ryan, Mary P. *Women in Public: Between Banners and Ballots, 1825–1880.* Baltimore: Johns Hopkins University Press, 1990.

Scharf, Lois. "The Great Uprising in Cleveland: When Sisterhood Failed." In Joan M. Jensen and Sue Davidson, eds., *A Needle, A Bobbin, A*

Strike: Women Needleworkers in America. Philadelphia: Temple University Press, 1984, pp. 146–66.

Scharf, Lois. "Helpmates and Housewives: Women's Changing Roles in the Western Reserve." *Western Reserve Magazine* (May–June 1978), 33–40.

Scharf, Lois. "Widening Their Sphere: Women in the Western Reserve, 1800–1870." *Western Reserve Magazine* (March–April 1978), 33–40.

Schatz, Ronald. "Review Essay: Labor Historians, Labor Economics, and a Question of Synthesis." *Journal of American History* 71 (June 1984): 93–100.

Scheiber, Harry N. "Alfred Kelley and the Ohio Business Elite, 1822–1859." *Ohio History* 87 (Autumn 1978): 365–92.

Scheiber, Harry N. *Ohio Canal Era: A Case Study of Government and the Economy, 1820–1861.* Athens: Ohio University Press, 1969.

Schlossman, Steven L. *Love and the American Delinquent: The Theory and Practice of Progressive Juvenile Justice, 1825–1920.* Chicago: University of Chicago Press, 1977.

Schofield, Ann. "The Uprising of the 20,000: The Making of a Labor Legend." In Joan M. Jensen and Sue Davidson, eds. *A Needle, A Bobbin, A Strike: Women Needleworkers in America.* Philadelphia: Temple University Press, 1984, pp. 167–82.

Scott, Anne Firor. *Natural Allies: Women's Associations in American History.* Urbana: University of Illinois Press, 1991.

Scott, Anne Firor. "On Seeing and Not Seeing: A Case of Historical Invisibility." *Journal Of American History* 71 (June 1984): 7–21.

Scott, Donald M. *From Office to Profession: The New England Ministry, 1750–1850.* Philadelphia: University of Pennsylvania Press, 1978.

Scott, James Allen. "The Businessman, Capitalism and the City: Businessmen and Municipal Reform from the Act of Consolidation (1854) to the Bullitt Bill (1885)." Ph.D. Dissertation, University of Delaware, 1974.

Seaman, Jeff, and Condran, Gretchen A. "Nominal Record Linkage by Machine and Hand: An Investigation of Linkage Techniques Using the Manuscript Census and the Death Register, Philadelphia, 1880." Paper presented at the annual meeting of the American Statistical Association, August 13–16, 1979. Available from the Philadelphia Social History Project.

Sears, Clara Endicott. *Days of Delusion: A Strange Bit of History.* Boston: Houghton Mifflin Co., 1924.

Sellers, Charles. *The Market Revolution: Jacksonian America, 1815–1846.* New York: Oxford University Press, 1991.

Shiels, Richard D. "The Feminization of American Congregationalism, 1730–1835." *American Quarterly* 33 (Spring 1981): 46–62.

Shiels, Richard D. "The Second Great Awakening in Connecticut: Critique of the Traditional Interpretation." *Church History* 49 (December 1980): 401–15.

Singleton, Gregory H. *Religion in the City of Angels: American Protestant Culture and Urbanization, Los Angeles, 1850–1930.* Ann Arbor, MI: UMI Research Press, 1979.

Sizer, Sandra. *Gospel Hymns and Social Religion: The Rhetoric of Nineteenth-Century Revivalism.* Philadelphia: Temple University Press, 1978.

Sizer, Sandra. "Politics and Apolitical Religion: The Great Urban Revivals of the Late Nineteenth Century." *Church History* 48 (March 1979): 81–98.

Sklar, Kathryn Kish. *Catherine Beecher: A Study in American Domesticity.* New York: W. W. Norton, 1973 (paper).

Skolnick, M. H. "A Computer Program for Linking Records." *Historical Methods Newsletter* 4 (September 1971): 114–25.

Smith, Thomas. "Reconstructing Occupational Structures: The Case of the Ambiguous Artisans." *Historical Methods Newsletter* 8 (June 1975): 134–46.

Smith, Timothy L. *Revivalism and Social Reform: American Protestantism on the Eve of the Civil War.* New York: Harper and Row, 1965 (paper).

Smith, Timothy L. "Righteousness and Hope: Christian Holiness and the Millenial Vision in America, 1800–1900." *American Quarterly* 31 (Spring 1979): 21–45.

Solberg, Winton U. *Redeem the Time: The Puritan Sabbath in Early America.* Cambridge, MA: Harvard University Press, 1977.

Spann, Edward K. *The New Metropolis: New York City, 1840–1857.* New York: Columbia University Press, 1981.

Spear, Denison, and Co.'s Cleveland City Directory, for 1856. Cleveland: Spear, Denison and Co., 1856.

Spirit of the Lakes, and Boatman's Magazine (January 1849–November 1850).

Spirit of the Lakes, and Boatmen's Reporter, Vol. 4, no. 4. Cleveland: Smead and Cowles, 1852.

Stansell, Christine. *City of Women: Sex and Class in New York, 1789–1860.* New York: Alfred A. Knopf, 1986.

Stephenson, Wm., comp. *Smead and Cowles General Business Directory of the City of Cleveland for 1848–49.* Cleveland: Smead and Cowles, 1848.

Stott, Richard B. *Workers in the Metropolis: Class, Ethnicity and Youth in Antebellum New York City.* Ithaca, NY: Cornell University Press, 1990.

Stuckey, James Herbert. "The Formation of Leadership Groups in a Frontier Town: Canton, Ohio, 1805–1855." Ph.D. Dissertation, Case Western Reserve University, 1976.

Taylor, Stuart, Jr. "U.S. Court Reinstates Rules on 'Industrial' Home Work." *New York Times*, Nov. 30, 1983, p. A11.

Thomas, George M. *Revivalism and Cultural Change: Christianity, Nation Building, and the Market in the Nineteenth-Century United States.* Chicago: University of Chicago Press, 1989.

Thomas, John L. "Romantic Reform in America, 1815–1865." *Ante-bellum Reform*. Edited by David Brion Davis. New York: Harper and Row, 1967 (paper).

Thompson, Russell. *The Young Men's Christian Association of Cleveland.* Cleveland: YMCA, 1901.

Tocqueville, Alexis de. *Democracy in America*. New York: Random House, Vintage, 1945.

Tracy, Patricia J. *Jonathan Edwards, Pastor: Religion and Society in Eighteenth-Century Northampton*. New York: Hill and Wang, 1980.

Trattner, Walter I. *From Poor Law to Welfare State: A History of Social Welfare in America*. New York: Free Press, Macmillan Co., 1974.

Truedley, Mary Bosworth. "The 'Benevolent Fair': A Study of Charitable Organizations Among American Women in the First Third of the Nineteenth Century." *Social Service Review* 14 (September 1940): 509–22.

Tyler, Alice Felt. *Freedom's Ferment: Phases of American Social History from the Colonial Period to the Outbreak of Civil War*. New York: Harper and Row, 1944 (paper).

Tyrrell, Ian R. *Sobering Up: From Temperance to Prohibition in Antebellum America, 1800–1860*. Westport, CT: Greenwood Press, 1979.

U.S., Manuscript Census, 1840 (Microfilm).

U.S., Manuscript Census, 1850 (Microfilm).

U.S., Manuscript Census, 1860 (Microfilm).

Upton, Harriet Taylor. *History of the Western Reserve*. Vol. 1. Chicago: Lewis Publishing Co., 1910.

Urann, Clara Augusta. *Centennial History of Cleveland*. Cleveland: Press of J.B. Savage, 1896.

U.S., Work Projects Administration, Ohio [Works Progress Administration in Ohio]. *Annals of Cleveland, 1818–1935*. 59 Vols. Cleveland: Works Progress Administration, 1936–38.

U.S., Work Projects Administration, Ohio [Works Progress Administration in Ohio]. Ohio Historical Records Survey Project. *Historic Sites of Cleveland: Hotels and Taverns*. Columbus: Ohio Historical Records Survey Project, 1942.

Utter, William T. *The Frontier State, 1803–1825*. Vol. 2 of *The History of the State of Ohio*. Edited by Carl Wittke. 6 Vols. Columbus: Ohio State Archeological and Historical Society, 1941–44.

Van Tassel, David D. and Grabowski, John J. eds. *The Encyclopedia of Cleveland History*. Bloomington: Indiana University Press, 1987.

Wallace, Anthony F. C. *Rockdale: The Growth of an American Village in the Early Industrial Revolution*. New York: Alfred A. Knopf, 1978.

Walters, Ronald G. *American Reformers, 1815–1860*. New York: Hill and Wang, 1978 (paper).

Walzer, Michael. *The Revolution of the Saints: A Study in the Origins of Radical Politics*. New York: Atheneum, 1967 (paper).

Weber, Timothy. *Living in the Shadow of the Second Coming: American Premillenialism, 1875–1925*. New York: Oxford University Press, 1979.

Weisenburger, Francis Phelps. *The Passing of the Frontier, 1825–1850*. Vol. 3 of *The History of the State of Ohio*. Edited by Carl Wittke. 6 Vols. Columbus: Ohio State Archeological and Historical Society, 1941–44.

Wellman, Judith M. "The Burned-Over District Revisited: Benevolent Reform and Abolitionism in Mexico, Paris, and Ithaca, New York, 1825–1842." Ph.D. Dissertation, University of Virginia, 1974.

Wellman, Judith. "Women and Radical Reform in Antebellum Upstate New York: A Profile of Grassroots Female Abolitionists." *Clio Was a Woman: Studies in the History of American Women*. Edited by Mabel E. Deutrich and Virginia C. Purdy. Washington, DC: Howard University Press, 1980.

Wells, Robert V. "On the Dangers of Constructing Artificial Cohorts in Times of Rapid Social Change." *Journal of Interdisciplinary History* 9 (Summer 1978): 103–10.

Welter, Barbara. "The Feminization of American Religion: 1800–1860." *Clio's Consciousness Raised: New Perspectives on the History of Women*. Edited by Mary S. Hartman and Lois Banner. New York: Harper and Row, Torchbook, 1974.

Welter, Barbara. "She Hath Done What She Could." *Women in American Religious History*. Edited by Janet Wilson James. Philadelphia: University of Pennsylvania Press, 1980 (paper).

The Western Pilot, Vol. 1 (January 1853–December 1853).

Western Seamen's Friend Society. *Annual Report, 1886*. Cleveland: W. R. Smellie, 1887.

Western Seamen's Friend Society. *The Bethel Work in the West*. Cleveland: Western Seamen's Friend Society, 1870.

Western Seamen's Friend Society. *Eleventh Annual Report of the Western Seamen's Friend Society, Presented at the Annual Meeting, Held in the City of Cincinnati, May 29, 1859*. Cleveland: Fairbanks, Benedict and Company, 1859.

Western Seamen's Friend Society. "First Annual Report." *Spirit of the Lakes, and Boatman's Magazine* (September 1848).

Western Seamen's Friend Society. "Fifth Annual Report." *Spirit of the Lakes, and Boatmen's Reporter*, Vol. 4, no. 4. Cleveland: Smead and Cowles, 1852.

Western Seamen's Friend Society. "Second Annual Report." *Spirit of the Lakes, and Boatman's Magazine* (November 1849).

Western Seamen's Friend Society. "Third Annual Report." *Spirit of the Lakes, and Boatman's Magazine* (October 1850).

Wheeler, Robert. "A Commercial Hamlet is Founded: 1796–1824." In *The Encyclopedia of Cleveland History*. Edited by David D. Van Tassel and John Grabowski. Bloomington: Indiana University Press, 1987, pp. xvii–xx.

Wheeler, Robert. "Commercial Village to Commercial City: 1825–1860." In *The Encyclopedia of Cleveland History*, ed. David D. Van Tassel and John J. Grabowksi. Bloomington: Indiana University Press, 1987, pp. xx–xxix.

Wheeler, Robert A. "Childhood in the Western Reserve." *Western Reserve Magazine* (Jan.–Feb. 1979), pp. 29–36.

Wheeler, Robert A. "Water to Steam: Industry in the Western Reserve, 1800–1860." *Western Reserve Magazine* (Sept.–Oct. 1978), pp. 27–34.

White, B., ed. *The Acts to Provide for the Organization of Cities and Villages, and the Revised Ordinances of the City of Cleveland*. Cleveland: Harris, Fairbanks and Co., 1855.

Whittlesey, Charles. *Early History of Cleveland, Ohio*. Cleveland: Fairbanks, Benedict and Co., 1867.

Wickham, Gertrude Van Rensselaer, ed. *Memorial to the Pioneer Women of the Western Reserve*. 3 vols. Cleveland: Woman's Department, Cleveland Centennial Commission, 1896–1924.

Wickham, Gertrude Van Rensselaer. *The Pioneer Families of Cleveland, 1796–1840*. 2 Vols. Cleveland: Evangelical Publishing House, 1914.

Wilentz, Sean. *Chants Democratic: New York City and the Rise of the American Working Class, 1788–1850*. New York: Oxford University Press, 1984.

[J. H.] Williston and Co.'s Directory of the City of Cleveland. Cleveland: J. H. Williston and Co., 1859–60.

Wilson, John F. *Public Religion in American Culture*. Philadelphia: Temple University Press, 1979.

Winkle, Kenneth J. *The Politics of Community: Migration and Politics in Antebellum Ohio*. New York: Cambridge University Press, 1988.

Winter, Gibson. *The New Creation as Metropolis*. New York: Macmillan, 1963.

Wishy, Bernard. *The Child and the Republic: The Dawn of Modern American Child Nurture*. Philadelphia: University fo Pennsylvania Press, 1968.

Wolf, Stephanie Grauman. *Urban Village: Population, Community and Family Structure in Germantown, Pennsylvania, 1683–1800*. Princeton, NJ: Princeton University press, 1976.

Wood, James R. and Houghland, James G. Jr. "The Role of Religion in Philanthropy." In Jon Van Til and Associates, *Critical Issues in American Philanthropy*. San Francisco: Jossey-Bass Publishers, 1990, pp. 99–132.

Wortman, Marlene Stein. "Domesticating the Nineteenth-Century American City." *Prospects: An Annual of American Cultural Studies*, 3: 531–72. Edited by Jack Salzman. New York: Burt Franklin and Co., 1977.

Wuthnow, Robert. "Religion and the Voluntary Spirit in the United States: Mapping the Terrain." In Robert Wuthnow and Virginia A. Hodgkinson and Associates, *Faith and Philanthropy in America: Exploring the Role of Religion in America's Voluntary Sector*. San Francisco: Jossey-Bass Publishers, 1990, pp. 3–21.

Wyatt-Brown, Bertram. *Lewis Tappan and the Evangelical War Against Slavery*. Cleveland: The Press of Case Western Reserve University, 1969.

Wyatt-Brown, Bertram. "Prelude to Abolitionism: Sabbatarian Politics and the Rise of the Second Party System." *Journal of American History*, 63, no. 2 (September 1971): 316–41.

Wyatt-Brown, Bertram. *Southern Honor: Ethics and Behavior in the Old South*. New York: Oxford University Press, 1982 (paper).

Yans-McLaughlin, Virginia. *Family and Community: Italian Immigirants in Buffalo, 1880–1930*. Ithaca, NY: Cornell University Press, 1977.

INDEX

Note: Numbers followed by a *t* indicate tables